CREATING ELEMENTAL JEWELRY

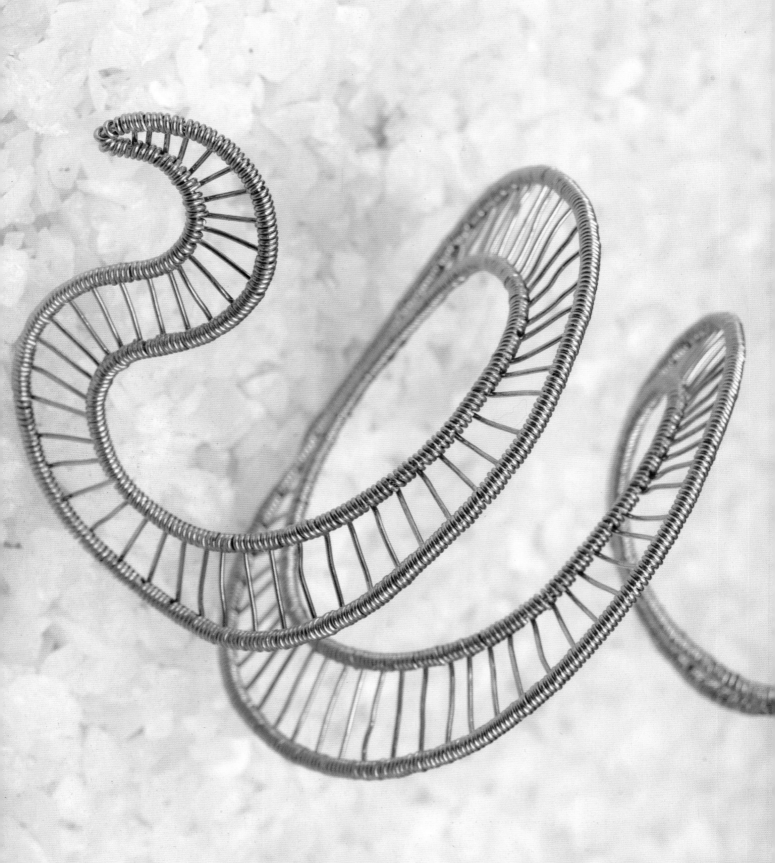

CREATING ELEMENTAL JEWELRY

20 PROJECTS CONJURED FROM FIRE, WATER, EARTH AND AIR

VICKY FORRESTER

NORTH LIGHT BOOKS

For Amber Stanza, with love

Creating Elemental Jewelry

Conceived, edited, and designed by Fil Rouge Press Ltd
110 Seddon House, Barbican, London EC2Y 8BX

Copyright © Fil Rouge Press, 2012
Text copyright © Vicky Forrester, 2012

Manufactured in China

Published by North Light Books, an imprint of F+W Media, Inc.,
10151 Carver Road,
Suite 200 Blue Ash,
Ohio 45242.
(800) 289-0963.
First Edition.
www.fwmedia.com

16 15 14 13 12 5 4 3 2 1

SRN: W7255

ISBN-13: 978-1-4403-2032-3

Fil Rouge Press
Publisher Judith More
Managing Editor Jennifer Latham
Designers Gaye Allen, Simon Goggin, David Jones
Editor Kathy Steer

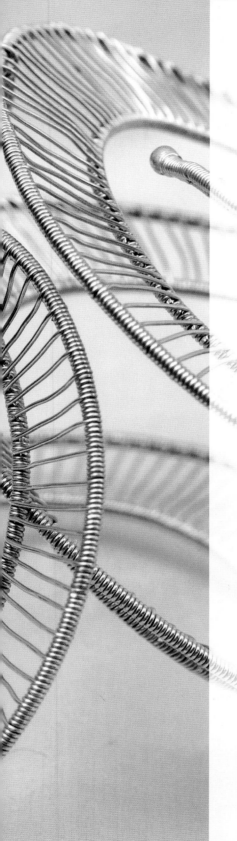

CONTENTS

FOREWORD

Nature and the elements provide an endless source of inspiration for my jewelry. When I first began my journey as a maker everything I created was small and "precious;" tiny leaves, perfect flowers. Designs were often literal representations of the world around me as most of my focus was given over to the "how" of jewelry making.

In time, I mastered the basic processes of the craft and the desire to develop new skills and to explore new techniques became second nature. At this point there was also room to consider the deeper and sometimes intimidating questions of "what?," "why?," and "who?."

Delving ever deeper, beyond self-doubt, these questions can become our friends, helping us to hone our ideas and refine our conclusions.

AN ELEMENTAL JOURNEY

This book is for anyone who is ready to seek answers to these deeper questions, and engage in the creative process. Here you will find 20 projects that aim to introduce new approaches to designing and making jewelry. I hope that in sharing my own experiences, processes, and conclusions, you can find parallels that will help you to engage with your own creative practice in new ways.

Presented in three purposeful sections—Ideas, Materials, and Techniques—the book aims to take you on an expansive journey through various approaches to designing and making jewelry.

Using Earth, Air, Fire, and Water as sources of inspiration, the step-by-step projects explore how these themes can provide potent undercurrents in conceptual, material, and technical investigation.

My intention throughout is to encourage a sense of play in the process. In my own experience, only through such extended periods of play—a combination of reflection, experimentation, and pushing the limits without concern for the preciousness of the outcome—can one begin to find a sense of fluidity with process and material. This kind of exploration leads to originality and personal authenticity in one's creative expression.

The process of designing cannot be formulaic if the outcome is to be original. However, there are common threads in the way we develop our ideas, and the sections in this book reflect the three most common starting points for developing creatively.

Working with ideas, responding to materials, or exploiting a technique—each of these approaches provides a valuable route to generating originality and authenticity in your jewelry designs.

HONING YOUR SKILLS

The first section—Earth, Air, Fire, Water, pages 12-59—explores how, from a generic point of inspiration, we can all find motivating and highly personal concepts that can become the driving force behind creative output.

Section two—Exploring Materials, pages 60-93—examines how materials can influence the process of design. Four inspirational jewelers share how the properties of their chosen materials can be exploited to harmonize with conceptual development. Imogen Belfield, Henrietta Fernandez, Nora Fok, and Louise Loder all take influence from the elements to produce a very diverse range of outcomes. You will find a gallery page for each, and an inspiring project for you to explore their personal approach to jewelry design.

The final section—Exploring Techniques, pages 94-177—focuses on technique. The first six projects are more challenging in technique, and lead to a specified outcome. The final six projects are exploratory and open-ended. They will provide you with a series of test pieces that can be used to make objects of choice. The principles are waiting to be exploited in your own context.

For all of us, I think, the art of making is a mindful process. More than just in the materials used, the skills undertaken, or the design of the piece, in this context our remit extends beyond the bounds of art or craft.

Jewelry is an unparalleled communicator. It fulfils our primitive urge to express, empower, protect. Replete with the maker's intentions, this creative impetus can invest the object with energy, meaning, and value. If a piece of jewelry is worn, it is never insignificant. Passing through generations, it becomes a record keeper of our social history and our personal family values. As makers of jewelry, we have the capacity to engage with humanity on many profound levels.

Whether you are an experienced jeweler or relatively new to the subject, I hope that these pages will enrich your personal dialog as a maker of powerful objects.

Vicky Forrester *London 2012*

THE DESIGN PROCESS

How do we make the leap from our excited first projects in jewelry making to become confident designer-makers with a recognizable style? I think our early experiences of making set the general structure for the way we design and evolve as makers.

What was it that hooked you when you made your first piece of jewelry? Was it the challenge of solving problems that excited you? Are you a "what if" kind of maker? Do you thirst for new techniques? Or did you fall in love with your materials? Are you inspired by color or texture, or the quality of your medium? Perhaps you are motivated to make jewelry for a person, a purpose, or an occasion. Do you have a personal message that you want to convey?

Designing jewelry is a multifaceted process for me. It becomes interesting when all of these threads come together. It is at this point that we as makers begin to express our creative identity through our work. The body, the idea, the material, and the execution—a good piece of jewelry will show consideration for each of these criteria. In addressing them all, a single piece of jewelry can confidently expand into a collection that continues to evolve according to your own inquiry.

To produce work that measures well against each of these principles is quite an undertaking, but by seeking out answers to the questions that arise from them you will find that in time the process becomes instinctive, and your own creative language will emerge.

THE CREATIVE PROCESS

In my own work, pieces often evolve in response to materials. I identify the interesting qualities of my chosen material and then develop techniques that exploit or enhance these qualities. The form itself is often suggested by the effect of the process on that particular material. I also consider how and where the emerging form can be worn, and the impact that gravity and movement will have on the piece.

Beneath this process-led practice there is always a conceptual undercurrent that both informs and impacts on my conclusions. This undercurrent is a distillation of all my experiences (thoughts, desires, feelings, sensory feedback), as distinct as my identity, and fluid enough to engage with new influences and new perspectives. What I feel, and what I want to communicate I often cannot describe well in words, but through the visual and tactile I find a more precise medium for expression.

EXPLORATORY QUESTIONS

Here are some questions that can help you to focus your ideas. Consider them as starting points for your next project. There is no right or wrong way to answer a question, and they can be rejected with validity if they have been considered.

- Who is your jewelry for? How should it be worn? Where should it be worn? When is it worn? Should it be comfortable?
- What are your influences? Are you making a political statement? Are you having a laugh? Are you telling a story? Are you evoking a mood or energy?
- What materials will you use? Why? What are their properties? How can you exploit these properties?
- What techniques can you use? Which materials can be used? Can you combine several techniques? Can you push the limits of your techniques to evolve new ways of working?

The beach is strewn with many varieties of seaweed (top left, third left); a shiny beach pebble (second left); mermaid stories (bottom); the bulbous root of a seaweed stem (opposite).

THE CREATIVE JOURNEY

How do we give form to our ordinary experiences of life? A walk on the beach provides a rich source of sensory input that will continue to emerge in many forms for my collections.

I pick up a pebble and it feels perfect in my hand; the right size, a pleasingly worn and smooth texture. I feel a connection with life that is hard to describe in words. There is a tangible energy in this solid, simple, ancient form and my hands absorb the physicality of this experience. Memories of all the other beaches I have visited—my own history—come to me, further adding to the power of this object in my hand.

Further up the beach, seaweed strewn across the pebbles reminds me of mermaid stories (childhood fantasy, sailor's caution!) I am drawn by the notion of freedom in casting off our human chains and diving to the depths of an other worldly beauty.

These incidents are stored in my subconscious, adding to my collection of experience and causing minute shifts in perspective. I take photographs to remind me of the details.

Back to reality, looking more closely at the form of the seaweed I notice how the fronds fall (in water they'd rise) from the main stem, and how the sea-wet surface glistens in the sunlight. The storm has torn up this plant from its bed and I find its root, a ball of tendrils looking for anchorage.

Starting with the concept Back in my studio, I want to weave my experiences into my work. I remember the pebble in my hand. How can I describe this sense of connection that seems so important to me? I want to express something of that whole powerful experience of holding the pebble on the beach. I think of literal uses first, and reject them. I try to analyze precisely what it is that I want to encapsulate. I realize that in the process of making I can invest, through my thoughts and actions, something of that power I felt. I work on the notions of suspension, of stillness, and movement. My hollow bead forms become vessels for the invisible in my Organic collection (see pages 18-19) and Adjustable Pebble Necklace (see pages 20-7).

From the Organic collection (see also pages 18-19), Pebble earrings (right) and Pebble neckpiece (below).

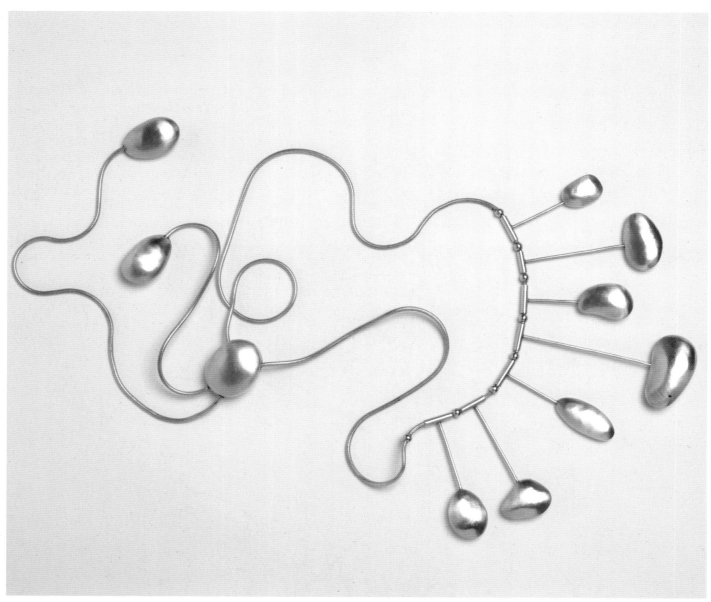

Starting with the material At a later point I find a piece of foxtail chain, and playing with the way the material curves I also notice a familiar glistening appeal—I am reminded of the mermaid; she becomes my muse as I knot a sea maid's net ... pearls are too obvious, but touches of gold hint at lost sea treasures.

From the Precious collection (see also pages 50-1), Siren ring (right), Siren necklace (below), Precious ring (bottom).

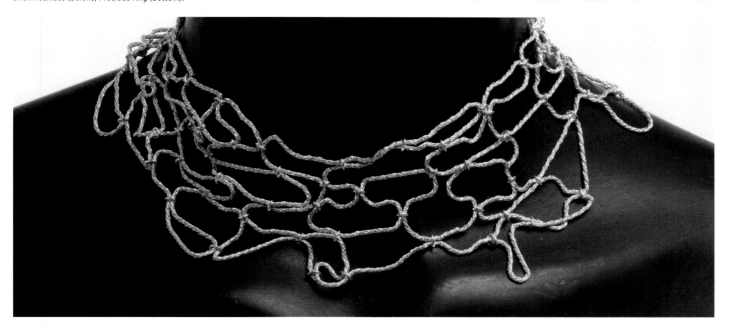

Starting with the technique Playing with wax one day I notice how the drips and molten streams are reminiscent of the seaweed roots. I look again at my photographs and I am curious to know more about sea forms. I plan a visit to the Natural History Museum in London to see other sea plants and I find an array of beautiful coral and sponge shapes that inspire me to make some hollow forms. After several days of play and experimentation, I find a technique to make my perfect shapes and I am pleased to find new ways to express my ongoing fascination with precious vessel forms.

COLLECTIONS

Three of my key pieces of jewelry have emerged from a beach walk, and these have seeded several collections that I continue to evolve.

I am not the first person to use tactile stone forms in my jewelry—we are often moved by similar experiences—but what makes my pebble collection uniquely mine is that it tells my story, my perspective, and this gives a sense of authenticity to my collection.

The following pages show how earth, air, fire, and water can provide a myriad starting points for your own designs to evolve. I encourage you to take time to develop your core concepts. Explore materials and techniques through the projects and push them further to find new ways to express your ideas. Examine the work of others to see how they have drawn conclusions from these same sources of inspiration. Feed your creativity.

The process should be pleasurable, and through play in time your own aesthetic will unfold to bring authenticity and originality to your creative voice. There is no wrong way to be creative. Just start. In my own experience, once I ask myself a design question, answers tend to arrive at the most unlikely moments; pen and paper should always be at hand!

CHAPTER **ONE**

EARTH, AIR, FIRE, WATER

WORKING WITH THE ELEMENTS

A walk through any natural history museum shows the most ancient jewelry to be made from found objects—shells, stone, horn, bones, teeth, feathers, gold—natural objects, honed by the elements, refined and worn by humankind. With passing time comes new perspective, and yet 90,000 years of human evolution cannot demystify our urge to express, describe, and rejoice in our natural and supernatural world. Earth, air, fire, water—their eternal rhythms pulse through our veins. In connecting with nature and the elements, we jewelry makers can conjure forms that resonate with the essence of life itself.

While we are captivated by the same elemental mysteries as our forebears, millennia of collective experience and innovation have transformed how we can respond to these sources of inspiration. Beyond the instinctive desire to string found natural objects into a necklace, how can we find ways to express a sense of self, a sense of our time in our jewelry?

WORKING WITH IDEAS

In addition to the physical manifestations that we readily use—from natural materials such as metal and stone, to manmade ones such as glass and plastic—the elements also provide us with a wealth of inspiration for our designs. Looking at earth, air, fire, and water in the widest contexts, we can find starting points for design ideas that can fascinate and that can inform our designs for a lifetime.

I like to use mind maps to broaden my perspective around a given theme (see my mind maps for earth, air, fire, and water on pages 17, 29, 39, and 49). In the process, I am often surprised by unusual connections that can enrich my appreciation of the world around me.

If you want to sharpen the conceptual element of your own design work, try mining the elements to find your form: consider earth, air, fire, or water as your starting point and write down as many associations as you can think of; find threads that resonate for you. Let them play in your mind. Use them to direct your research—draw, read books, collect images, take photographs, make collages, talk about the ideas that fire your imagination! Allow these ideas to grow into three-dimensional form.

The following pages show how I look for threads of inspiration from the elements, and how I have used these influences in my work.

THE DESIGN PROCESS

If you are new to the process of designing, you may find it helpful to follow a more methodical approach to developing ideas. We can break the design process into a series of stages that can lead to an effective solution for any design brief.

- The brief—the problem you need to solve, for example, design a jewelry item based on "Flowing Water."
- Analysis—write down as many ideas and questions as possible to help identify what you need to fine out about. Who? What? Where? Why? How?
- Research—explore the ideas your analysis created; sources include books, museums, the Internet, people, etc.
- Stimulus material—collect additional materials that can help to develop ideas (usually visual, but could be verbal or aural too, or even tactile).
- Specification—having identified the areas that interest you most, make a list of statements that explain and limit the direction of your project.
- Initial sketches—develop some quick models or drawings based on your initial research conclusions. Use any medium that helps you to express your ideas—clay, wax, collage, pen, paint. Photograph all your delicate and three-dimensional work for your sketchbook record.
- Development—pursue the ideas you like the most. Look more closely at ergonomic/aesthetic/technical issues; also scale. Make models and initial test pieces to explore ideas further.
- Chosen idea—make a tighter drawing or a model of your intended design.
- Planning—work out your materials and measurements; outline the order of making.
- Making—ideally you should keep notes and take quick photographs as you go, so you can recall how to do it again—or not, if mistakes occurred!
- Evaluation—ask questions to determine the success of the piece. Compare it to your original intentions. Does it work? Why? Can you wear it? Will you wear it?

These beautiful fossils provide a window into our planet's history.

FROM MATERIAL TO CONCEPT

Starting points for your designs can arise from any source. Here is an example of how material and concept can be drawn together to create a unique story.

If this rough opal chip (see below) was yours, how would you use it? Look at the opal. Do you like its rough form, or would you want to file those edges smooth? You could carve it into an entirely different shape; can you see a form that wants to emerge?

Do you think of fire when you look into those colors, or is there an ethereal mystery to them? How can you enhance the opal's elemental nature? You could surround it in golden flames, or set it into a protective, earthy, rough slice of bog oak; it could be a watery pool half hidden beneath reedy rushes, or you could smooth and streamline it, set into an airy swirl.

What other associations are there for you? Do you know where the opal comes from, how it is mined? Do you know how the stone forms, and what it is made from? How can you weave these ideas into the design?

A rough opal chip, 15 x 15 x 8 mm in size.

DESIGN INSPIRATION FROM THE EARTH

Materials we associate with earth are plentiful—stone, metal, wood, leather, bone—they all derive from her. We could argue that all materials available to us are by default of this earth and therefore relate to this element. However, at a deeper level, how we choose to use our materials becomes critical in how they are interpreted. So, for example, a piece of wood shaped in the form of a boat makes us think of the sea.

To make a piece of jewelry that invokes the earthiest of earthy energies, we should give this piece of wood a suitable context. We could carve the wood into a tree, but perhaps this is too literal; what other inspiration can we draw from our planet? Here are some thoughts on earth.

EARTH IS OUR HOME

The earth represents the visible, the tangible. To be earthed is to be connected, rooted, balanced, solid. What keeps us on the planet? The earth's magnetic force pins our feet to the ground, holds the moon in orbit, keeps our balance, gives us rhythm. The earth's rotations include night and day, the seasons, the life cycle of fertilization, birth, growth, death, and decay. This planet is teaming with life. It engages all our senses.

Gaia, mother, nurturing protector, giver of life. Womb-like warmth and protection; fertile ground. In the soil, the seed takes root and grows strong, food and shelter for animal life to flourish.

Symbiosis. Life supports life, give and take, equal and opposite. Yin/yang, male/female.

Organic matter. Organisms: the structure and function of cells, how things grow, how things move. The human body, needing fire, water, air to survive. Animal, vegetable, mineral. Mega, micro, macro.

Back to the soil. The smells, colors, and textures of earth, its constituent parts. In the ground, insect life.

Underground. Caves, caverns, rock. The earth's crust; mining for treasures. Metamorphic rock (pressure and heat). Gems! Sedimentary rock (erosion). Fossils!

fossils   treasures
sedimentary
rock
underground   time   sun   moon
                              magnetism
                      cycles

                          rotation   calm
solid matter   planets   stillness
structure   silence
cells   fibers   balance
organisms
colonies   yin/yang

EARTH

life   mother
embryo   womb   gaia
                                          receptive

growth   death   home
animal   nest
insects   decay   set
vegetables   burrow caves
pods   sanctuary
trees   seeds
wood   nourishment   sense
        fertile ground   hear   touch
            activity   smell feel
                soil   see

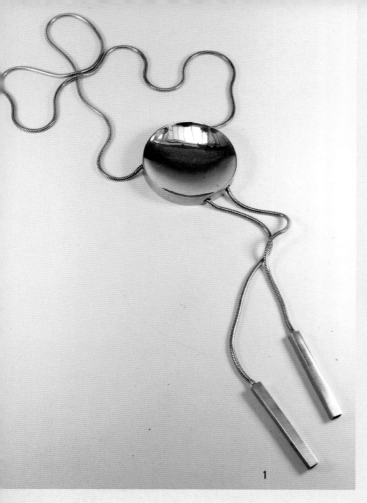

1

THE ORGANIC COLLECTION
Style: Dress down
Impact: Classic beauty
Mood: Easy living, being in tune with nature
Story: Life by the sea, beachcombing, the process of transformation in nature, talismans, personal investments into objects

Reference: The natural world, stones, bones, seeds, pods, twigs, flotsam and jetsam
1 Mirror pendant
2 Organic rings
3 Pebble stack rings
4 Pebble stack pendant
5 Moon pendant (bottle)
6 Bone pendant

2

ORGANIC
COMBINING EARTHY FORMS WITH MOVEMENT

The Organic collection reflects earthy influence in its tactile, solid forms. Soft, matte textures or oxidizing treatments of the metal give subtle focus to shapes and colors reminiscent of pebbles, bones, and twigs.

    The pieces in this collection often incorporate the potential for movement; stacks of pebbles rotate around their invisible axes, or pendants can be positioned as desired along chain, suspended magically by internal forces, or held in balance by gravity's pull.

3

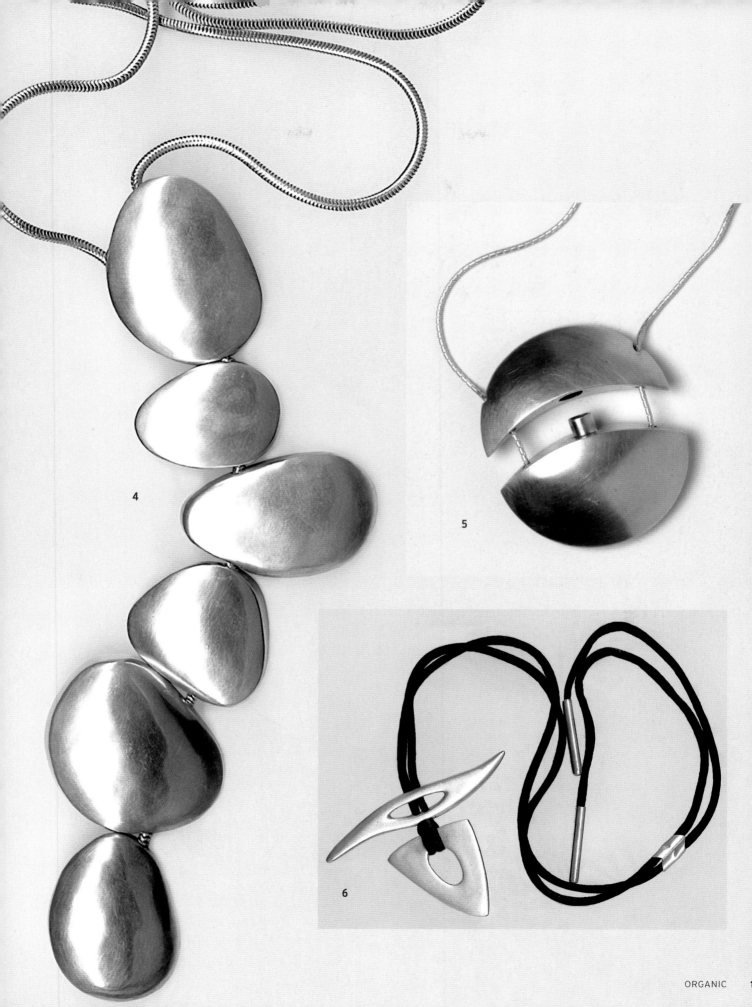

4

5

6

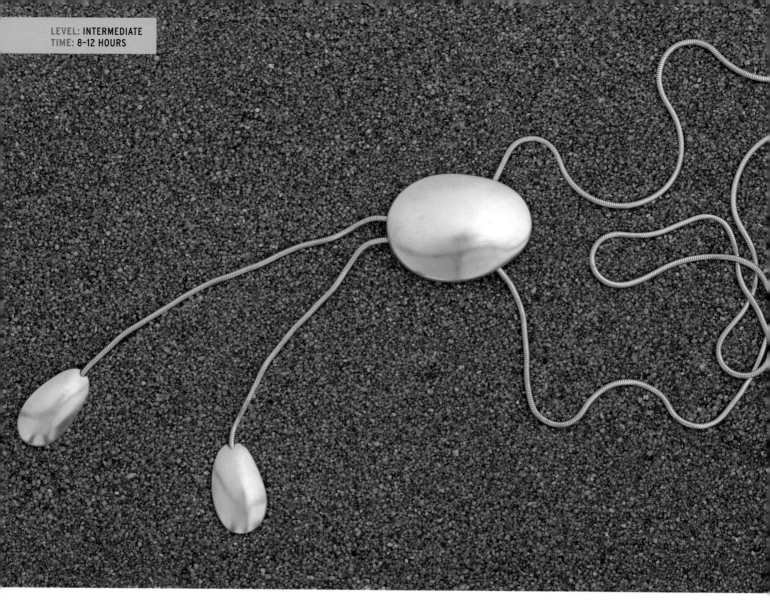

ADJUSTABLE PEBBLE NECKLACE

My mind spends a lot of time trying to find ways to avoid making precision work—catches in particular—and being a jeweler this is something of a fool's task, but occasionally I hit on a eureka solution that can impact on a whole collection. In my pebble collection I exploit gravity (and the behavior of the snake chain) to magically suspend the pebbles on the chain in any position, thus making the pieces adjustable to suit mood, style, or dress.

Internal tubing is the secret. The snake chain must pass through curved tubes that are hidden inside the large pebble. When relaxed, the chain can move freely through the pebble, but in the worn position gravity provides sufficient tension and friction to stop the chain's movement through the necklace. Smaller pebbles at the ends of the chain provide an elegant conclusion to the piece, also providing additional gravitational pull.

It's important to get the balance of form right with this necklace—there exists a complex relationship between the three major elements because they can all move in proximity. The sizes are important, too, in relation to the dimension of the snake chain—too big will look clumsy, too small will look just wrong.

I like to work in metal paper first. Looking at my pebbles for inspiration, I cut out a range of shapes that I think work together. I use wall putty to stick them onto the chain so I can get a sense of how each form will look.

If you are the kind of person who likes to pick up stones and pebbles on your vacation walks, you will know the kind of shapes you like, so base your pebble shapes for your own necklace on these. There is also a template for my pebble design on page 186.

MATERIALS

1. Small length of wire, 1.5 mm diameter, to support tubing while bending it
2. Sterling silver snake chain or foxtail (see below right), 1.6 mm diameter, 3 ft (1 m) long
3. Sterling silver sheet, 0.8 mm thickness, 3 x 2 in (80 x 55 mm)
4. Sterling silver tubing (see below right), 1/10 in (2.5 mm) external/1.65 mm internal diameter, 4 in (100 mm) long
5. Sterling silver sheet, 0.8 mm thickness, 4 x 1/6 in (105 x 3.5 mm)

You will also need:
- For modeling: metal foil or card (see below right), wall putty, and binding wire
- Two-part epoxy glue

TOOLS

- Binding wire, steel rule, and dividers (see pages 183 and 178) for measuring the size of the pebble
- Snips (see page 178)
- Files (see page 179): flat file; large rough file and large smooth file for surfacing
- Fine-line permanent pen
- Piercing saw (see page 178), 3/0 blade
- Soldering equipment (see pages 182 and 183): flux (borax), brush, hard solder, easy solder, torch, tweezers, soldering block, and pickle
- Wall putty for assisting in holding the pebble forms when surfacing on wet and dry papers
- Wet and dry papers (see page 184): 450 and 800 grit, plus fine ones for polishing
- Scribe (see page 178) for scoring and marking
- Hardwood block and wooden doming punches (see right and page 181) for forming curved pebble shape
- Mallet (see page 180)
- Steel block (see page 181)
- Bow drill (see page 179), 1.5 mm drill bit and 1/10 in (2.5 mm) drill bit
- Graver (see page 178)
- Broacher (see right and page 179), size 2-3 mm
- Nylon-tipped pliers (see page 180)
- Pendant drill (see page 182), split pin
- Steel wool (see page 185)
- Pin vise (see page 179) for hand twisting drill bits; for delicate de-burring, and drilling jobs

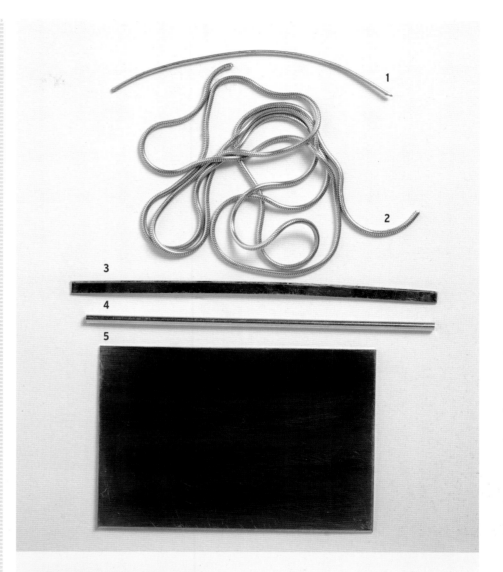

MATERIALS AND TOOLS TIPS

CHAIN AND TUBING When purchasing the chain and tubing for this project it is important that the chain fits the tubing perfectly—not too tight, not too loose. Dimensions given by the supplier might be slightly inaccurate. Check for fit, and if necessary go up or down a size in chain and tubing dimensions until you find a good match. Scale your designs accordingly.

METAL PAPER This thick foil is an excellent modeling material for jewelry where the design utilizes sheet metal. It cuts easily with scissors, and although not quite so malleable as sheet metal, it nonetheless has some ability to hold form. With the appearance of metal, this will help you to consider how light and reflection will affect your designs.

HARDWOOD BLOCK My hardwood block (see Step 4, page 22) has become an essential workshop tool over the years and its surface describes my repertoire of preferred shapes and forms. Every time I have wanted to make a new hollow form I have carved the desired shape into the block by hand using chisels and routing tools. If you don't have access to a fly press or a hydraulic press, the old and low-tech methods work well, and you can exploit the process to add texture to your pieces.

BROACHERS These are invaluable tools for making holes to a precise diameter (see page 179). Their scraping action speedily opens a small hole to size, so if you have a set of these tools you can get away without having to buy an extensive range of drill bit sizes.

PREPARING THE WAX SHAPE

1 The large pebble is the one that holds all the magic, and will take most of the time to make. Once you have the shape you like, bend some binding wire around the outline, then cut open and straighten the wire with snips to work out the length required to make the wall. In this example, I needed 4 in (105 mm) in length.

Cut the strip to length and file the ends square with a flat file. Solder (H) into a ring. Pickle and dry before shaping it with your fingers into the original pebble outline. There's no need to file the seam yet. This wall defines the final shape of the main pebble, so it's important to get it right.

2 Sand flat the top and bottom of the pebble wall ready for soldering to the front and back of the pebble, using the coarse 450 grit wet and dry paper on a flat surface.

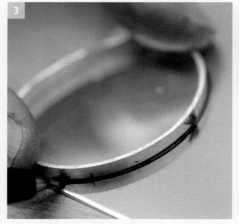

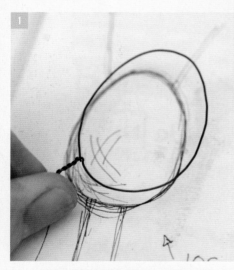

MAKING THE BACK AND FRONT

3 Place the shaped wall onto the large sheet of silver, as economically as you can. Draw around the outside of the wall with your pen. This should give you an additional 0.5 mm distance from the actual edge, enough to allow for the forming of the metal. Flip over the wall (the front and back are likely to be different) and draw the other side in the same way. Score an "x" in the middle of each of these with a pen to denote the inside top and bottom—this is the side you will punch out into a soft dome.

4 Cut with a piercing saw, anneal, and pickle these two sides. Find a sympathetic indented form in the hardwood block (or make one) and, with the "x" facing upward, tap the two sides into the form, using the wooden punch and a mallet. Don't go for too much shape, or they won't fit the wall well.

5 Check the pieces for flatness against a steel block. Tap gently with a mallet from the top rounded surface to bring all the edges down flat onto the block. Where an edge remains high, hold this raised edge near the side of the steel block and strike with the mallet to force it inward and downward.

6 To make the surfaces perfectly flat for soldering, use a piece of wall putty to grip the formed sheets and rub against 450-grit wet and dry paper. Check each side for fit against the pebble wall. You should aim for full contact with the flat surfaces.

7 Take the necessary health and safety precautions before you begin soldering (see page 183). Solder (H) the bottom piece to the wall. Use binding wire if necessary to hold both elements together. I put a few large pieces of solder on the inside—it doesn't need to be pretty, and it keeps the solder from flowing unnecessarily to the outside of the piece. Pickle, but don't do any filing yet.

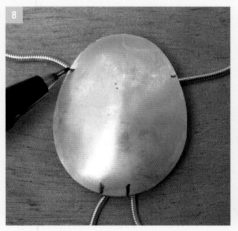

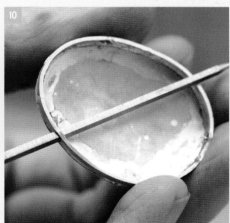

PREPARING FOR THE TUBING

8 You need to shape the tubing into a curve and then solder this into the wall of the pebble. You will also need to drill some holes to house the tubing. Start by placing the pebble over the snake chain to decide where the tubing will fit. Make sure the positioning is as symmetrical as you want it to be. Mark the positions with a pen.

9 To drill these holes in a central position, set the dividers to half the width of the wall (1.75 mm) and mark the centerpoint with a graver. To make the hole, I use my trusty bow drill for the job. First, drill a 1.5 mm pilot hole, then use the $\frac{1}{10}$ in (2.5 mm) drill to widen it.

10 Use a broacher to ease the hole to fit the tubing. You can see now the curve required to get the tubing to come from this hole.

CURVING THE TUBE

11 Anneal the tube and pickle. Feed some well-fitting wire into the tube, then ease the tube into a bend with your fingers, as close as you can to the end; repeat at the other end. Keep the middle as straight as you can.

Check that the snake chain can still pass through the tubing. It should be very slightly resistant, but not tight.

12 Hold one side of the tubing in position against the wall of the pebble and mark where its exit hole should go. Also mark the tubing just below where it will exit the wall. Cut the tube at this point. Drill and broach the hole as before. Repeat for the second piece of tubing.

13 Drill a small hole (0.8 mm or less) into one of the tubes—this is the breathing hole for normalizing the air pressure when soldering. Make sure to remove any burr from the inside of the tube using the tip of a drill bit.

14 Fit the tubing into the holes, first pushing the tubing into the bottom hole, then wriggling the top ends into the upper holes. Pass this whole assembly over the 450-grit wet and dry paper a few times to make sure that the wall edge is still flat.

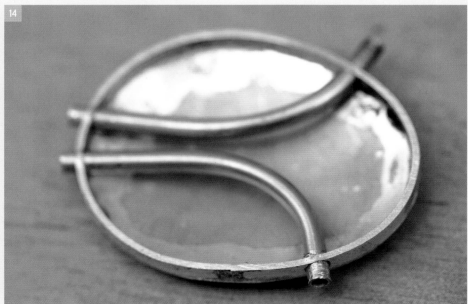

SOLDERING THE TUBING AND FRONT

15 Flux the inside of the wall and around the tube/wall joints. Use binding wire to hold the front face in position (see Step 7). Add tension loops to the wire to assist in tightening it.

Flux all the seams from the outside. Add small pallions of solder beside the tubing joint, and cut a few long, thin strips of the same solder ready for feeding into the seam when it's hot enough. Heat the whole thing and when the solder begins to melt around the tubing joint you are ready to add solder to the final seam. Touch your solder strip against the wall/front seam and watch the solder suck along the joint. Use the heat to draw the solder around the seam—make it travel as far as you can—adding a little more when required.

Leave to cool, but **do not immerse in pickle** as it will fill up through the breathing hole you made, and then you are in trouble!

16 Once it's cool enough to handle, file away all the excess silver (collecting all your filings for a casting or texturing project), then sand down and polish. Use the pendant drill, with wet and dry paper on a split pin mandrel to speed up the process. Remove any burrs that might have built up around the tubing. Gently scrub the surface all over with steel wool to give a soft sheen. This piece is now complete. Thread your chain through the pebble.

MAKING THE END BEADS

17 Use the foil pebbles as a template for cutting out your end beads—I like the two to be similar but not the same—and form as before in the hardwood block (see page 22). Remember you need mirror images when you shape them, especially if you are going for quirky shapes.

18 Tap back on the steel block to get flat edges and make flat on the 800-grit wet and dry paper. File a "v"-shaped groove at the top end of each side (so they match up) to allow a breathing hole, but at the same time marking where the chain will enter the bead.

19 Wire up and solder together—I use the feeding method again for this. Once more, do not immerse in pickle. Remove the binding wire and file the edges back and roughly clean up the surface of the bead.

20 Using the piercing saw and 3/0 blade, cut a "v" shape into the top of the soldered bead, where you made the breathing hole, approximately 1.6 mm wide at the top edge, going to a point 2 mm into the bead. Use a round file and then the 1.5 mm drill bit (held in a pin vise) to open up this "v" shape until the chain fits tightly into the bead. Clean up the surface and polish as before. If you want a shorter length of chain than the full 3 ft (1 m), now is the time to cut it to length. Remember it needs to be long enough to pass over your head!

21 Finally, mix the two-part epoxy glue, and using a needle, push a good amount into the hollow beads. Further coat the chain ends and then insert, making sure to wipe away all excess as you go. Leave to dry. Hey presto!

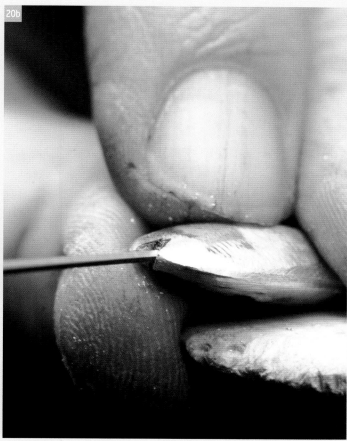

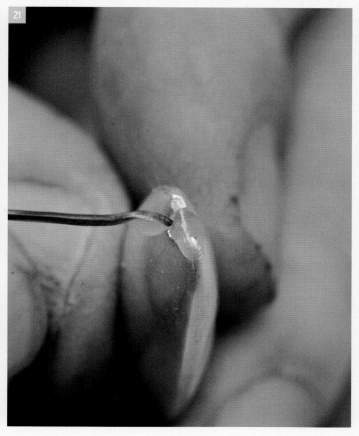

DESIGN INSPIRATION FROM AIR

Air is the least tangible of all the elements; there is no physical material for us to work with here other than invisible and unbounded gas. We must call on earth's material wealth to contain it or describe it. To invoke air in our designs, we need to rely on thought and wit—two of air's great offerings. Here are some thoughts on air.

AIR—SYMBOLIC OF SPIRIT, OF BEING ALIVE

Air's life-giving properties are in its constituent parts: oxygen and nitrogen. Its quality can change: respiration, expiration. Contamination; other gases can poison us. What does it look like? Invisible air, gaseous bonds. Atomic structures. Positive and negatively charged particles. Electricity.

CREATIVITY, INSPIRATION

The evolution of humankind began with questions. Why? How? Where? What? Who? The power of thought: electrical impulses communicate ideas in the brain and to the body to fashion our world. Technology changes everything. New beliefs. New materials. New problems.

Are we too big for our boots? Science and the thinking man versus nature and the elemental forces; man seeks dominion over all that exists. On a lighter note, consider how sound waves travel through the air, and how this affects us. We hear the voice, the drums, music, melody; bird song, a sweet mystery. Consider the animated conductor, sculpting a symphony of sound from the air, and how the heart quickens or falls to the beat of his whim. Air delivers our weather: a gentle breeze on a summer's day, fall leaves caught in an eddy; visualize the heady dance! Spin, sway, swing, swivel, bend, twirl, twist, vibrate, weave, wheel, whirl, wind, yaw, zephyr …. More weather—whirlwind, tornado, storm, rage!

Traveling through air—flight, birds on the wing, in formation, kite flying, airwaves, aerodynamics, travel in space, planets, other worlds, other dimensions. Heaven. Home of the Gods. Mercury, the messenger, winged feet, mobility, communication, quick-thinking, ideas, technology. Speed.

magic

power

electricity

airs and graces

mood

ambience

technology

tornado

wind

intangible/invisible

weather

thought

ideas

breeze

dance

communication

change

rhythm

movement

AIR

sound

flutter

music

voice

flight

breath

birds

lightness

life

feathers

flocking behavior

gas

quantum physics

atomic structures

mercury

speed

health

sky

the heavens

space

asteroids

science fiction

planetary activity

ATHENA
CONJURING FORM FROM CONCEPT

The Athena collection draws from several airy elements. Lightweight, shape-shifting forms combine a mercurial airiness with rhythmic lines, curves and punctuations–elements we might associate with music, flight, movement, wind, invisible energies, magic. The collection also takes influence from its namesake Athena (thought to derive from Aether, air and earth, ether), the warrior goddess, strategist, wise woman, and goddess of the weave. (Her symbols are the owl and the olive branch; Medusa on her shield.) The Athena collection infuses the wearer with her grace, her resplendent, sublime, commanding energies.

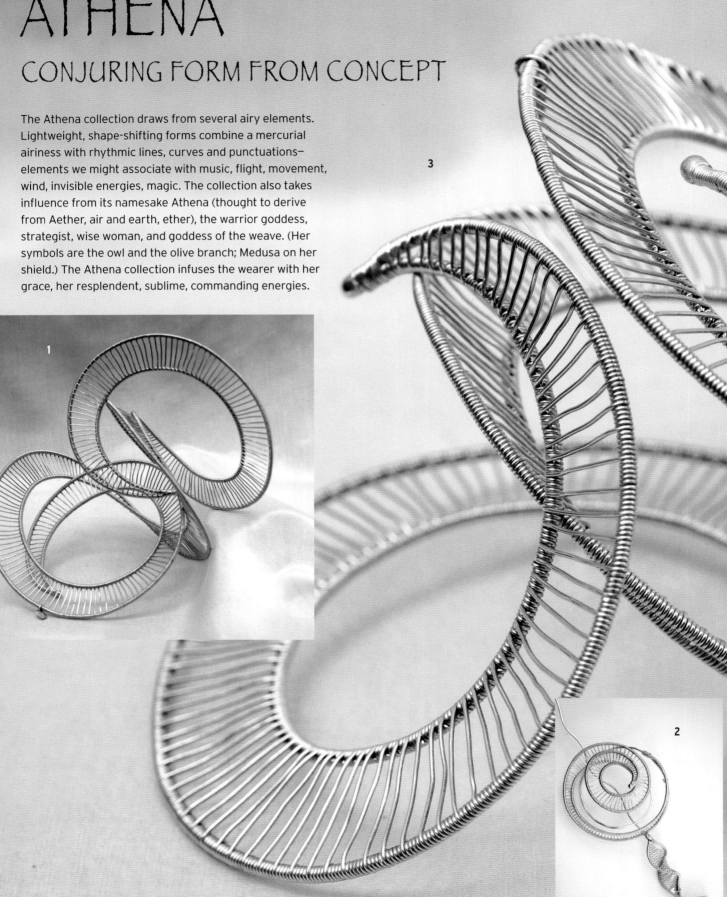

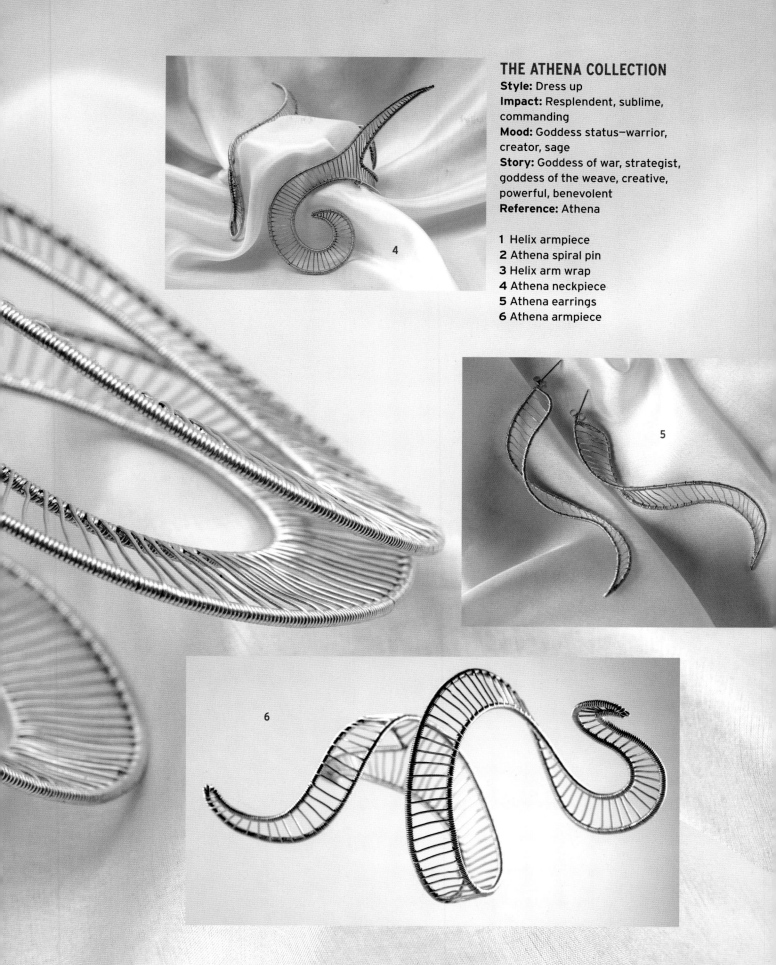

THE ATHENA COLLECTION

Style: Dress up
Impact: Resplendent, sublime, commanding
Mood: Goddess status—warrior, creator, sage
Story: Goddess of war, strategist, goddess of the weave, creative, powerful, benevolent
Reference: Athena

1 Helix armpiece
2 Athena spiral pin
3 Helix arm wrap
4 Athena neckpiece
5 Athena earrings
6 Athena armpiece

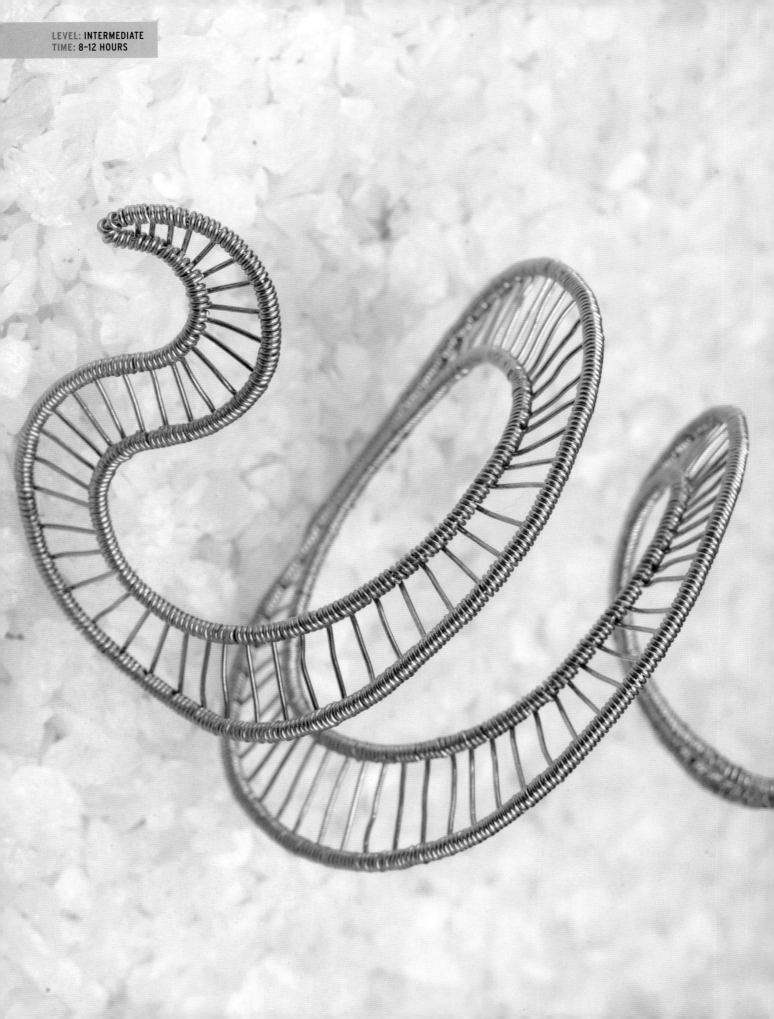

ATHENA ARMPIECE

This armpiece is made entirely from sterling silver wire, and with the exception of one small solder joint (to join the external framework together), the process of making requires only a few regular tools (see list below), a flight of fancy, and half a pound of patience!

One of the most difficult issues with this technique is dealing with wild-minded and long wires; over time I have learnt to wind these lengths into tidy coils. Held with simple binding wire twists, this allows you to extract any length of wire as required without mess or difficulty.

You don't need to stick to the precise pattern shown here—allow the process and the emerging form to interplay with your own intentions. For the making, it is better to start with more wire than you need. This approach also gives ample opportunity to let loose your spiraling form once you have found your rhythm. Personally, I enjoy the meditative state that the repetitive process induces. Here there is space to weave mindfully your intent into form.

If you are interested to see how this armpiece might look in gold, it is possible to have it plated, as I have done here. I like to use 22 karat gold plating, as this gives a beautifully rich color to the metal.

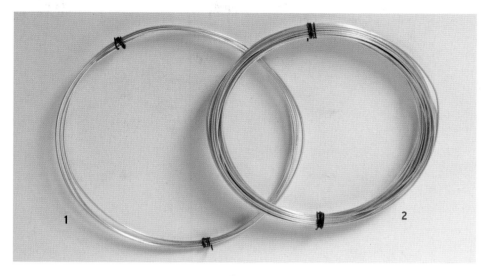

MATERIALS
1. Soft sterling silver wire, 0.7 mm diameter, 49 ft (15 m) long, in coils or reels, for making radial wires
2. Hard sterling silver wire, 1 mm diameter, 5 ft (1.5 m) long, for making core wires

TOOLS
- Small round objects for forming the core wires—e.g. small bottles, lids, and jars
- Pliers (see page 180): flat-nosed pliers, snipe-nosed pliers
- Wire cutters (see page 178)
- Needle file (see page 179) for filing the core wires prior to soldering
- Soldering equipment (see pages 182 and 183): flux, brush, hard solder, hard solder paste syringe (a ready mix of powdered solder with flux, sold in a syringe for precise placement, indispensable when soldering small wires together), soldering block, torch, tweezers, and pickle
- Wet and dry paper (see page 184), 1200 grit or emery papers

UNDERSTANDING THE WRAPPING PATTERN

The numbers in brackets relate to the number of wraps for each radial wire, with the first (bold) number being for the wire furthest away from you, and the second being the wire nearest to you. Where there are two sets of numbers, this refers to an alternating pair, so for example 10(**4**/7,**7**/8) would mean that you make a 4/7 then a 7/8, and you need to repeat this pattern 10 times.

NOTES
CORE WIRE This is the 1 mm wire, which you use to create the framework for wrapping.
RADIAL WIRE This is the 0.7 mm wire, which you use to span between the framework, and also to wrap it.

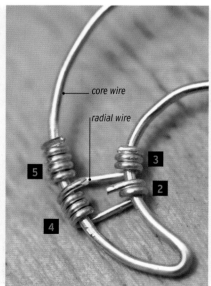

core wire

radial wire

Start 3/8 in (10 mm) from end, this pattern is for the shape shown yours may vary.

1 x	(**4**/2)
2 x	(**5**/3)
4 x	(**6**/2)
1 x	(**6**/3)
1 x	(**5**/3)
2 x	(**4**/3)
1 x	(**5**/5)
1 x	(**4**/6)
1 x	(**3**/6)
2 x	(**2**/6)
11 x	(**3**/6)
10 x	(**4**/7,**5**/7)
6 x	(**5**/6,**5**/7)
7 x	(**5**/7,**4**/7)
7 x	(**5**/7,**4**/6)
4 x	(**4**/6,**5**/6)
4 x	(**4**/6,**3**/5)
15 x	(**5**/4)
10 x	(**3**/4)
1 x	(**3**/3)

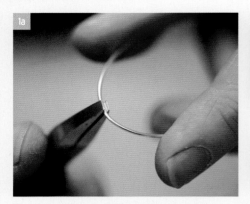

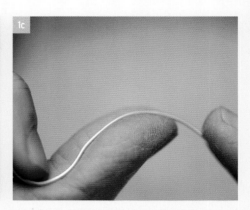

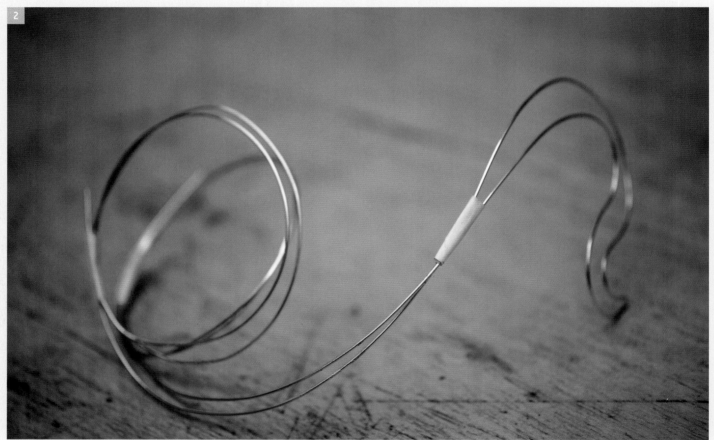

MAKING THE FRAMEWORK

1 Before you begin, if you're working with new pliers, use an 800-grit wet and dry paper on a stick to rub the sharpness off the edges of new pliers to avoid damage to your wire. For wirework, it's important that your pliers fit comfortably in your hand. (Buy the best that you can afford, you will love them, and anyway cheaper versions tend to give you blisters as well as working loose at the pivot!)

Start with a sharp bend in the middle of the core wire; this bend forms the uppermost point of the serpent-like spiral for the armpiece. The flat pliers are very good for sharpening this bend to a pleasing, tapering shape. Make coils from the ends of your wires, to keep them tidy and manageable.

2 Now sketch out the general curves for the next 6 1/4 in (160 mm) of the core wire. The first curves from this folding point should writhe like a snake, so keep them tight. Allow the core wires to get gradually wider apart as these curves evolve. Don't be too precise about your initial form—you can make changes along the way. It's helpful to use masking tape to hold these wires in place as you work into the form (see above). I use a combination of finger and thumb pressure to make my curves, also sometimes working around curved objects such as bottles or jars. As a general rule, the core wires should be **up to** 3/4 in (20 mm) apart. (You can make this distance wider, but the radial wires you put in to span this gap will be more vulnerable to mis-shaping.)

BEGINNING THE BINDING

3 You need to establish first a comfortable working position. Left-handers should hold the framework in the right hand, with the open ends flowing to the left. Right-handers will find it easier to hold the framework in the left hand with the open ends flowing to the right. Your wraps should always rotate away from your "holding" hand. The length of wire required to make each segment will depend on the number of wraps you need to make, and the distance you need to span between the two core wires. Work directly from the coil of wire for each radial; this helps to get the length right for each one. As a rule, it takes about 1/4 in (5 mm) of this 0.7 mm wire to make one wrap around the 1 mm framework. Begin your first radial at least 3/8 in (10 mm) from the tip of your spiral. You will complete all the tips at the very end.

4 From the reel of wire, stretch out about 3 in (80 mm) for your first radial. Using your index finger and thumb, hold the radial (0.7 mm) wire against the outside core (1 mm) wire. Allow 1 1/4 in (30 mm) of this wire to extend beyond, and using snipe-nosed pliers in your dominant hand, bend this "tail" over the core wire and wrap tightly four times. Make sure that there are no gaps between the coils. Pull the excess toward you. DO NOT TRIM. You may need this extra length later to adjust the tension.

Holding the radial wire across the gap between the two core wires, allow 3/5 in (15 mm) to extend beyond the internal core, then cut the radial wire from the reel. Now wrap as before, two times, and push the remaining end back toward the far side. DO NOT TRIM. You may need this extra length later to adjust the tension.

The next radial requires five wraps (allow 1 1/4 in/30 mm) on the far side, and three wraps closest to you (allow 3/4 in/20 mm). Repeat this process twice, making sure that each time the wrapping is on the same side of the wires. I always hold the radial wire underneath the core wire. Follow the tapering curves, allowing your radials to get wider or thinner according to your desired shape.

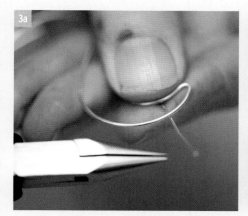

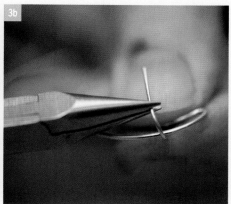

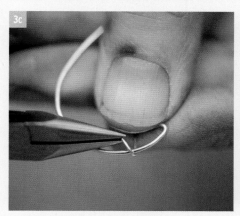

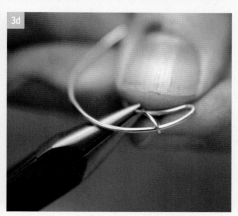

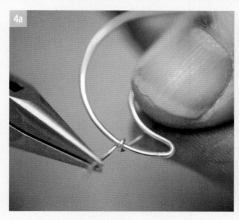

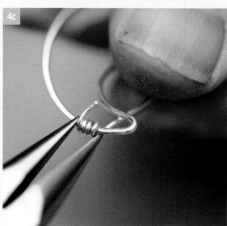

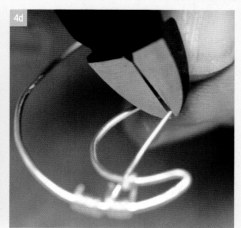

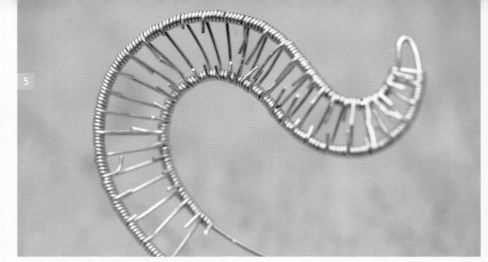

FORMING THE SHAPE

As your snake writhes and twists, the outside curve will become the inside curve, so move with it. You will need to adjust the numbers of wraps for each wire, according to the curve you are making. From 5/3 you will gradually need to drop to 4/2, then as the curve reverses increase your wraps to 4/5 and 3/6. Straighter sections work better with a 5/6 or 5/7 ratio

The next 9 1/2 in (240 mm) of your core wires need to perform a function. This part of the armpiece provides the gripping form that will make the piece wearable, rather than just a beautiful sculpture!

5 Choose the inside core wire to follow the form of your arm. Shape as before, either by hand or using other round objects, to create a curve that is faithful to your arm. Mine turns out to be quite oval in shape.

6 Allow the outside core wire to follow the same general curve, at a distance of 3/5–3/4 in (15-20 mm), according to your preference. Play with the way it can move from a horizontal to vertical plane, in relation to the inside core. When you have found the shape you like, use masking tape at various intervals to help tie these curves together.

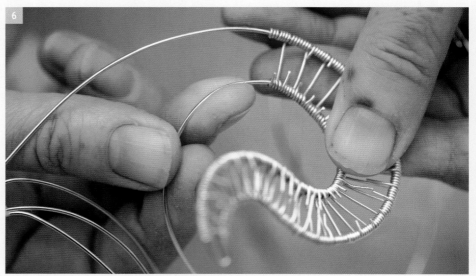

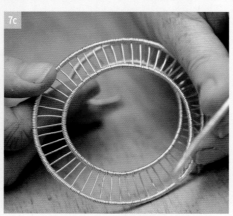

7 Start to fill in the shape with radials, following the same technique as before. Now that you are working with your radials all at the same length, once you have made a few you can begin to spread them out along the core wires in place of the masking tape. You may find that your framework begins to pull together as you work; insert the tips of the pliers between the core wires and force them open to widen areas where the core wires are not parallel.

Periodically you need to check over your work for tightness and regularity. Use the extra lengths of the radial tails to add extra coils if necessary, to keep the radials in line. You can always insert extra radials where necessary to adjust the shape or the curve balance.

From this point your core wires are getting closer and closer together, finally to the position where you will solder the two together to complete the form. Bend them into pleasing curves, and at an appropriate place bend one of these wires to make a sharp point, as you did at the very beginning in Step 1 (see page 34).

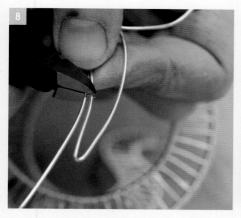

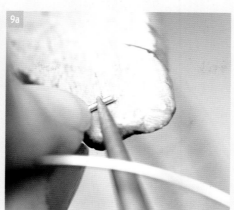

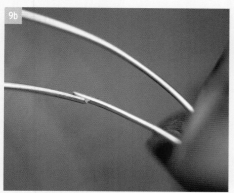

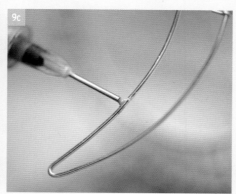

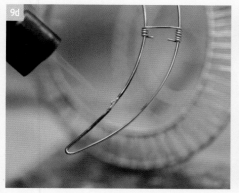

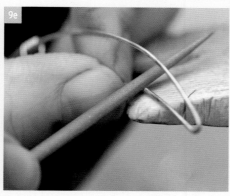

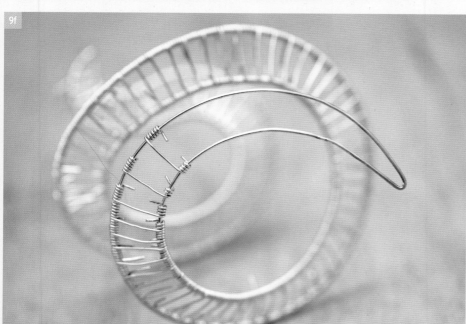

SOLDERING AND FINISHING

8 At some point you will find that the core wires cross. In a minute you need to cut them at the most appropriate point, and solder them together, but to make this job easier for you it's a good idea to add some more radials between the framework of core wires you have just created. These radials will give structure to the wires, making the soldering job easier.

9 When you are entirely happy with the overall form, cut the wires and file both parts to make a perfect lap joint. Add additional radials if necessary to help keep these ends together for soldering. Take the necessary health and safety precautions before you begin soldering (see page 183). Solder using hard solder, and keep a pair of tweezers handy! Clean up the joint with files and wet and dry papers—you should get away without having to put the piece in pickle. Continue to fill the framework now with radials until the form is entirely complete. The last places requiring attention are the two points you have made. Carefully work your radial wire around each to blend with the wrap-work.

10 Use side cutters to trim all the excess ends. (Keep trimmings to melt down for a casting project.) Use the flat-nosed piers to smooth the newly cut ends down and around the core. You should find that they tuck neatly inside the gap made by the next radial along. Check the armpiece for size. You can gently readjust the form to fit if necessary. Days have passed. Feel good about your beautiful creation. Wear it with pride!

DESIGN INSPIRATION FROM FIRE

From fire's embers we can extract beautiful materials to make our jewelry. Silver and gold, obsidian and diamonds, metals, and precious stones spew from our earth's fiery core. Fire is the jeweler's friend as we transform with a torch our raw materials into purposefully shaped items of adornment. Here are some thoughts on fire.

FIRE—THE STATE CHANGER

Our power of fire distinguishes us from all other animals. It is the source of our evolution. Providing light, heat, and protection, this element is the source of irreversible transformation, in multiple contexts.

Fire needs air to burn; it boils water and scorches earth's life forms, releasing gases in the process, yet water can quench it and earth can smother it. These qualities we also attribute to our fiery emotions: lust, passion, tempestuous outbursts. Fireworks! Crackle, pop, bang!

From lust to love, to the hearth, and the warmth, comfort, and security that fire affords us. Looking into the embers, we lose ourselves in story, mythical creatures rise from the flames: the dragon, the phoenix.

Dancing around the bonfire, we invoke the spirit world—primal magic, purification rituals. Celebrations. By this same hand of fate, the witch is exorcized, she is burnt at the stake.

The Greek goddess Hestia, known by the Romans as Vesta, guardian spirit of the hearth, home, and family. The pagan goddess Brigid (her name means "fiery arrow"), ruling over all things of high dimension, including forging.

Raking through the ashes of the bonfire, we find all else that was not released to the spirit world: lumps of fused glass and nuggets of metals ....

Magma spews from earth's fiery core, a molten mass of minerals that cool to form igneous rock. More heat combined with pressure further transform to create metamorphic rock. Among the rock, our favorite minerals form, precious metals and gemstones. From the softest opaque drawing material (graphite) to the hardest, most lustrous (and lusted-after) gem, carbon becomes diamond.

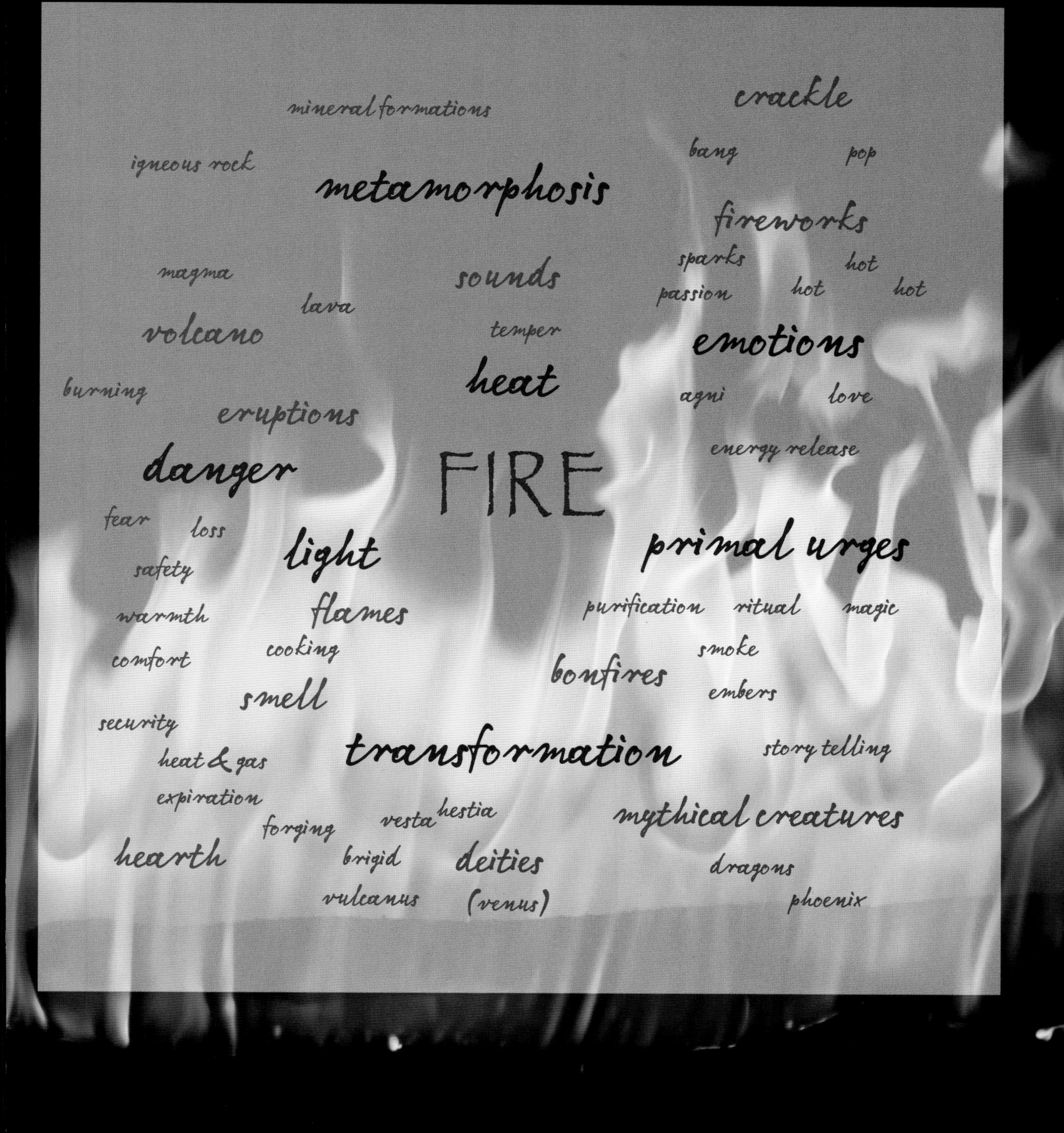

mineral formations

crackle

igneous rock

bang   pop

metamorphosis

fireworks

sparks

magma

sounds

passion   hot   hot   hot

lava

volcano

temper

emotions

heat

burning

agni   love

eruptions

FIRE

energy release

danger

primal urges

fear   loss

safety

light

purification   ritual   magic

warmth

flames

smoke

comfort

cooking

bonfires

embers

smell

security

heat & gas

transformation

story telling

expiration

forging   vesta hestia

mythical creatures

hearth

brigid

deities

dragons

vulcanus   (venus)

phoenix

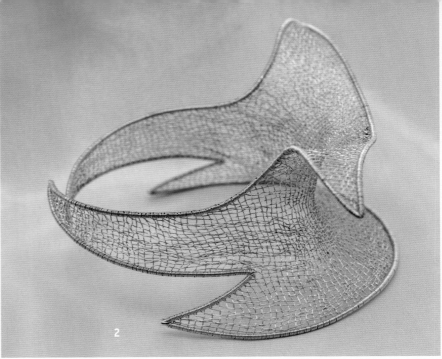

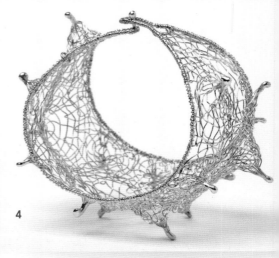

THE VENUS COLLECTION

Style: Dress up
Impact: Elegance, desire
Mood: Goddess status: playful, seductive, abundant
Story: Weaving magic into form; wrapping the body with sparkling threads; to be unwrapped

Reference: Venus; Elizabethan collars, corsets

1 Galaxy pendant
2 Goddess neckpiece
3 Rose neckpiece
4 Spiky bangle
5 Venus collar
6 Venus ring
7 Venus star bracelet
8 Venus star reticule

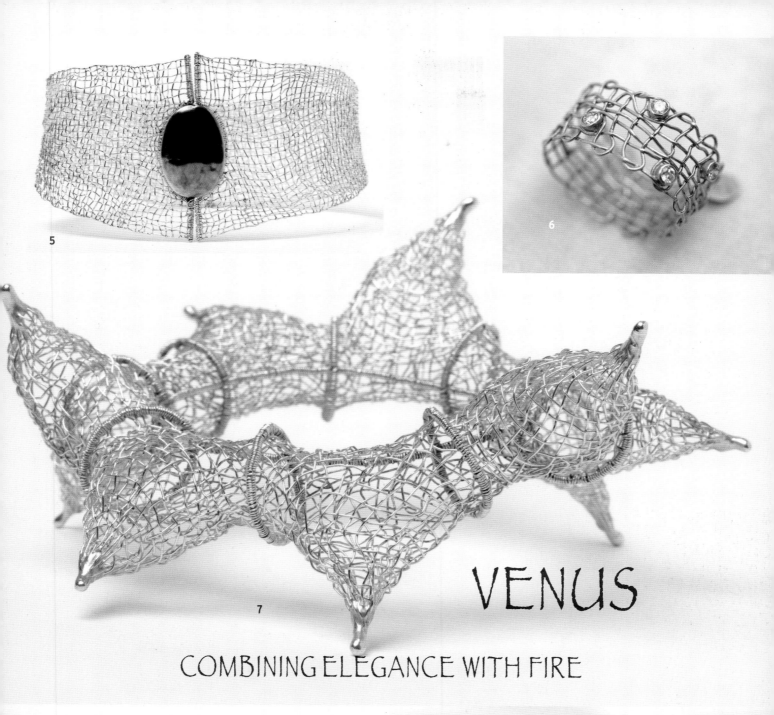

5

6

7

VENUS

COMBINING ELEGANCE WITH FIRE

The Venus collection suffuses earthly beauty with fire's sparkling and transformative energies. Fine silver and gold wires interweave to create dramatic, shimmering forms. Here and there, embedded in the weave, a scattering of tiny diamonds breathes life into a ring, or a half-hidden treasure dances inside its protective, spiky shell.

In keeping with fire's story-telling tradition, this collection draws from myth and fairy tale, also referencing historical costume, and so in the making, each piece weaves a beginning, a drama waiting for the wearer to unfold.

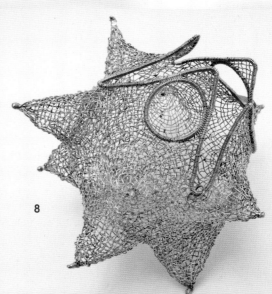

8

VENUS RING

I have made endless variations of this ring over the years; the first gold and diamond version became known as the Cinderella ring as so many hopeful ladies tried in vain to fit it—eventually she came, and her handsome prince (husband) slipped it on her finger forever. I'm not sure that he also realized that his gift was a freedom pass from the kitchen chores ....

The beauty of this ring lies in the fineness of the woven wires and the sparkle of the stones. It's a delicate and powerful piece, designed for a refined hand out on a night of seduction; if you wear it while cleaning house and putting the trash out it will lose the will to live!

To make the Venus ring more durable, if you get the hang of working with solder paste, you can add strength and structure to the ring by soldering all the weave joints in turn—but you will need to take extra care not to melt the silver wires while you are soldering.

MATERIALS

1) Sterling silver tubing, 2.2 mm external diameter, 3/4 in (20 mm) long
2) Sterling silver wire, 0.5 mm diameter, 3 ft (1 m) long
3) 5 x cubic zirconium or other stones, 1.75 mm diameter

TOOLS

- Steel rule
- 30 panel pins to use as pegs when weaving
- Honeycomb soldering board (see below right and page 183) for weaving the silver wire
- Snipe-nosed pliers (see page 180)
- Wire cutters (see page 178)
- Fine-line permanent pen
- Soldering equipment (see page 183): flux (borax), brush, solder paste, torch, tweezers, soldering block, and pickle
- Ring mandrel (see page 181)
- Mallet and boxwood mallet (see page 180)
- Tube cutting jig (see below right and page 181)
- Needle file (see page 179)
- Piercing saw (see page 178), 4/0 blades
- 1.75 mm stone-setting burr (see page 182)
- Pin vise (see page 179)
- Loupe (see page 182)
- Wall putty (see below right)
- Pusher (see below right and page 182)
- Burnisher (see page 182)

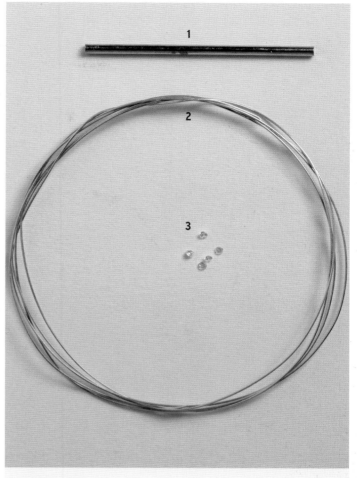

WORKING WITH STERLING SILVER WIRE

I like to use sterling silver wire when I weave, because the slight hardness of the metal helps to give structure to my final form. During the weaving process, sterling silver tends to become uncooperative and stiff after the shortest of working times, and it will give you sore fingers. It is also possible to use fine silver for weaving, but being so pure this type of silver is also soft, and even the gentlest hand pressure will distort the final outcome. However, fine silver is easier to manipulate and it requires no annealing during the working process (and it doesn't get fire stain through heating processes).

TOOLS TIPS

WALL PUTTY I always use wall putty rather than setters wax when I'm handling stone— it's easy and clean to work with and has sufficient stickiness to pick up a stone without leaving a residue.

PUSHER When you buy a pusher usually the tool face is rough, and the edges sharp and unfinished. Use wet and dry paper on a stick to remove the sharpness of those edges, and polish the whole of the tool end to a high shine.

TUBE CUTTING JIG This tool is a fantastic aid when you have lots of pieces of tube to cut to a specific size. The tool also guides your blade to cut a nice 90-degree angle, and if you remove the end stop you can use it to file the tube ends square and flat too.

HONEYCOMB SOLDERING BOARD This type of board is intended for soldering; the tiny holes that run through the block allow heat to dissipate as you apply the flame to your metal, so it gives added temperature control for tricky soldering jobs. Of course we can also use those holes to assist in binding or pinning objects for soldering, and for this project we use them as a means to assist in the weaving of the ring. If you go on to design more complex items using this technique, you have the added bonus of being able to solder with everything held in place.

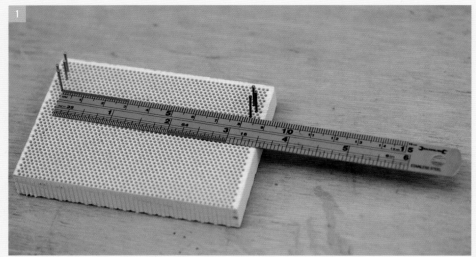

WEAVING THE RING

1 Measure your ring size and convert it to the circumference length, so you know before you start what you are aiming for. Now place three pins in staggered holes at the top end of the honeycomb board, and three more in alignment at the other end. This should give around 2 3/4 in (72 mm) distance between them.

2 Wrap the end of the sterling wire around the first of the pins, then take it down, and wrap around its aligned partner at the bottom. Continue back and forth until you have five lengths of wire—these are the warp wires. Don't cut the wire. You work with them as a continuous length, making the woven strip easy to handle as you weave it.

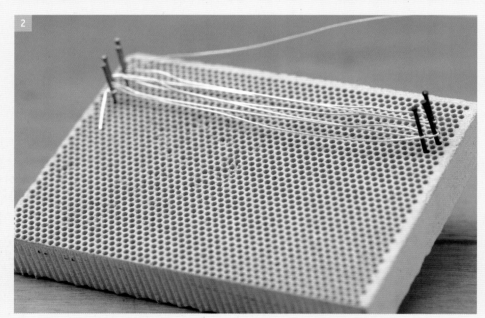

3 Wrap the wire an extra time around the last pin to affirm the changeover from warp to weft, then fold the remaining wire about one-third of the way from the end. This makes the weft (horizontal) wire easier to weave through the warp (vertical) wires.

4 Starting from left to right, begin to weave through the vertical wires. As you weave through these wires, use the tips of the snipe-nosed pliers to help push each weft as close to the last as possible. Don't expect it to behave—it will take a wobbly form of its own as you work your way down. This gives the ring character. At the end of each weft, put a pin into the appropriate hole of the honeycomb board and use this to keep your edges relatively uniform.

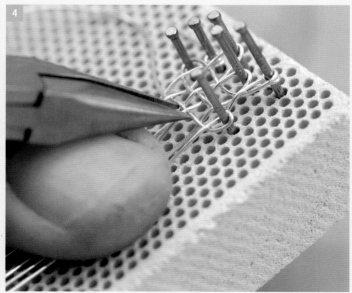

5 Soon, you will find that the warp wires are so taut that you can't push the weft wire through them. To solve this problem take the end pins out and move them in by a line to provide some slack. Continue weaving in this vein until you have reached your target length—in my case, 2 in (56 mm). This length is measured from the first weft line to the last, and you need to make this last weft wire travel from right to left. Mark the length—start and finish—onto the warp wires with a permanent pen.

6 Using wire cutters, cut the warp wires with 1 mm extra at each end. This extra length provides you with enough overlap to intertwine the wires to make the band. Use the pliers to manipulate the ends into a comfortable (and invisible) position ready for soldering.

7 Take the necessary health and safety precautions before you begin soldering (see page 183). Use the solder paste to solder these ends into position. Pickle clean, and file away any visible excess. Make round using finger pressure on the ring mandrel, and tap gently with a mallet to make the ring bigger if necessary.

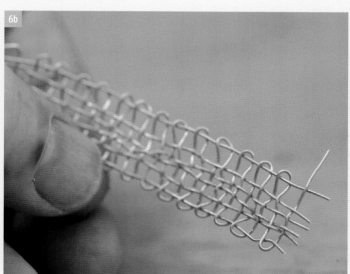

MAKING THE STONE SETTINGS AND SETTING THE STONES

8 Cut five (or more, depending on how many stones you wish to set) pieces of tubing 2 mm in length, using the tube cutting jig to assist in measuring equal lengths and ensuring straight cuts. These pieces of tubing are held in place by the tension of the woven wires—push each one into a gap in the weave, making sure that you are creating a good pattern.

9 Apply solder paste around the pieces of tubing wherever there is contact with the woven wires, at the same time with your finger making sure that the tubes are flush with the internal surface of the ring so that it will be comfortable to wear. Solder and pickle clean.

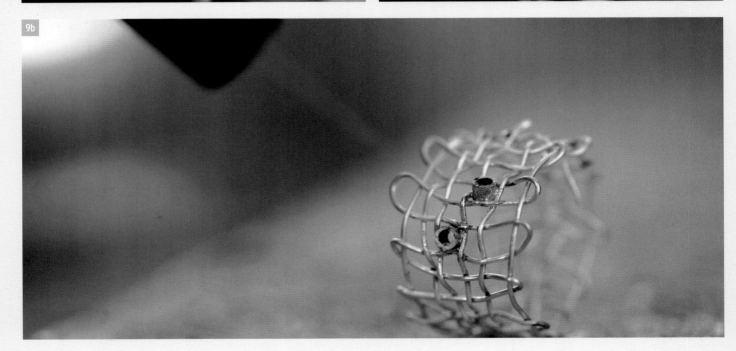

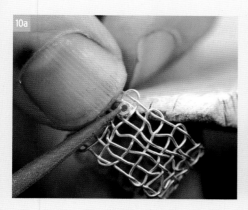

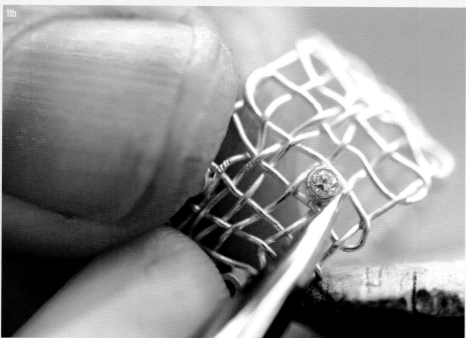

10 File the tubes so they rise 0.5 mm above the surface of the woven band. Drill into the tubing with the 1.75 mm stone-setting burr. I mount the burr in a pin vise and drill the tubing by hand, for optimum control.

11 Check the stones for fit—use a loupe if you need to—there should be at least 0.3 mm of the silver wall rising above the girdle of the stone to be set. Set the stones, one at a time. Use a pusher to coax gently the wall down onto the stone (north/south/east/west). Finish the job using a burnisher to give an even, shiny appearance to the sparkly stone. Check with wall putty whether the stone is sufficiently held in place.

12 Finally, gently tap around the whole ring on a mandrel, using a boxwood mallet, to toughen up the silver weave. The ring is now ready to wear.

DESIGN INSPIRATION FROM WATER

Water brings many treasures for the jeweler to enjoy: everything from pearls and coral to a shark's tooth. The boundaries blur between the water and the earth as we scour the water's edge for inspirational materials. I cannot think of water without it also invoking sound …. Here are some thoughts on water.

H_2O-LIFE DEPENDS ON IT

This shape-shifter element exists in multiple states: fluid as water, hard as ice, and gaseous as steam. Hot water rises and yet ice will float on it. We like to float on it too. Flotsam and jetsam. Having no pre-determined form itself, water fills any cavity, permeates all porous substances in its desire to get to the bottom of the earth's gravitational pull. And yet the sun and the moon will pull it back.

Where does water come from? Springs, lakes, streams, rivers, estuaries, the sea. Through evaporation to precipitation, the cycle is without beginning or end. Drawn by the moon, the sea's tides ebb and flow across our shores. Rhythmic waves can soothe our senses and yet gentle ripples become ever larger and terrifying under the influences of forceful weather patterns or earthquakes.

WATER'S TREASURE

Pearls, shells, and coral: a pirate's hoard! The process of flow wears the roughest, hardest surface to smoothness over time; water freezes and expands to crack rock into ever smaller pieces, and so earth's gems are released to us by nature's force. Hot waters, bathed in love, steamy romance, quenching the flames of passion, floods of tears, drowning in misery, washed clean, cold as ice. So many associations exist for life-giving water.

Home to the emotions and intuition, water also provides shelter to aquatic life. Salt water and fresh water, creatures swim, wriggle, leap through the mind's eye. Primordial soup—we came from it.

Drip, trickle, splish splash splosh, stamping in puddles! Childhood games, never mind the rain. The smell of damp clothes. Holy Water, it's a blessing.

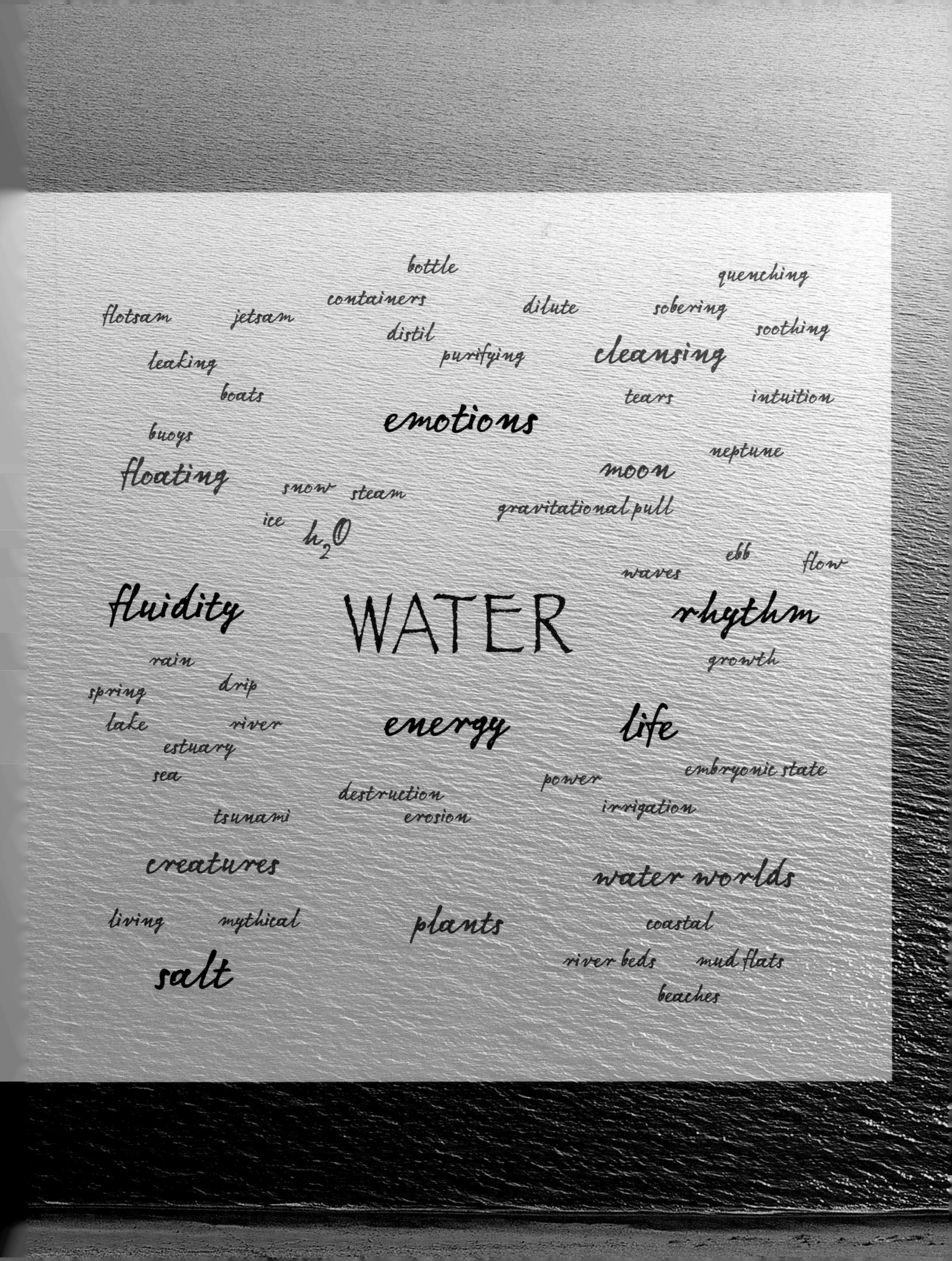

bottle

flotsam   jetsam   containers   dilute   sobering   quenching

distil   cleansing   soothing

leaking   purifying

boats   emotions   tears   intuition

buoys   neptune

floating   snow   steam   moon

ice h_2O gravitational pull

waves   ebb   flow

fluidity   WATER   rhythm

rain   growth

spring   drip

lake   river   energy   life

estuary

sea   embryonic state

destruction   power

tsunami   erosion   irrigation

creatures   water worlds

living   mythical   plants   coastal

river beds   mud flats

salt   beaches

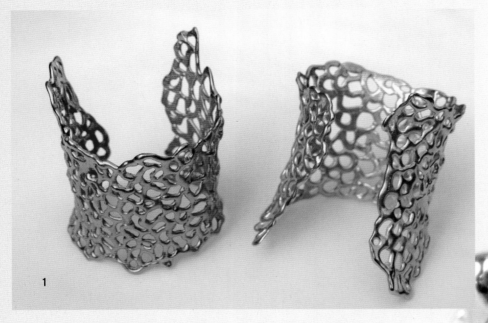

1

2

PRECIOUS

FLUID FORMS INSPIRED BY THE OCEAN

The Precious collection takes inspiration from the ocean's treasures. Rapturous forms are sculpted in silver and gold, their internal precious spaces filled with gems (or secrets)—a siren's delight! Suggestive of coral and sponges, the pieces in this collection express a delight in the fluidity of the technical process and pleasure in the preciousness of the material. They are joyous and playful objects to wear.

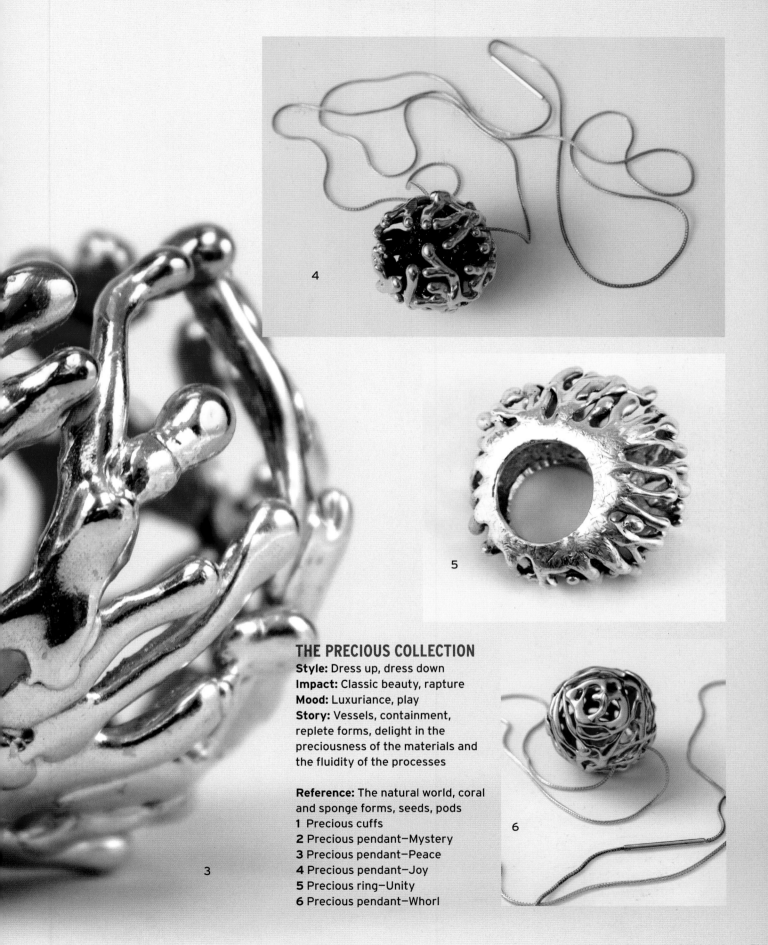

THE PRECIOUS COLLECTION
Style: Dress up, dress down
Impact: Classic beauty, rapture
Mood: Luxuriance, play
Story: Vessels, containment, replete forms, delight in the preciousness of the materials and the fluidity of the processes

Reference: The natural world, coral and sponge forms, seeds, pods
1 Precious cuffs
2 Precious pendant—Mystery
3 Precious pendant—Peace
4 Precious pendant—Joy
5 Precious ring—Unity
6 Precious pendant—Whorl

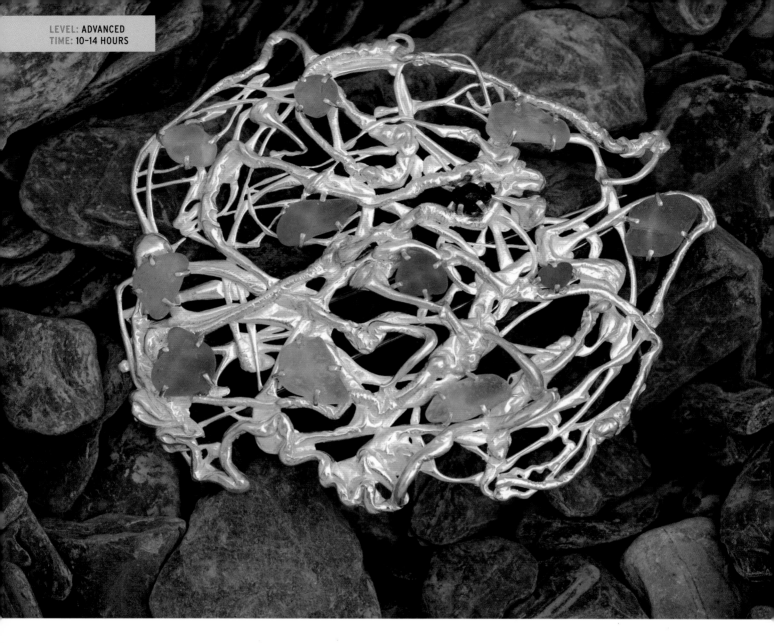

ROCK POOL PIN

Treasures! Rock and seaweed, limpets and barnacles, pretty shells and sparkly pebbles; anemones swaying in gentle currents caused by a light breeze, a scurrying shrimp, a shifty crab scuttles from niche to crevice. Green, pink, white, brown, black, red and shiny, colors are so vivid in salty water and sunlight. Half-forgotten childhood games float by ... I can lose myself in a good rock pool.

In its making, the rock pool pin recalls that sense of play as you pour hot wax onto water to make attractive ribbons of seaweed, and glistening surface ripples. Once cast, the pin is embellished with treasures—in my case diamonds (sea glass if you don't believe in magic), gathered in the moonlight from the shores of Tenerife.

Your treasures can be any precious stones, shells, or other found objects that suit your pin, and when finished, your whimsical piece will look unique.

Once you have made the wax for the pin, it will need to be cast. I had mine cast in silver, but you can cast yours in brass or bronze. This form of casting requires expensive equipment and the process itself is very complex, messy, and dangerous. There are experts who know how to get the best possible results from my waxes and it makes sense to utilize their expertise. However, it is extremely useful to know how the casting process works in order to get the most from this technique (see box opposite). Remember to calculate the casters' turnaround time into the making time for this project.

MATERIALS

1. 2 x sterling silver wires, 1.5 mm diameter, 1½ in (40 mm) long, and 0.8 mm diameter, 20 in (500 mm) long
2. Sterling silver tubing, 1 mm internal diameter, ³/₈ in (10 mm) long
3. Stainless steel wire (see below right), 1 mm diameter, 7 in (180 mm) long
4. 9 karat yellow or red gold wire, 0.8 mm diameter, 1¼ in (30 mm) long (optional)
5. Jeweler's wax (see below right), green or blue wax
6. Sea glass, collected from beaches, or other sea treasures

TOOLS

- Heavy-bottomed pan for melting the wax
- Hot plate for heating up the wax
- Ladle for ladling the hot wax into water
- Large dish, three-quarters filled with water
- Bristle brush and pumice (see page 185) to clean up the casting
- Piercing saw (see page 178), 0, 8/0 blades
- Pendant drill (see page 182), diamond-tipped grinding wheels, and polishing wheels
- Files (see page 179): three-square file; half-round needle files; thin (slotting) files, 0.36 mm, 0.46 mm
- Wire cutters and snips (see page 178)
- Soldering equipment (see pages 182 and 183): flux, brush, hard solder strip, easy solder paste, torch, tweezers, soldering block, and pickle
- Planishing hammer and steel block (see pages 180 and 181)
- Pliers (see page 180): snipe-nosed pliers, round-nosed pliers, flat-nosed pliers, and parallel pliers
- Sprung tweezers (see page 183)
- Ruler and fine-line permanent pen
- Thermo-gel for protecting delicate items from excessive heat
- Wet and dry paper (see page 184), 880 grit
- Pusher (see page 182) for setting the sea glass
- Burnisher (see page 182)
- Diamond-tipped burr (see page 182)

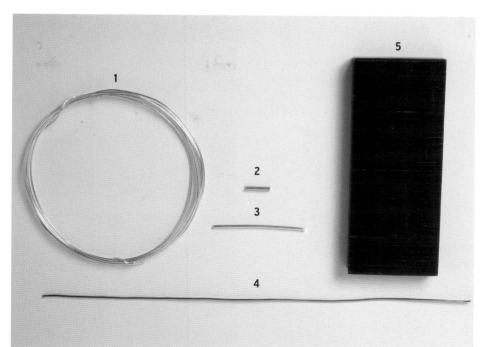

MATERIALS AND TOOLS TIPS

STAINLESS STEEL This metal makes for a good fastening, because it is suitably hard and won't corrode. Don't try to cut it with your snips—it will ruin them. Instead, use the edge of an old three-square file to cut a groove into it. The same goes for filing—keep special files for this kind of work, as it will wear down the cutting teeth of your ordinary tools. Diamond-tipped tools will work well.

WAXES To be sure of the best possible result from your original, it is best to use professional jewelry waxes, which are known to burn out without leaving residue in the mold. The standard waxes are available in green, blue, purple, and red. Each has its own distinct set of behaviors, with green being the hardest (and brittle), to red being almost plasticine (soft). Experiment with each to see how you can exploit their characteristics. All these waxes have a plastic content, and melting should be carried out in a well-ventilated area, and make sure that you don't heat them to smoking point!

LOST WAX CASTING OVERVIEW

For the lost wax casting process, your wax model will have one or more sprues added to it before being coated in investment (plaster). It is put in a can, dried, then the can is put into an oven to burn out the wax, leaving a cavity in the shape of your design (hence the term "lost wax"). The can is mounted onto the receiving end of the arm of the centrifugal casting machine, your metal of choice is melted, and at the critical temperature is flung into the mold via the sprue. The arm rotation creates a throwing action to make sure that the whole cavity is filled with the metal.

CREATING THE BASE

1 Melt the wax in your pan, keeping an eye on the temperature–do not to let the wax get to smoking hot. Turn the temperature down when the wax has become liquid, then pour a ladleful of the wax onto the water in the dish and let the stream of wax squiggle across the surface. Stop pouring when there seem to be enough interesting shapes.

2 Let the wax solidify for a few moments before removing it from the bowl and turning it over to see its most interesting face. Put it to one side and do another. Be ready to try several times before getting a result you like. Try fast/slow/sweeping curves/jiggly movements to see what you can conjure up. There's no wastage here, in that once dried, the less interesting waxes can be put back into the melting pot.

Take your favorite piece to the casters, making sure that you tell them to sprue the piece from the side that you consider to be the back.

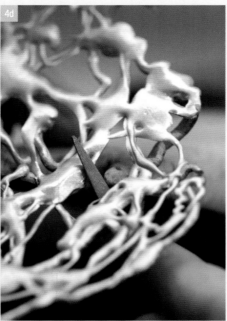

CLEANING UP THE CASTINGS

3 Your piece will come back from the casters with sprue stumps on the back, which, very annoyingly, you will have to remove with a piercing saw and 0 blade; it's a horrible job. Before tackling the sprues, give the front surface a bristle brush (with a little soap and pumice, if you like). Avoid cutting too close to the pin surface, and check you aren't causing damage with the blade elsewhere.

4 Once cut, use a diamond-tipped grinding wheel in the pendant drill to grind down the remaining stumps. I find this job deeply rewarding after the last 5 minutes of strife.

Use latex/grit wheels to smooth down these last grinding marks, making the slight bumps more integral to the squiggles of your rock pool. Using a needle file, file any rough edges if necessary.

ARRANGING YOUR TREASURES

5 This is where the fun starts. Find the right pieces to nestle into your forms, also paying close attention to balancing the colors. Take several snapshots of the arrangements, if you would like to remind yourself later.

Once you know which pieces you are going to use, you need to make the claw settings for them. In my pin, I used mostly silver, but, to emphasize the small piece of obsidian (the stone sitting on the pin, front left), my most precious find, I used 9 karat gold wire for this one.

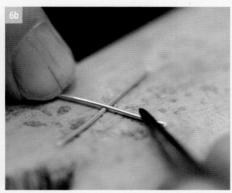

MAKING THE CLAW SETTINGS

6 Cut the 0.8 mm wire into ³/₅ in (15 mm) lengths. Use the slotting files to make a groove in each wire, to halfway through. Overlap the two wires at the grooves to make a cross formation. Take the necessary health and safety precautions before you begin soldering (see page 183). Add a little solder paste to the joint and solder them together.

7 Flatten at the joint using a planishing hammer on a steel block. Place the cross under one of your stones, then using finger pressure, push the claws around to hold the stone tightly. Complete all the settings in this way. You may find pliers helpful (I used flat-nosed pliers here) to grip the stone in position against the crossed wire as you bend. Set aside.

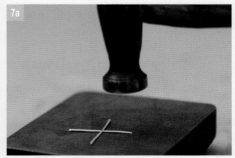

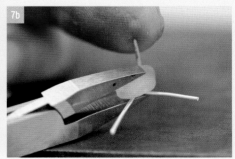

MAKING THE HINGE AND CLASP FOR THE FASTENING

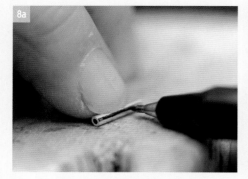

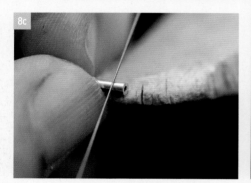

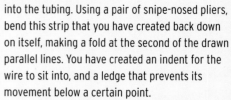

8 The hinge for the double fastening needs to be made first. You want to give some upward spring to the fastening once it is in the hinge. Draw a line 2 mm from each end of the tubing, and also two lines along the length of the tubing, about 2 mm apart. Take one end and, using a piercing saw and 8/0 blade, cut vertically into the tubing down the top parallel line, until you reach the perpendicular line. Now cut the perpendicular line from this first cut down to the second parallel line you drew. This gives you an "L"-shaped cut into the tubing. Using a pair of snipe-nosed pliers, bend this strip that you have created back down on itself, making a fold at the second of the drawn parallel lines. You have created an indent for the wire to sit into, and a ledge that prevents its movement below a certain point.

Repeat for the other end of the tubing, and file to tidy it up. Don't worry if that little strip breaks off when you bend it; the indent you have made will function in the same way, but will be slightly less robust.

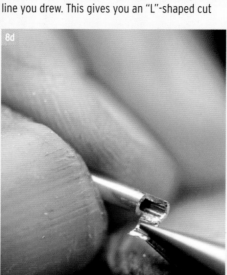

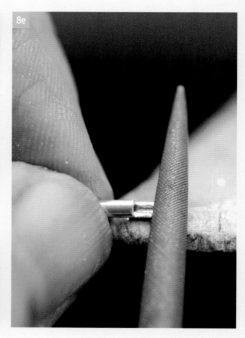

9 Next, you need to find a suitable place for the hinge to be soldered on to the back of the pin.

It's unlikely you will find an even surface to solder your hinge to. Find a good place for it, mark the position with your pen, and make a groove with a diamond wheel on the pendant drill, which allows the hinge to sit securely and straight on the pin.

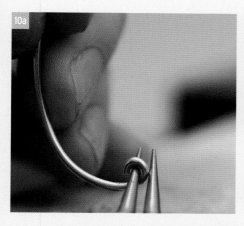

10 To make the clasp for the pin fastening, take a piece of 1.5 mm wire and bend into a curly "c" shape using round-nosed pliers. Using a piercing saw and 8/0 blade, trim as necessary to make it symmetrical.

11 You will probably need to grind a groove to solder this piece onto the back too; find a good spot parallel and in line with the hinge groove that will give enough distance from it to make the fastening function well.

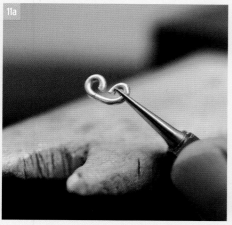

12 Solder the hinge and clasp into their positions in the grooves you made on the back of the pin, taking care to position them correctly. When positioning the hinge, the ledge that you cut (see 8d, opposite) should be face up (12a, below left)—imagine how it should give leverage to the fastening.

For the clasp, you are likely to need to set up the job with some support so that it doesn't fall over in the process of soldering. In this instance, I have used a pair of sprung tweezers mounted on a "third hand." Clean up after soldering, check the parts for a good joint, and apply some thermo-gel to protect them for the next soldering job.

PIN FASTENINGS

These should always sit above the gravitational halfway line of the pin in order to avoid the pin hanging forward when it is pinned to a garment. The size and style of the fastening needs to be chosen to suit the pin itself. A large and heavy pin like this one should be worn on stiff or thick fabric and will sit more securely with a double fastening, while a slim tiebar requires something more discreet, and should be fine enough not to snag on silky threads.

POSITIONING THE CLAW SETTINGS

13 This is the tricky part, as it's time to put the claw settings in place. Turn to the front of the pin and find positions for your treasures. If you took a photograph before, you can refer back to it now. Or, you may want to make some changes now that you have a measure of the settings. You can place the treasures on the silver ribbons or nestle them in the gaps between; in all cases you should look for good contact for soldering, with at least three of the claws touching part of the pin.

Once you have a satisfactory arrangement, it's a good idea to take a snapshot again, so you can identify the stones with the settings after you have soldered them.

Remove the treasures from your settings, one at a time, and replace the settings as you had them. It's a bit of a balancing act. Add some easy solder paste as you go to all points of contact. This will help to keep one in place while you fiddle with the next. When all the settings are in position, carefully apply heat to solder them on. As cast silver is slightly porous it tends to suck in solder, leaving insufficient amounts for the joint to become strong, so you may find that you need to add extra solder. Bear in mind that the claws you have made are thin and vulnerable to melting, so build up the heat in the body of the pin before attempting to focus on a single solder joint.

MAKING THE FASTENING

14 To construct the fastening, measure the distance between the hinge and the clasp on the back of the pin and double this length (it's a double fastening), adding an extra $3/8$ in (10 mm) to pass through the hinge and another $3/5$ in (16 mm) to allow for the fastening tips to come through the clasp (i.e. $5/16$ in/8 mm per fastening).

File both of the ends to a point. I find the easiest way to make a good point is to file the wire to a tapering square, then when a good sharpness has been achieved I file off the corners to make it round again.

Rub the filed surfaces smooth with 800-grit wet and dry paper. If the wire is soft rather than hardened stainless steel, you will need to work it on a steel block with a hammer to harden it.

15 Find the center point of the fastening and mark $1/4$ in (5 mm) either side of this point to identify where the bends will need to go. Make one of these a right angle bend now, using a pair of parallel pliers, then very slightly bend the second point, leaving it wide enough to flex through the tubing. Once you have fed it through, bend it to the full 90 degrees.

16 Check the fastening fits securely in the clasp, making adjustments as necessary with pliers. The fastening should naturally spring against the outer curves of the clasp, giving some tension.

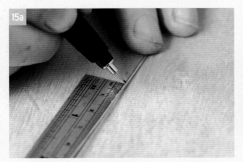

SETTING THE STONES

17 Now it's time to set the treasures into their claws. Refer back to the last snapshot if you need some help remembering what goes where and fit each piece carefully into its setting, making sure it won't be able to slip out of any spaces between the claws. Use flat-nosed pliers and gentle leverage to press each claw against the side of the piece, or to move the claws to a better holding position.

Using wire cutters, trim each claw to about 2 mm above the point where it no longer touches the object—you may make this smaller if your pieces that are to be set are tiny, and file the end round using a needle file.

18 Give each claw tip a final rub over with a fine wet and dry paper to remove file marks, then use a pusher to press them all firmly down until they lie against the treasure. Burnish the tips for a final, bright finish.

CHAPTER **TWO**

EXPLORING MATERIALS

THE MATERIAL QUESTION

Because we jewelers are preoccupied with three-dimensional forms, the specific qualities of our materials are of great significance to us in our design process. We need to handle our materials, play with them, test them to the limits in order to really understand them, and in the process we can find direction for exploring the techniques that will enhance (and support or protect) them to the full. This kind of understanding can lead to a productive dialog with your favored material that seeds a lifetime's work.

THE CHARACTERISTICS OF MATERIALS

The visual element might immediately conjure up the style of design that best shows off the material, but more than just how it looks, we must also consider the tactile qualities of the material, its weight, strength, durability, and its specific working properties. So for example, while we can say that both fine silver and sterling silver are malleable and ductile, fine silver is much softer and so it's relatively easy to weave. The tiny copper content in sterling silver gives it hardness and so it's tougher to manipulate in this way. However, if you are willing to devise a suitable approach to the technique, your finished woven form will maintain its final structure far better.

Alternatively, if you are inspired by the fiery beauty of a rough-cut opal, it's important to know that this stone is chippy and easily scratched, and it can be damaged by changes in humidity. So in your jewelry design you must contrive to protect the opal's vulnerable surfaces, and in the making of the piece you must avoid exposing the opal to detrimental chemical treatments. (This is information you also need to pass on to the future owner of your finished piece.)

THE DEEPER MEANING OF MATERIALS

Materials are often chosen for their deeper significance, and it is worth considering the cultural and historical associations for materials you like to use.

In addition, it's important to consider the wider ethical implications when selecting materials. We must take responsibility for the message we impart—it is possible that our jewelry will be visible to a wide audience over many future generations (see right).

There are many materials available to us that don't cost the earth. New materials and new technologies spur each other on to make ever more sophisticated products for us to use. Rapid prototyping and three-dimensional printers produce minimal wastage and require little physical interaction, and developments in nanoelectronics make sensory and responsive jewelry (wearables) an exciting new frontier for us to explore.

Rubber, silicone, and nylon and other plastics also become useful to us, as producers recognize that their initial industrial applications can extend to other uses in the creative industries.

Designing jewelry with recycled materials in mind (paper, cardboard, wood, metals, found objects, plastics, and textiles) can add an interesting dimension to your work, and of course you can readily recycle metals and stones from items of unwanted jewelry.

Bev Holden exploits the opposing behaviors of silicone and silver to bring structure and flexibility to her jewelry.

THINKING ABOUT COST

We must consider the cost of our materials—not just what we pay in cash to purchase the material, but the cost to animal welfare, to our planet, and to people's lives. Some materials, such as ivory, should simply not be used, but for many of us it is hard to imagine not using precious metals and beautiful stones in our jewelry.

THE ISSUES AROUND MINING

Mining is a notoriously dirty process and if you use these materials in your work, you must acknowledge the impact that your purchase has on the individuals and communities involved in the processes of extracting these treasures, and the poisonous, destructive effect that it has on their landscape.

A growing number of mining communities do process metals and gemstones using ethical methods and their products are certified as Fairtrade and Fairmined. Though we are still limited by the range of products available to us, in purchasing as many of our materials as we can, and in asking for more from these sources we are promoting changes in the mining industries. (Silver is not currently available from ethical sources, but it is possible to purchase recycled silver in sheet and wire form.) You will find references and sources for these materials on page 188.

Above: Materials for making jewelry can come from the most unusual sources—in this case, closer inspection of a broken television revealed the unexpected beauty of components that conjure our audiovisual experience; in playing with these electronic components, a whole range of jewelry emerged. Interestingly, people often comment on the ethnic influence of my "Irresistible" bracelets and necklaces.

Top right: In these rings Nic Webb achieves a pleasing marriage of materials by utilizing the malleable nature of silver to form around rings of wood.

Middle right: Sarah Eyton combines manmade materials with new technologies in her Perspex, laser-etched cuffs.

Bottom right: Inspired by Omamori (Japanese amulets), Yuki Sasakura Assiter combines materials that are infused with symbolic meaning—carefully chosen fabrics, metallic ribbons, and precious beads—to give this bangle quiet energy.

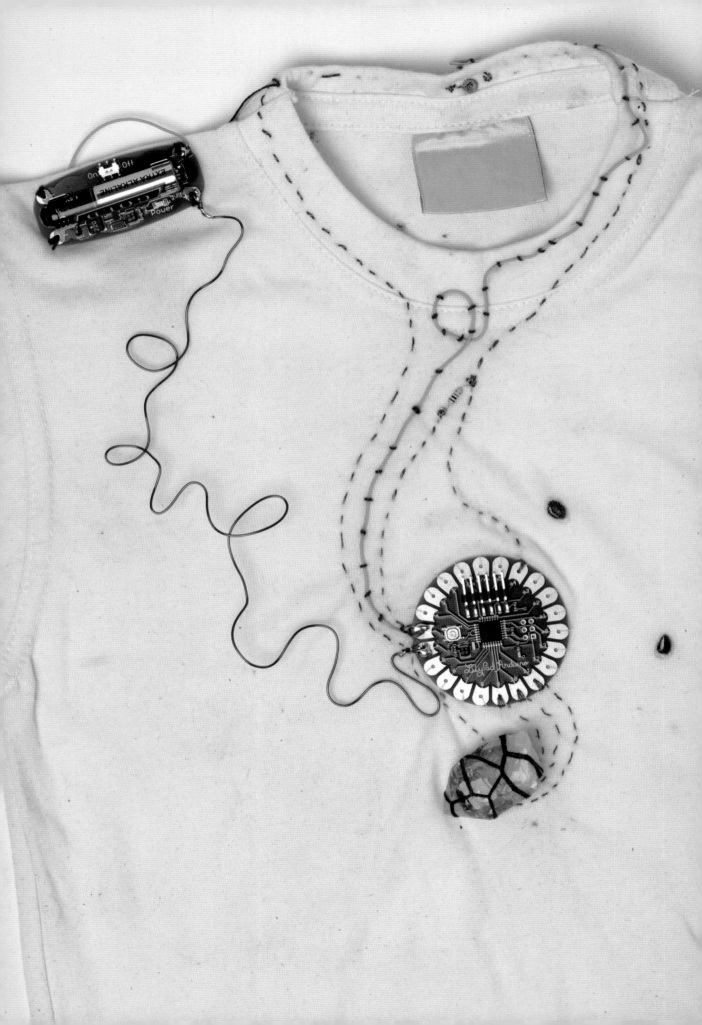

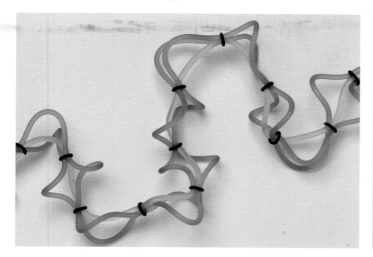

Silicone rubber is tough enough to withstand extensive tension and torsion. Here I have used rubber "O" rings to grab these twisted and stretched lengths of silicone to make interesting, rhythmic forms.

If you are planning to smelt all that scrap yourself, do make sure that the metals you put together are of a known quality, and be sure to remove non-precious springs or rivets from clasps and hinges beforehand.

MATERIALS FOR EARTH, WATER, AIR, AND FIRE

MATERIALS WE CAN ASSOCIATE WITH EARTH: solid, earthy materials—fossils, rocks, and pebbles, pigments, metals, minerals, soil; vegetable/animal materials—wood, bone, leather, horn, seeds, pods, fibrous materials. Stimulating the senses of touch, sight, smell, and taste.

MATERIALS WE CAN ASSOCIATE WITH WATER: animal/vegetable materials—pearls, shells, fish bones, seaweed, coral; found objects—eroded and weather-worn beachcombing finds; materials in a liquid state. Stimulating the senses of touch, sound, and sight.

MATERIALS WE CAN ASSOCIATE WITH AIR: the intangible—sound, electricity, flight, movement (electronics/feathers/clockwork parts); manmade materials—plastics, latex, monofilaments. Stimulating the senses of sound and smell.

MATERIALS WE CAN ASSOCIATE WITH FIRE: bright and lustrous materials—gems and metals, for example, ores, rough stones, cut gems; materials resulting from heat: glass and hot enamels. Stimulating the senses of sight, sound, taste, and smell.

Left: The Arduino Lilypad is a programmable device that can be used to transform a given input into a specified output. Here I wanted to explore how a piece of crystal, ideally incorporated into a pendant, might change color (expressed as light; red for hot, green for calm, blue for chilled) to describe one's mood (temperature). A sensor at the back of the neck transmits temperature data to the lilypad, and this controls the color and speed of pulse of the LED under the rock crystal.

THE CONTRIBUTORS

On the following pages four jewelers describe their working practice. Drawing influence from multiple sources, each one has evolved their own creative language that communicates through their work. In all of these jewelers, I perceive an elemental connection that is seamlessly integrated between idea, choice of material, and process. Each jeweler has also contributed a project based around their theme.

Earth Henrietta Fernandez takes her inspiration from the natural world; working mainly with silver and gold, she infuses her pieces with earthy tones using oxides and cold enamels (see pages 66-73).

Water Louise Loder manifests fluidity in both the form and the function of her work. Having a responsive approach to her materials, this also influences her choice of technique; elements are bound together, or groups of objects are made to relate to each other and these pieces invoke a sense of ancient ritual (see pages 74-81).

Air Nora Fok is renowned for her ethereal, sculptural jewelry and body pieces, which she constructs from nylon thread. Describing her process of making as instinctive, there is also a scientific element to her practice as she looks beneath the immediate visual experience of the world around her to understand the structure, symmetry, and punctuations that make them (see pages 82-7).

Fire Imogen Belfield creates luscious, golden forms reminiscent of lava and raw crystal structures. Her jewelry often incorporates uncut minerals or porcelain chips that are encapsulated by molten metal (see pages 88-93).

HENRIETTA FERNANDEZ
(EARTH)

The jewelry that I design and make is most definitely a reflection of the world I live in—things I see around me that kick-start the process of an idea, which develops into a piece of something wearable and precious.

Growing up in the 1960s and surrounded by lots of visual and eclectic stimuli that my parents collected I developed a love of pattern and graphics. These still influence my style today, as does my garden of flowers and vegetables.

My work is contemporary, graphic, and modern, but is softened by the natural elements that inspire it. My daisy necklace, for example, (see my "Flower" collection, opposite), is modern and graphic, but was inspired by a fairly old-fashioned and traditional image.

In the context of this book of elemental jewelry, I see my designs loosely as earth ... the plants and patterns I draw inspiration from all starting their life as tiny seeds deep in the soil. The design of the piece I've chosen to make for this book (see pages 69-73) has risen not only out of the ground, but has been influenced by the internet and a phone app—a first for me!

DRAWING ON THE EARTH

Treatments I use in my work are also earth-related. I use oxidization in some of my work, and this treatment of blackening silver is drawn directly from the earth, as it uses sulphur. Sulphur occurs naturally in the environment, being the thirteenth most abundant element in the earth's crust. I use a commercially bought oxidizing solution (see Resources, page 188) that is easy to use, which gives my jewelry a richness and an "earthiness," too. Silver and gold are also metals that are derived from the earth, and these are the materials I rely on most heavily in my work.

USING COLOR

I love color and try to use it in my jewelry designs, sometimes only as little touches, but ones that add depth and luxury to a piece—a tiny highlight of gold, or the gorgeous purple of a semi-precious stone such as amethyst, or the rich red-brown of a carnelian, perhaps combined with a detail of opaque enameled color.

Enamel is a good way of adding color and combines brilliantly with silver, which works well with some of my designs. Traditional vitreous enamel is also a by-product of the earth. It is great to use but needs a kiln, high temperatures, and a lot of patience and knowledge for success. I use cold enamels for their ease of use. They are available in a range of colors, and with some knowledge can be used very effectively when combined with silver, for example.

The cold enamel I use in my work is actually an epoxy resin. It doesn't require to be heated in a kiln and is used with a ratio of two parts color to one part hardener. It is odorless and non-toxic when used in small quantities, and forms a long-lasting, hard, colorful material, which is very similar to vitreous enamel.

There is a fairly new material on the market called Bio resin. This resin is plant-based and non-toxic and is derived from natural triglyceride vegetable oils (e.g. rapeseed, soya, and sunflower oil). It is therefore a sustainable and renewable product. At the time of writing, it is only available in fairly large quantities and has been used as a casting material in jewelry making, but not yet for cold enameling. I am keen to experiment with this new product when time and the right equipment allows.

PIECES DISPLAYED

1 Petal ring
2 Tulip ring
3 Daisy necklace
4 Tulip necklace
5 Starflower gold necklace
6 Carpenter ear studs

HENRIETTA FERNANDEZ

SWEET PEA PENDANT

This summer I joined Instagram, a photograph-sharing app on my smartphone. It is very addictive. I have taken some gorgeous photographs of the countryside and the flowers in my garden to share. The app has allowed me to be very creative in ways that I haven't tried before, and I have been so inspired by some of my photographs that I felt I had to use them in my work. This piece is a silver and enamel necklace based on an Instagram photograph I took of some sweet peas. It is graphic in its approach and is similar to a commission I recently carried out, which I made in a

similar way. Both were made by layering and soldering silver to form negative spaces, which cold enamel could be poured into. Although this is a fairly lengthy process, a similar project could be achieved with perhaps a simpler, smaller design.

I encourage you not to copy my design, but to go out and take your own photograph of a beautiful flower, seed head, or pattern—anything that gets your creative juices flowing, and that you think could translate into a piece of enameled jewelry. Make it your own design that is unique and special to you.

MATERIALS
1. Cold enamels with hardener (see below right)
2. Silver sheet, 0.8 mm thickness, 1 x 1 in (25 x 25 mm),
3. Thin gauge silver sheet, 0.5 mm thickness, 1 x 1 in (25 x 25 mm)
4. Rectangular wire, 2 mm x 1.6 mm x 3 in (83 mm)

You will also need: a jump ring

TOOLS
- Circle template
- Masking tape
- Tracing paper and pencil
- Double-sided tape
- Scissors
- Piercing saw (see page 178), 2/0 blade
- Files (see page 179): half-round file, flat file, round needle files, and large flat file
- Soldering equipment (see pages 182 and 183): flux; brush; solder, hard and easy, plus solder pallions; torch; insulated reverse action pincers; pick; honeycomb soldering board; and pickle
- Large ring mandrel (see page 181)
- Wet and dry papers (see page 184), 400, 600, 800, and 1200 grit
- Buff stick (see page 184)
- Small bowls for mixing cold enamel colors with hardener
- Mixing sticks for mixing colors and hardener
- Latex gloves for wearing while mixing and applying the enamels
- Lengths of wire to apply enamel
- Steel wool (see page 185), grade 0000
- Mop for polishing (optional)
- Silver polish and cloth (see page 185) (optional)

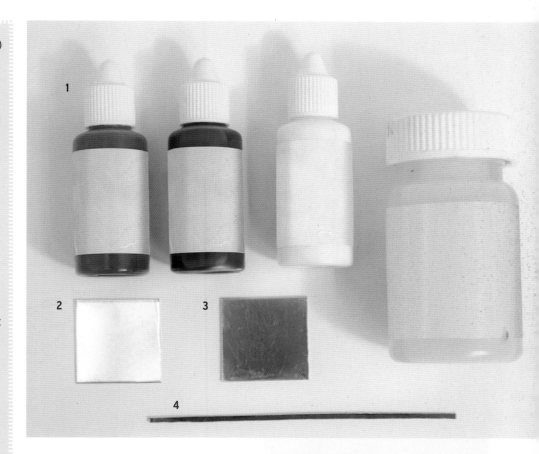

MATERIALS TIP

ENAMELS Always refer to the manufacturer's health and safety instructions on the bottle when using cold enamels. The ones used here (see Resources, page 188) require good ventilation and care must be taken to avoid getting enamel onto the skin. Wearing latex gloves is recommended, and you may also want to wear an apron to avoid enamel dripping onto your clothes.

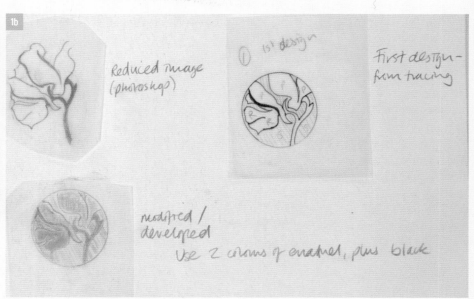

Reduced image (photoshop)

1st design

First design – from tracing

modified / developed

Use 2 colours of enamel, plus black

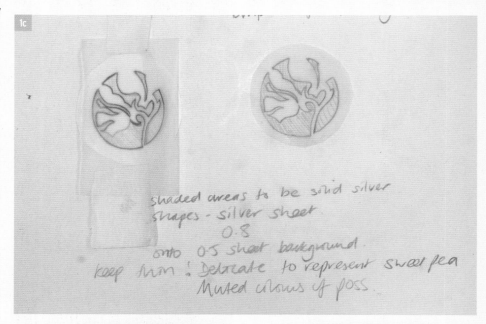

shaded areas to be solid silver shapes - silver sheet.

0.8

onto 0.5 sheet background.

keep firm! Delicate to represent sweet pea

Muted colours if poss.

CREATING THE DESIGN TEMPLATE

1 My inspiration for this piece is a photograph of my sweet peas. I used my computer as a light box by loosely attaching some tracing paper to my screen with masking tape. I traced the outline and shapes of the sweet pea flower, then reduced the drawing using Photoshop until I was happy with the size. I then refined and developed the design in my sketchbook. I opted for a size that is fairly large; using a round shape suits the design.

2 Use a 1 in (25 mm) diameter circle template to draw the circle onto the thin gauge 0.5 mm thick silver sheet. A circle template is easier to use than a compass. Then draw and cut out another 1 in (25 mm) circle onto the thicker ³/₈ in (8 mm) sheet for the base plate.

3 Adhere double-sided tape to the back of the sweet pea design template so that each part of the design can be cut out separately, and stuck directly onto the 0.8 mm thick silver sheet.

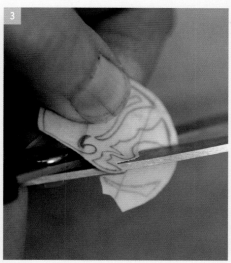

PREPARING THE DESIGN TEMPLATE

4 Carefully cut out each piece of the template on the outside of the design, using a piercing saw with a 2/0 saw blade. Try to use the silver as economically as possible.

5 Using a range of needle files—here half-round, flat, and round files—file each small piece back up to the line that is still visible. Check each piece over carefully for any imperfections. It's much easier to do this now rather than when it has all been soldered.

6 It's a good idea to check that all your pieces match up, so arrange them back onto the original design in your sketchbook to make sure.

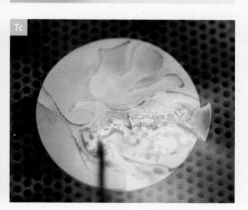

SOLDERING

7 Take the necessary health and safety precautions before you begin soldering (see page 183). Solder each piece, one by one, using hard solder and sweat soldering. Turn over the first piece to be soldered, add flux, and put a few solder pallions on the back of it in strategic places—enough so that the solder will flow over without being too much. More can be added later if there isn't enough. Heat the piece until the solder just flows, and move the solder gently around with a pick to spread it, while keeping the flame there so that it stays molten. Now lay each piece onto your fluxed base plate and solder into place one by one. Continue in the same way with all the pieces, making sure that they stay in position while soldering, all using hard solder.

LEVEL: INTERMEDIATE
TIME: 14 HOURS

MAKING THE OUTSIDE RING

8 Make a ring using the rectangular wire and solder together using hard solder. Use a large mandrel to form the ring, which should fit around your base plate circle exactly.

9 Push fit the ring onto your base plate, flux, and add small pieces of hard solder around the inside edge. Apply heat evenly and solder into place, making sure the solder flows all around and that there are no gaps.

10 Using reverse action insulated tweezers to hold the ring, sweat solder a piece of solder onto the ring first, then carefully heat it back again. Add the jump ring when the solder reflows.

ENAMELING

11 Before enameling, the pendant needs to be finished. Use a large flat file to make the front, back, and sides smooth and flush, then surface with wet and dry papers and a buff stick. Use a coarse grit 400 paper, then go down to a finer grit of 600, and don't use water.

12 Mix the cold enamel colors in small separate bowls, using two parts color to one part hardener. It's important to be precise with these ratios, otherwise the enamel may not set. Leave to stand for 10 minutes to allow any air bubbles to settle. The enamel mix will start to harden after an hour, so bear this in mind when working with this material.

When you have added the enamel, it's a good idea to check back over your piece regularly for an hour or so, to make sure that there are no air bubbles present in the enamel. If there are, remove them with a fine needle or broken saw blade.

There are different methods in applying cold enamels—I have chosen to use the over-filling method, which requires sanding back to the level of the metal so that the enamel is flush with the metal, leaving a semi-matte finish. (An alternative is to fill the enamel so that it just sits below the level of the metal—no sanding back is needed, and the enamel stays shiny.) Leave the enamel to dry for 24 hours, then use 400-, 600-, 800-, and 1200-grit wet and dry papers with water to sand down and remove high areas of enamel, where it has been overfilled. Always use water with wet and dry papers at this stage, as metal particles and grit particles from the paper can infiltrate the enamel and make it look dirty.

13 Finally, use a very fine steel wool, grade 0000, to fine finish the enamel. Polish can also be used with a mop and a plastic/acrylic compound if a high finish is required, then burnish again with silver polish and a soft cloth.

LOUISE LODER
(WATER)

I work predominately in silver. My work includes jewelry, tableware, sculptural wall pieces, plus the more playful "Tools for Building Sand Castles," where I mix silver with driftwood. I like to make functional, tactile, evocative objects, often drawing on rituals, personal experiences, and play to inform my design process. The intangible charm of imperfection, irregularity, and impermanence fascinates me, and I have always been drawn to the irregular—to objects with character.

TOOLS FOR BUILDING SAND CASTLES

As a regular beachcomber, I enjoy the ritual of collecting and sorting. The beauty of everyday scraps transformed by the sea into enigmatic little treasures always fills me with wonder—each piece exposing intricate markings and evocative forms. Often their beauty lies within their fragility and sense of history.

I try to retain and recreate these qualities while adding silver and experimenting with the finish to make sand castle tools. "Tools for Building Sand Castles" were originally developed while doing my Masters of Arts degree. My daughter was young, and we spent the summers on the beach. As a maker, I needed to be active with my hands so mirroring my own childhood I indulged in sand castle building. It struck me that despite the time and energy put into building the castle, the tide would always come in and wash it away, so the activity was all about the process.

After the initial inspiration I went on to make limited edition boxed sets of "Tools for Building Sand Castles," which consisted of about seven to nine tools in a beautifully designed box with a lift-off glass lid and a hallmarked silver plaque, which can be played with like a small beach as a solitary pleasure, or enjoyed with friends. The Brighton & Hove Museum, England, commissioned me to make the tenth set, which became the last in the series. This practice has greatly influenced the way I deal with silver.

DESIGNING WITH SILVER

Silver is, of course, a precious metal and I love its inherent qualities, but after making the vital decisions regarding the design I often use silver in a non-precious way. This allows me the freedom to enjoy an intuitive dialog with the material by adopting the same mind-set used when building sand castles on the beach. A good sand castle should be enjoyed with family and friends, maintaining its structure and aesthetic for as long as possible while the sea travels around it slowly deconstructing it—pure joy!

I have often been asked to turn these little tools into jewelry, but in some cases part of their beauty is their fragility. This, however, doesn't allow an object to be practically worn, and this is how the idea behind the little buckets on a leather string evolved (see pages 76-81).

Scoops and pins are inspired by pieces of broken tree bark found in the woods while out walking. Often the beauty lies within its fragility, tenuously holding its form, ravaged by the elements. The intangible charm of the irregular, the imperfect, and the impermanent never ceases to inspire me.

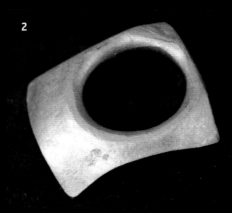

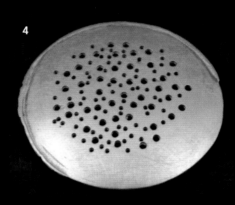

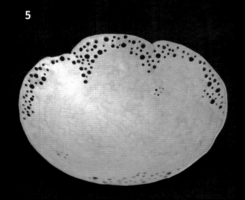

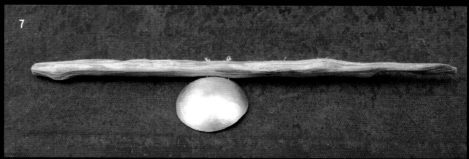

BUCKET NECKLACE

I love these little buckets. They can be worn hung on colored leather as a necklace or displayed as an ornament. They have proved to be very popular with my friends and clients. Each one is hand made and has its own character. They are made from sterling silver and I achieve the patination effect by experimenting with the firescale through the heating process.

Some of the patterns are like miniature landscapes. I like to make the buckets in batches and to save time I order individually cut silver tube (see Resources, page 188). Of course, the tube could be made from sheet, but I am quite lazy and prefer spending the time creating the painterly effects rather than on tube making.

MATERIALS
1. Length of leather cord on which to suspend the bucket; to add some color, try using different colored cords
2. Silver wire, 0.6 mm diameter, ³/₄ in (20 mm) long, for attaching the handle to the bucket
3. Sterling silver tube, ³/₄ in (19 mm) diameter, ³/₄ in (20 mm) long
4. Sterling silver sheet, 0.5 mm thickness, ³/₄ x ³/₄ in (20 x 20 mm) for the base of the bucket; the corners make good solder resting places that I cut off after soldering
5. Silver wire for the handle, 1.2 mm diameter, 2¹/₄ in (60 mm) long
6. Art masking fluid and brush for patination of the bucket (see right)

TOOLS
- Cardstock, fine-line permanent pen, compass, and ruler for making the template
- Dividers (see page 178)
- Center punch (see page 179)
- Bench drill, 1 mm, 0.6 mm, and 0.7 mm drill bits
- Doweling (wooden rod) to help with drilling holes
- Files (see page 179): 6 in (150 mm) half-round slim file cut 2, 6 in (150 mm) flat file cut 0, assorted needle files
- Selection of wet and dry papers (see page 184)
- Piercing saw (see page 178), 2/0 blade
- Small raising hammer (see page 180)
- Pliers (see page 180): flat-nosed pliers, small round-nosed pliers
- Wooden mallet (see page 180)
- Scraper (optional)
- Soldering equipment (see page 183): Degussa flux (see Step 7, page 80), brush, torch, tweezers, soldering block, and pickle
- Soft cloth and Renaissance wax (see page 185)

TOOL TIP

MASKING FLUID The masking fluid is painted onto the bucket after it has been soldered and left to dry (see page 81). This forms a semi-waterproof barrier when the bucket is then immersed in the safety pickle. I often get impatient for the masking fluid to dry, so in the winter I paint it on then leave the bucket on the radiator or use a hairdryer to speed up the process. In the summer, it can just sit in the sunshine and it dries very quickly.

MAKING THE HOLES FOR THE HANDLE

If you want to make a roll-top bucket, I suggest doing this before drilling the holes for the handle (see Step 3, below).

1 First, mark the silver tube at the top where the handle will be attached to the bucket. To make sure that the holes are evenly placed it is best to make a template. Take a piece of cardstock and draw around the tube with a pen, then use a compass and ruler to draw a line across the center. Put the tube back in place on the cardstock, then with the pen, continue the line up the side of the tube for ¼ in (5 mm). Using your dividers, set at ⅙ in (3 mm), mark from the top of the tube down the line. This is the place to use the center punch over a stake or piece of wood.

2 Drill a hole using a 1 mm drill bit. To stop the tube collapsing, I pack the tube with two pieces of doweling pushed inside. They are shaped at the end so they can be used in various sized hollow forms. Clean up the edges using a small fine needle file or wet and dry paper.

MAKING A ROLL-TOP BUCKET

This is a variation on the flat-topped bucket.

3 Using a "pointy" stake and raising hammer, stretch the top, then hammer down the sides using a wooden mallet, easing the edges together. Try to maintain a bit of a roll on the top rather than flattening completely.

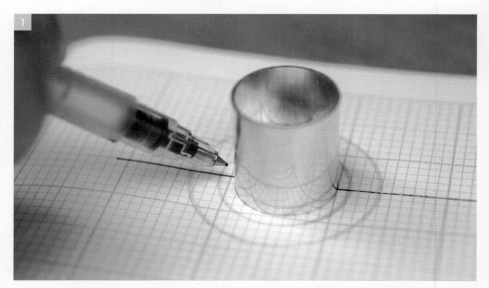

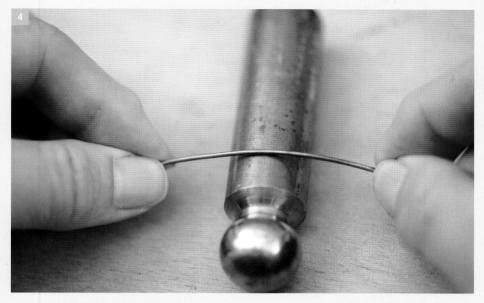

MAKING THE HANDLE

4 I always make and prepare the handle components at this stage even though they are not needed yet. This helps me get a perspective of the bucket shape and decreases the risk of scratching the final surface pattern. Anneal the 1.2 mm x 2¼ in (60 mm) silver wire, then flatten each end using a small raising hammer over a stake. You will be drilling a hole through this, so try to flatten it as evenly as possible.

5 Use the center punch and a 0.6 mm drill bit to mark the point to drill. It is important to get this as central as you can because there is not much material either side. Drill a hole in each end in the center of the flattened piece, using the 0.7 mm drill bit. Clean up with a half-round file and round off any corners. Bend and gently hammer the wire over a stake similar in size to that of the bucket, then using a pair of flat-nosed pliers, flatten out the ends slightly. Adjust where necessary to fit the bucket. All my buckets seem to have slightly different-shaped handles, but I like this. It gives them different characters. Put the handle to the side, ready to attach later.

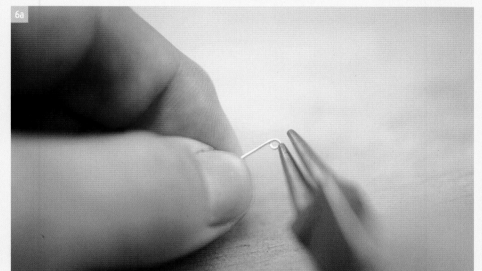

FITTING THE HANDLE

I suggest fitting the handle AFTER the patination process (see page 81) because the wire holding it on is quite thin and prone to melting if overheated, but I would prepare the components beforehand and then the final job is just fitting them together.

6 Take the thin wire (0.6 mm x ¾ in/20 mm) and cut it in half, giving you two pieces of ⅜ in (10 mm) wire. This is used to attach the handle to the bucket. Using small round-nosed pliers, bend just one end a couple of times around to create a ring, then flatten with the pliers to tuck in the end so that it does not catch. Each piece of wire is threaded through the hole on the handle and then the bucket. Use the same technique each side and to secure on the inside of the bucket.

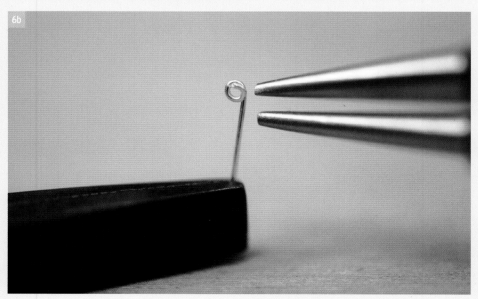

PUTTING A BASE ON THE BUCKET

7 Sand the bottom of the tube ready for soldering by holding the top of the tube in an upright position and using a circular motion over coarse to fine wet and dry papers, each one stuck firmly to a flat piece of wood. As I use ready-cut pieces of tube this doesn't take much time, but if you made your own tube, you will probably have already done this. I like to finish off around the edge with my scraper.

Rub the tube and base down with wet and dry paper to prepare the surface for soldering and to rough up the surface for the final surface texture.

For soldering, I use Degussa flux, which is a paste I buy in Germany. It is ready to use and can be removed after soldering by immersing in very hot water. This allows me to keep the firescale but remove the flux.

Take the necessary health and safety precautions before you begin soldering (see page 183). Solder the tube to the base ensuring it is the correct way up (i.e. with the drilled holes) for the handle at the top. You can use a disk for the base, but I like to use a square so that the corners can make good resting places for the solder.

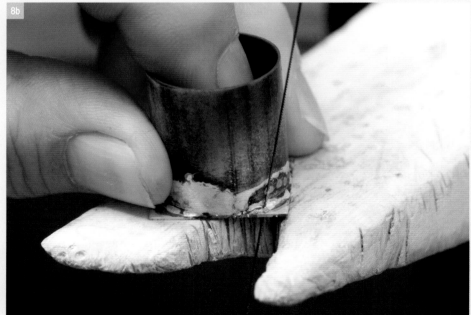

8 Using a piercing saw, cut off the excess base and file with a half-round slim file. The file marks will contribute to the final pattern, so you can use a heavy file, but keep the marks to the lower part of the bucket. Using emery paper (experiment with different grades, from coarse to fine, to create different effects), rub in a circular motion over the file marks—the aim is not to obliterate them but blend them and add uniformity to the rest of the surface. Run around the top with your scraper or small file then heat again to bring the oxides to the surface.

PATINATING THE BUCKET

You may have noticed that I have not immersed the bucket into pickle and it will have a patination of blackened firescale covering it. I have always found the patterns and colors created during the soldering process very inspiring. I love the randomness of the patterns created from the flame bringing the oxides to the surface of the metal, and through experimentation I have developed different techniques to control the pattern. This is the point where there are choices to be made regarding the coloring of your bucket. I will take you through one process, but part of the fun is playing around.

9 Wash the bucket, but do not pickle. Apply an art masking fluid with a paintbrush around the bottom of the bucket, covering the area of blackened firescale you wish to keep. The fluid when dry will protect it from the pickle.

10 Once the masking fluid is dry, either stand or suspend the bucket in about ³/₈ in (10 mm) of warm safety pickle for 5-10 minutes so that it will remove the firescale from parts of the bucket not covered with the fluid. If possible, do not completely immerse the bucket as pickle can seep underneath the masking fluid.

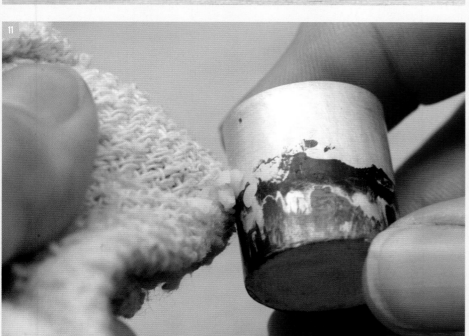

11 Rinse the bucket thoroughly before removing the latex mask. Wash and dry the bucket with a soft cloth, then attach the handle (see Step 6, page 79). Give the bucket a final light heating to blend it with the colors of the handle. Be careful not to heat it too much or the thin wire holding on the handle will melt, but heat it enough for any file marks to blacken. Then apply some Renaissance wax with a soft cloth to protect the finish and enhance the blackness. Attach a leather thong and you are good to go.

NORA FOK
(AIR)

Contemporary jewelry is a vast subject and takes on many forms, as this book demonstrates. Individual artists have their own interpretations and ways of creating jewelry that are unique to them. As an artist and jewelry maker, I value artistic experimentation, craftsmanship, and the uniqueness of my own hands as my major tool. Most of my work consists of one-off pieces, and some are made as limited editions. I enjoy different challenges and my jewelry pieces satisfy my curiosity about the world around me as well as my need to create.

THE ART OF WABI-SABI

I draw inspiration mainly from the natural world, and my jewelry also reflects my emotions and thoughts. I want to celebrate the beauty of organic forms and their imperfections using my own hands. I would borrow the Japanese word *wabi-sabi* to describe this, a term that encapsulates a number of subtle concepts, including an appreciation of the transient, the joy of simplicity, and even the recognition of the perfection in imperfection. I see beauty in everyday things and have great pleasure in studying and

interpreting them in my work. I love experimenting with materials and exploring new ideas to make wearable objects that are in harmony with the female body. These pieces can take on a different identity as sculptural decorative ornaments when displayed in an environment.

SIMPLE MATERIALS, SPECIAL EFFECTS

The material of my choice to create my objects is non-precious, low-cost nylon monofilament, a relatively new substance, most commonly used as fishing line. It's light in weight, soft, supple, warm to the touch, and after over 30 years of working with it there are still many possibilities to be explored and discovered.

Each of my pieces has its own individual identity and meaning and often tells a story. However, these jewelry pieces are not complete until they are worn. The enjoyable sensation experienced by the wearer is an important outcome of my creative process. Wearing my jewelry makes the wearer feel very special and happy. Although my jewelry is mostly suitable for special occasions, it is always comfortable and fun.

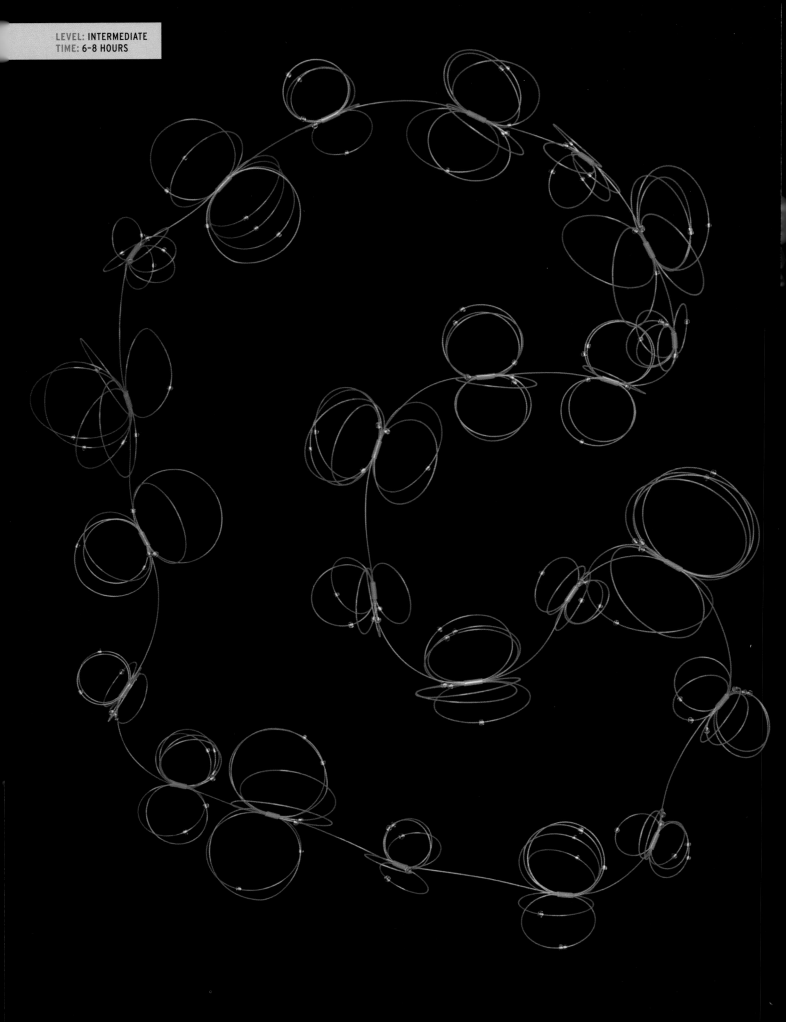

DANCING ELECTRONS NECKPIECE

I was asked to think about using "air" as an inspiration for a piece of jewelry, which seems an abstract concept, and would be difficult to achieve. However, looking deeper into the subject it was intriguing: something we can't see or feel, it exists as airbound minute particles, microwaves, sound frequencies, and the ghostly subatomic particles called neutrinos, so small that they pass through our bodies without us knowing—a magical world of the extremely small.

I like the idea of using something in the air as my starting point and to interpret this piece of jewelry as light and airy as the material will allow; letting energy flow around the neckline. Gentle waves create ripples and vibrations invisibly traveling in space or through water and as images of atoms and molecules came to me, I started to look at the traveling paths of electrons around the nucleus.

This electron neckpiece idea is based on the diagram of an atom and shows the electrons orbiting the nucleus, creating space and movement. I chose strong, bold-colored nylon in contrast with the invisible circular paths, and the result is like drawing with nylon in three dimensions.

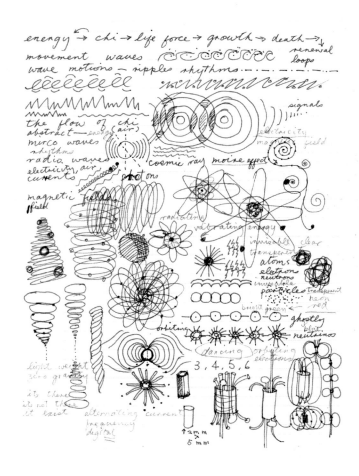

I sketched ideas in my sketchbook for this dancing electrons neckpiece (see left). I also made an early experiment with nylon and unraveled wool yarn.

MATERIALS

1. Red nylon monofilament, 20 lb (9 kg) in strength, 0.40 mm diameter, about 28¼ ft (8.6 m) long; these monofilaments are fishing lines, the red one is called Ultima red ice, also shown is the Daiwa sensor black fishing line
2. Red PVC tubing (scoubidou braiding cord), 2 mm diameter, 4 in (100 mm) long, cut into 16 pieces of ¼ in (5 mm) long, also shown is black PVC tubing; PVC tubing is available from all good craft stores
3. A selection of glass beads, available from all good craft stores

TOOLS

- Ruler or tape measure
- Scissors
- Tweezers
- Candle and/or tea light
- Matches

1 The aim is to make 16 electrons, each one taking up about a 21³/₄ in (550 mm) length of nylon, and allowing 2-3 in (50-75 mm) of nylon between each electron. To start the necklace, find the center of the 28¹/₄ ft (8.6 m) length of nylon monofilament; it is easier to work from the middle, creating eight electrons on one side and then eight electrons on the other. Cut the PVC tube into 16 (or more) sections, each between ¹/₄ in and ⁵/₁₆ in (5 and 7 mm) in length.

2 Thread one piece of PVC tube and a glass bead as far as the center of the nylon monofilament, and build the first loop of the electron on that side of the nylon. Take the whole length of nylon through the PVC center, each time trapping a bead in the loop before threading. Continue to thread through, making up to a maximum of six loops and a minimum of three loops per electron. Use tweezers to help to push the nylon through for the fifth and sixth loops.

Start a new electron between 1¹/₂ in and 4 in (40 mm and 100 mm) apart from the first, and continue until one half of the length of nylon has been used up. Now work on the other half of the nylon length to create a further eight electrons.

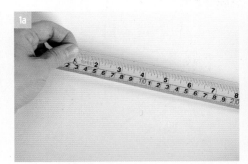

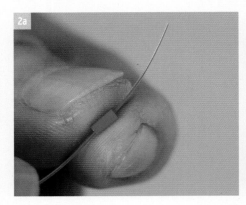
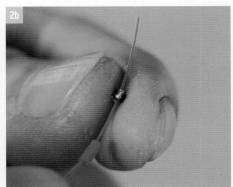
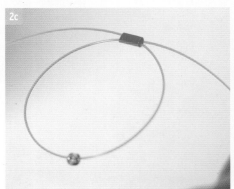
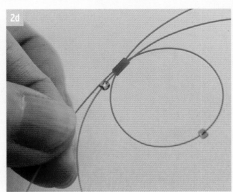
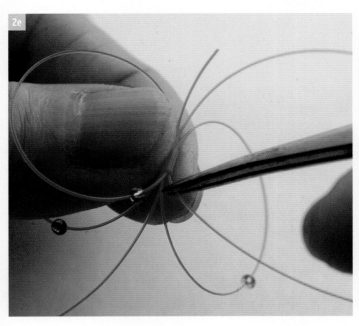
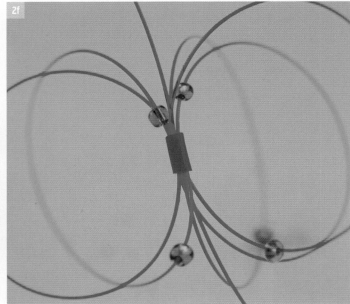

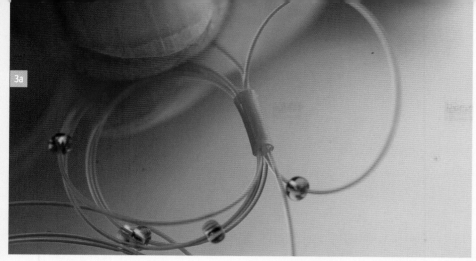

3a

3b

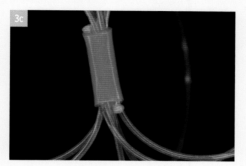

3c

3 Thread the two ends of nylon through the last electron center tube in opposite directions. Heat fuse both ends in the candle flame. Hold the nylon tightly, leaving a 1/4 in (5-6 mm) end, and gently move the nylon end toward the lowest and coolest part of the flame. Keep the end about 1/4 in (5 mm) away from the flame, and take special care not to burn the nylon. Melt the tip to form a molten bead as a stopper to secure the joint neatly.

Caution When fusing the end of the nylon with a candle, take extreme care not to hold the nylon too close to the flame. Always work in a well-ventilated room.

VARIATIONS ON A THEME

There are many possibilities for this looping technique (see right, below right, and below left). Use clear nylon to build pieces and dyes to achieve multicolor effects. Replace the glass beads with small freshwater pearls or gem chips. Try using PVC tubing with a larger diameter to hold more loops.

DANCING ELECTRON EARRINGS These earrings are fun to make and to wear (below left). Use two 25 in (625 mm) lengths of nylon monofilament to form two single electrons, leaving a 6 in (150 mm) length of nylon at the end of each electron; cut the tips of the nylon ends at a 45-degree angle to sharpen them. To wear, thread the nylon through pierced ears, then make a loose half knot behind each ear to secure.

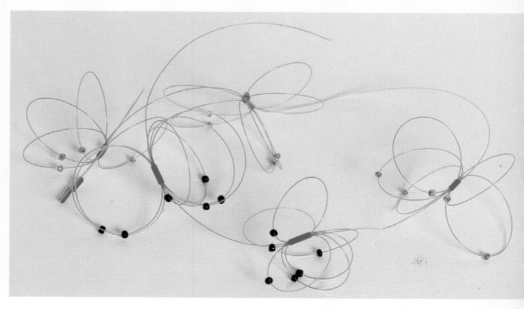

IMOGEN BELFIELD
(FIRE)

I aim to create bold and beautiful jewelry sculptures for the body, with each piece being designed and crafted in my London studio. I'm inspired by my surroundings, creating experimentalist jewelry that takes influences from both architecture and nature—from the tallest building to the smallest flower, working with bronze, sterling silver, rose gold and yellow gold, raw minerals, and gemstones. The key sources of inspiration for my work—architecture and organic forms—are combined with aspects from my fine art background. I describe my work as little sculptures that adorn the body. These evolved from the large sculptures I created while at school, which over time became smaller and smaller as they formed a stronger synthesis to the body. Architects such as Santiago Calatrava and Zaha Hadid, and artists such as Gustav Klimt have been a big influence on my work.

SOURCES OF INSPIRATION

My ideas can grow from anything, starting from the fruit stalls in London's Brick Lane market, and the vast array of incredible natural forms and shapes on display. I have found some amazing fruits and vegetables in this market, including the kerala (a bitter gourd) and the custard apple (a tropical fruit). I love the fact that these forms are so completely natural and untouched, yet provide such a source of inspiration and a plethora of ideas. Equally, an idea can be sparked from the towering buildings and angular edges of the city's skyscrapers.

My design process always begins with a three-dimensional object. I'm an avid collector of rocks, and I try to emulate their natural formation in the work I create, which relates to the texturing effects I create through manipulation of materials. I begin by making paper or wire maquettes, and plaster models by casting directly from these three-dimensional objects. Developing my work is as much an organic process as the work I produce is organic.

I spend time scouring the amazing raw minerals at London's Natural History Museum, which is where I source a lot of my stones. These beautifully rough, uncarved, unpolished stones can spark the inspiration for the final piece of jewelry.

Carving, scoring, filing, sanding, heating, burning, and melting are all processes involved in my work. For me, it is all about taking a material to its extreme, adding texture and completely transforming its shape.

THEMED COLLECTIONS

Each collection I create carries a different theme. The "Rockoco" collection brings a new, darker, more menacing edge to my organic style. The collection is inspired by the fluid nature of the Rococo art movement combined with the natural and raw state of rocks and minerals. Indicative titles such as "Jagged rocks" convey the sharp spiked points of the rings, and the delicate "Waterfall rocks" intimates the contrasting soft curves of the pendants. Shards of nuggets clustered in mounds are reminiscent of a mass of bubbles, delicate and temporary.

The "Equilibrium" collection draws on space: from star clusters and bubbling gases, to spiralling milky ways and angular meteorites. The incredible colors and shapes seen in the solar system have inspired and evolved my designs, expanding my repertoire into pieces of dramatic molten-like formations in rose and yellow gold-plated bronze and sterling silver. Like moltenous and lava-like forms, all created by heat, I also use heat, fire, and flames to create the globular and volcanic forms in my work.

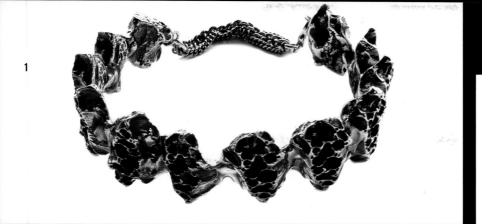

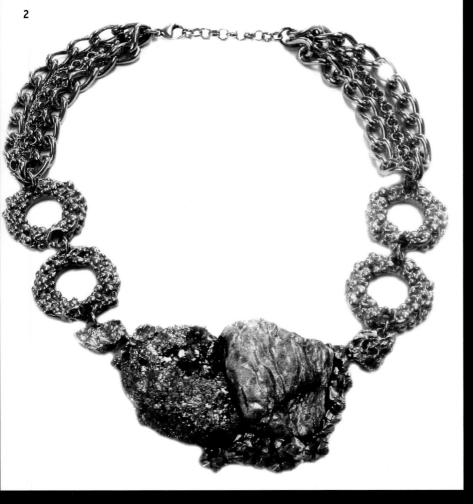

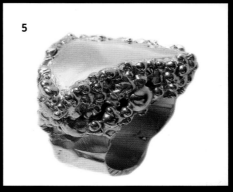

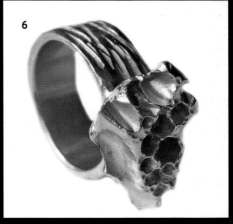

PIECES DISPLAYED

1 Poseidon bracelet
2 Fool's wreath necklace
3 Fool's bow bracelet
4 Jagged rocks ring
5 Plasma ring
6 Little ridges ring

ANGULAR CARVED RING

I enjoy creating pieces that have a strong textural quality, and carving into jeweler's wax enables me to form bold pieces with surface interest. Here, the ring has a raw, hewn appearance, the marks resembling those made by a rough saw. This ring is a strong, modern piece, yet it is also reminiscent of something ancient, even elemental—the work of a Bronze Age artist, perhaps? The design of the ring is closest to my Diffusions range, which focuses on striking metal and gemstone work, resulting in eye-catching statement pieces. The ring would have worked equally well without the stone, but I like the juxtaposition of the naturally faceted, geometric stone—like a small nugget found lying in some mountainous region—and the pronounced grain of the ring.

I had the ring cast in silver, and then decided it would add an extra component to have it gold-plated. The weight and look of the ring demanded this final touch, and the result gives the piece an interesting masculine edge. Note: The time given to make the ring does not include the time for casting and gold-plating.

MATERIALS

1. Round wax tube

2. Small pyrite stone (also known as fool's gold) for ring

You will also need:

- Silver, about 1/2 oz (12 g) in weight, for the ring
- A short length of wax rod to create the sprue for casting
- Two-part epoxy glue for securing the stone in the setting

TOOLS

- Scribe (see page 178)
- Ruler
- Wax saw blades (see page 184)
- Ring gauge (see page 178)
- Ring enlarger (see page 184), optional
- Files (see page 179): large industrial rough file for helping to create texture on the ring's surface; selection of other files
- Scoring tools (see page 184) for scoring the wax ring
- Soldering iron, a small soldering torch for welding the wax rod to the wax tube
- Piercing saw (see page 178), wax blades (see page 184), and 2/0 blades
- Rough burr (see page 182) to recreate textures in the ring lost from the casting process
- Pendant drill (see page 182) with collet inside for holding the split pin in place
- Wet and dry papers (see page 184), 400, 800, and 1200 grit
- Barrel polisher (see page 185) for polishing the ring
- Burnisher (see page 182) for polishing the edges of the ring
- Small container for mixing the glue in
- Wall putty for holding the ring in position when setting the stone

CREATING THE RING SHAPE

1 Measure ³/₈ in (8 mm) on a ruler, then mark the same width on a wax tube. Score around the tube to create an accurate and even measure around the ring. Using a wax saw blade, saw just outside the scribed line, the whole way around the tube.

2 Measure your ring size, then use a ring enlarger to adjust the size if necessary. Make sure that the blade is facing the right way to remove the wax from inside the ring.

CREATING TEXTURE

3 To create texture on the surface of the ring, first use a large industrial rough file to file one side of the ring at an angle to create a slight curve, then file the opposite side until flat and smooth.

4 Using the scoring tools, carve very light lines and angles into the outer surfaces. A ruler can be used to create the straight lines more accurately, then use the large file again to skim across the top surface of the ring to create a textured effect. If the edges feel sharp, go around them lightly with the file, until smooth. The more finishing work done in the wax now the easier the job will be to clean once it has been cast.

5 To create a setting for the stone, use an engraving tool to make a small hole in the wax. The tool has the perfect angle on the blade to scoop out a hole in the wax.

FORMING AND REMOVING THE SPRUE

6 Using the soldering iron, carefully melt the wax rod, between 3/5 in and 3/4 in (15 mm and 20 mm) long, onto the outer surface of the ring. This will create your sprue for casting. The ring is now ready to take to the casters.

7 When the ring is back from the casters, saw off the sprue with a piercing saw and 2/0 saw blade.

8 Using a smoother file, file over the area where the sprue stump is left until there is a completely even and smooth curved surface on the top side of the ring.

9 The casting will have removed some of the definition from the textures that you created in the wax. To redefine them, burnish over with a rough burr, using a pendant drill. Check for any other sharp edges that may need to be filed down.

10 Again using the pendant motor, start to sand the ring with the coarser wet and dry paper. Once all the edges have been smoothed, move onto the finer paper to get a smoother finish.

11 Using a barrel polisher, polish the ring, then finally, burnish the edges to create a subtle accent on each of the edges. At this stage, the ring is sent to be gold-plated.

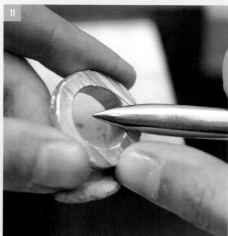

SETTING THE STONE

12 To set the stone, mix some two-part epoxy adhesive in a small container. Hold the ring in position with a large piece of wall putty and carefully place a large dab of glue in the setting.

Using a pair of tweezers, position the stone in the setting. Adjust the position of the stone if necessary. Leave the stone to set for 12 hours.

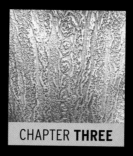

CHAPTER **THREE**

EXPLORING TECHNIQUES

A QUESTION OF TECHNIQUE

Craftsmanship is a very important element of the jeweler's work. The quality of jewelry is usually measured by how well it is made, and the greatest idea can be lost at the last moment by a poorly cut line or a pitted solder joint. Virtually every technique requires the application of the core skills of jewelry making—cutting, filing, soldering, finishing—and however well you think you have mastered them, there is always room for improvement.

Beyond the quality of application, it's important to look to the relationship between technique, material, and intention. Consider how effectively the chosen techniques exploit the materials in the finished piece and how well both elements integrate with the intention of the design. You will find that in time the process becomes instinctive, and your own creative language will emerge.

Technique can in itself become the focus for your work—you might find an affinity with "folding" (see pages 164–9), which spurs you to develop your own unique and recognizable style, for example.

EXPLORATION AND EXPERIMENTATION

Whether your starting point is from the technique, the material, or the idea, research and experimentation are key to finding the most powerful way to bring your intentions into three-dimensionality. In this process of investigation, you should be open to examining information from a variety of sources. Your research might take you to your library or to the zoo, to the museum, or to the toy store.

So, for example, if you want to incorporate movement into your work, to find the most appropriate method to achieve this you need to consider how other things move. Rather than reinventing the wheel, you should explore how and why the wheel works and how over time the wheel has lent itself to the cog and cam. An axle is a pivot—where else is this type of movement in action? Consider leverage, and perfect balance. You might also experiment with magnetic forces of attraction and repulsion. Or your own movement—how do your joints work to provide so many different kinds of movement? All the time you should be looking to see how the principles can be applied in interesting ways in your work.

Research might also lead you to look through your inherited jewelry, or to take a trip to an antiques market. Feeling and examining an object will tell you so much more than just looking from a singular point of view.

Make notes about your discoveries—what works and does not work? Make some quick samples and try out your ideas in other materials that can give you quick initial answers.

PROJECTS AND EXERCISES

The first six projects in this section are a challenging set of assignments that apply jewelry-making techniques in unexpected ways.

ONE-PIECE BROOCH Making a pin from a single sheet of metal using only hand tools (see pages 98–101).

PEWTER AND ACRYLIC PENDANT The ply/Perspex casting method: making a pendant from pewter and Perspex using balsa wood as a mold (see pages 102–107).

SAND CAST RINGS Making a ring from scrap silver using the delft sand-casting technique and incorporating stones in the casting process (see pages 108–13).

MOOD PENDANT Using thermo-conductive film and silver to make a precious version of the lucky bag ring (see pages 114–19).

FORGED RAINDROP EARRINGS Making a pair of earrings from forged silver wire, incorporating movement (see pages 120–5).

CACTUS BOX RING Making a complex box ring construction form, incorporating a stone setting (see pages 126–31).

The last six projects in this section are in the form of experimental, open-ended exercises exploring technique and providing the opportunity for unpredictable (personalized) outcomes.

ETCHING PROCESSES Three approaches to etching in the studio: low-tech photo etching, nail polish applications, and stencils from parcel tape (see pages 132–9).

MARRIED METALS Creating a multicolored or patterned metal from combined metals for use in other processes, as well as developing cutting, and soldering skills (see pages 140–5).

FUSION How to create a range of surface textures, with a focus on heat control (see pages 146–53).

LOW-TECH BATCH FORMING Use of polymorph to create plastic molds for sinking metal sheet to create repeatable forms. Use of flypress; hammers/mallets; other low-tech processes for forming, and some tool-making tips, too (see pages 154–63).

FOLDING METALS Scoring metal for folding, starting with cardstock, exploring planes, angles, and curves to create architectural/structural forms (see pages 164–7).

LINKAGES Exploring ways to join elements together to create movement (see pages 168–77).

Incorporating influences from her painting and fine art background, the etching process (top) provides Rebecca Dockree with an excellent means to convey words, stories, and imagery in her work.

Alex Yule maintains a sense of movement and fluidity through her jewelry collections (above), whether literal or suggested. Her inquiry has led her to explore various ways to incorporate a kinetic element in her pieces, as in these forget-me-not rings that were inspired by daisy chains.

The Totem Collection (above) takes inspiration from bones, and my original interest was to mirror the movement of the spine. By using two jump rings to join links together the degree of mobility between them is limited. In contrast, single connections between key links brings a dynamism to the piece and the wearer's movements are mirrored in the Totem's dance.

Natascha Kotsopoulou (right) uses vitreous enamel on abstract copper forms to explore the interaction of the elements themselves—the fusion of the earth's components through fire. She says about her work, "What I love about using these materials is essentially the attempt to overpower and control the elements, as well as the beauty of letting them take over. This partnership leads to intriguing results and a never-ending study where ideas keep changing and growing while new ones are born, fuelling innovative and creative work."

ONE-PIECE PIN

I like to work with limitations, and often my best pieces have developed from pushing against boundaries, or as a result of stretching tight constraints. In many cases, limitations are imposed by circumstance, but given the world and all its resources to play with, conversely this limitless opportunity challenges me to know where to start. In the absence of external impositions I seek my own brief—a challenge to myself, to see how ingenious I can be! Here's a nice pin project for you to try, and feel free to develop your own design rather than following this precise pattern.

MATERIALS

- Sterling silver sheet, 1.2 mm thickness,
  1¾ x 1 in (45 x 25 mm)

TOOLS

- Tracing paper, pencil, and fine-line
  permanent pen for marking out
- Bow drill (see page 179), 0.5 mm drill bit,
  for drilling holes for piercing
- Piercing saw (see page 178), 0/3 blades, for
  cutting out the shape
- Files (see page 179): half-round file and
  needle file for making edges smooth
- Scribe (see page 178) for pushing out the
  pin ready for filing
- Nylon-tipped pliers (see page 180)
- Wet and dry papers (see page 184), 1000
  grit, and buffing sticks
- Steel wool (see page 184) or other
  polishing material

TOOL TIP

CUSTOM POLISHING STRIP A great tip I found on the Ganoksin website (see Resources, page 188) is to stick glass-fiber tape (used for taping parcels, available from hardware or art stores) to the back of some wet and dry paper, then to cut thin strips with a scalpel. Use these in your saw frame as you would a blade (but sideways) so that you have a super thin and flexible polishing strip for getting into those really difficult gaps.

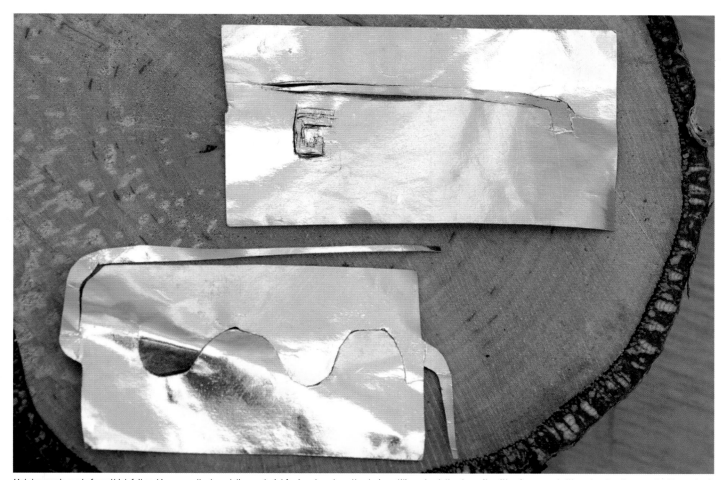

Metal paper is made from thick foil and is an excellent modeling material for jewelry where the design utilizes sheet. It cuts easily with scissors, and although not quite so malleable as sheet metal, it nonetheless has some ability to hold form. Also, having the appearance of metal this also helps to consider how light and reflection will affect your designs.

MAKING THE BASIC PIN

1 Trace the pattern from the template (see pages 186), and transfer it to your sheet of metal.

2 Mark the holes for drilling, as indicated by a dot on the pattern, and drill these holes with a bow drill with a 0.5 mm drill bit.

3 Feed the saw blade into the holes and carefully cut the lines. You only get one chance to get this right, so concentrate on a clean cut. I have used a fairly thin blade here because I love the "drawn" quality of the line it gives. Because the metal is thick, you need to pay particular attention to keeping your saw perfectly perpendicular to the surface of your metal.

Once the inside lines have been made, saw the external lines. Cutting these last gives you a chance to redraw the form, if you made any serious mistakes with your inside lines.

4 File the outside edges smooth. A half-round file does the job nicely.

MAKING FASTENING AND HOOK

5 Push out the fastening using the tip of a scribe, and use a pair of nylon-tipped pliers to bend it out completely for easy access for filing (see below, Step 7). File this strip of metal to a nicely tapered, round, thin wire. Rough file marks will snag in any fine fabric fibers, so rub your fastening with 1000-grit wet and dry paper to make it smooth.

6 Now the fastening is out of the pin, clean up any wobbly inside lines, either with a file, or with a strip of tape-backed wet and dry paper (see Tool tip, page 99) threaded into your saw.

7 Bend out the hook in the same way you did with the fastening. Push out the fastening with the tip of a scribe, and use a pair of nylon-tipped pliers to bend it out completely, this time bringing it to a full 90 degrees from the pin. File minimally to make smooth.

8 Using the pliers, manipulate the fastening so that it lies parallel with the pin back, pointing toward the hook. You may need to tweak the hook now so that the two elements function well.

9 Give your one-piece pin a final polish, and wear it!

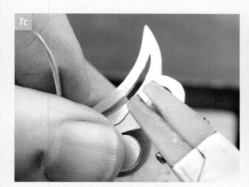

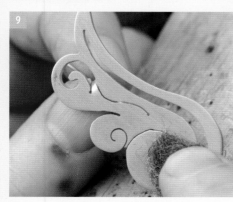

PEWTER AND ACRYLIC PENDANT

Lead-free pewter is a fabulous metal to work with for casting. Made almost entirely from tin, it has a low melting point, making it easy and safe to use. It has a superb silver color and the metal retains its shine and finish without tarnishing. It's considered a hypoallergenic material for jewelry purposes. The metal is soft though, so works well for low-impact jewelry such as earrings and pendants, but rings will deform relatively quickly. An advantage of pewter having a low melting point is that other materials can be easily combined inside the mold without fear of shattering or burning up. Here we are using acrylic sheet.

This method of casting is simple and effective, and if you are careful with the preparation of the mold you should be able to reuse it many times to produce multiples of the same shape. When designing the mold, always consider how the metal will fill it—we are using gravity to fill the mold, so imagine it filling like a cup from the faucet. Certain shapes cannot work because air will become trapped and the resulting item will be incomplete. Consider this in relation to the acrylic inserts, too. Most shapes are resolvable if you think logically about them. For instance, an "n" shape will capture air and prevent metal from filling into it, but if it's upturned to become a "u" the metal will flow all around it without problems.

You can add variety to your pendants by interchanging the colors and shapes of the acrylic sheet, or try other materials, as long as it maintains the same thickness as the balsa wood mold.

MATERIALS

1) Acrylic sheet, $\frac{1}{6}$ in (3 mm) thickness, 2 x 1$\frac{1}{2}$ in (50 x 40 mm); a smaller sheet would do for this design
2) Leather or cord to hang the pendant from
3) Balsa wood, $\frac{1}{6}$ in (3 mm) thickness, 4 x 4 in (100 x 100 mm)
4) Lead-free pewter, half bar (approx. 2 oz/50 g)

You will also need:
- Two sheets of MDF (or plywood), $\frac{3}{8}$ in (10 mm) thickness, 4 x 4 in (100 x 100 mm) each

TOOLS

Bear in mind that tools for use with pewter should be kept separate (see Tools tips, right).
- Tracing paper, pencil, and fine-line permanent pen
- Piercing saw (see page 178), 8/0 blades, and wax cutting blades for cutting out the acrylic shapes
- Needle files (see page 179): half-round needle file, three-square (triangular) needle file
- Double-sided tape
- Vise and quick-release clamps (see page 181)
- Aluminum pans, hot plate, and old baking tray for melting the pewter
- Center punch (see page 179)
- Drill (see pages 179 and 182), 2.5 mm drill bit
- Countersink or larger drill
- Wet and dry papers, (see page 184) 400, 600, and 1000 grit
- Polishing method of choice (see page 185), hand polish/tumbler/bench polisher

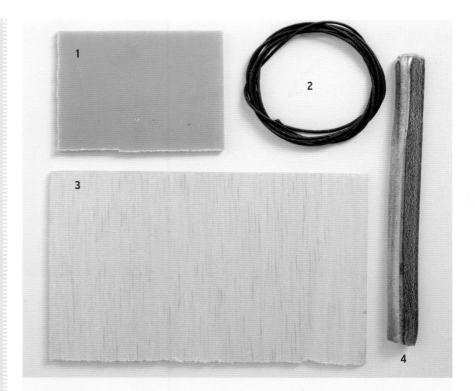

TOOLS TIPS

WAX CUTTING BLADES These are heavy-duty twisted blades, so they can cut in any/all directions without you needing to turn the saw. They cut beautifully through the thick acrylic sheet without breaking, and with minimal risk of cracking the plastic.

AVOIDING CONTAMINATION WITH PRECIOUS MATERIALS Pewter is a tin-rich, low-melt, soft and dense metal. It will make a mess of your precious metals if it gets a chance to—a crumb of pewter on silver, when heated, will burn a hole through it, so you need to avoid any possible contamination. This is not too difficult to organize if you follow some basic rules: keep separate files, blades, and drill bits for pewter work; brush down your bench and work surfaces during and after using pewter.

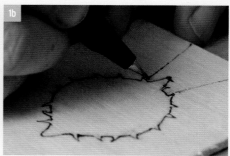

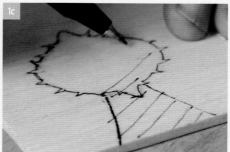

MAKING THE MOLD

1 First, you will need to make the mold from the sheet of balsa wood. Draw a line ³/₄ in (20 mm) from the top of the balsa wood sheet, parallel to the edge. Copy the chestnut design onto a sheet of tracing paper; rub the pencil over the back and then lay it onto the balsa wood with the pattern below the ³/₄ in (20 mm) line, and roughly central from the sides. Draw over the line to leave a tracing of the chestnut.

Draw over the line with a pen, correcting any wobbles in the tracing as you go. From the top, draw two lines, which will form the sprue, or mouth, for the metal to enter the balsa mold. Don't worry if you "lose" some of the chestnut pattern—you can cut this back into the pendant when you have cast it in metal. Shade in this area to be removed so that you are clear, as you cut, what your purpose is.

2 Cut out the shaded area in one continuous line, using the 8/0 blade. Pay attention to the angle of your saw—keep it vertical.

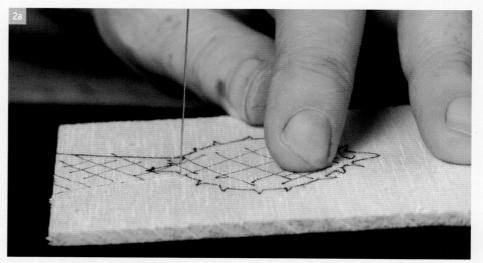

MAKING THE ACRYLIC INSERTS

3 Leave the protective plastic sheet on the acrylic when tracing and cutting as it picks up the pencil line very well. Trace the acrylic shapes from the center of the pattern, and cut them out using the wax blades. Note how thick these blades are; cut on the waste side of the line to maintain the original sizes of the inserts. Once cut, file the edges smooth.

4 Heated acrylic becomes slightly rubbery, and as the molten pewter pours around it in the mold the pewter will not stick to it as you might imagine. To make the acrylic stay in position once the pewter is cast, a jigsaw effect needs to be created so that the acrylic is wedged into place. Do this by grooving the edges with a three-square (triangular) needle file.

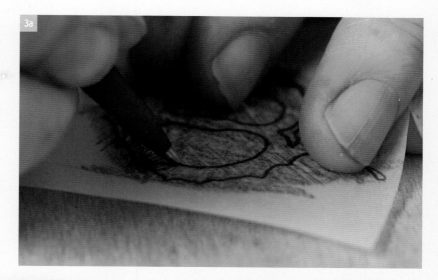

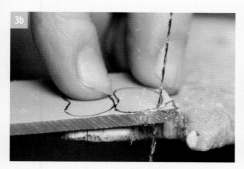

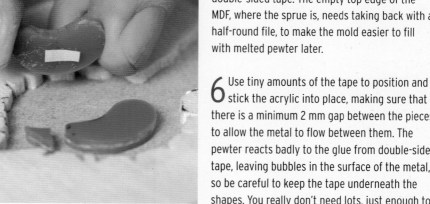

ASSEMBLING THE MOLD

5 Stick the balsa wood mold onto a sheet of MDF or plywood, using a small amount of double-sided tape. The empty top edge of the MDF, where the sprue is, needs taking back with a half-round file, to make the mold easier to fill with melted pewter later.

6 Use tiny amounts of the tape to position and stick the acrylic into place, making sure that there is a minimum 2 mm gap between the pieces to allow the metal to flow between them. The pewter reacts badly to the glue from double-sided tape, leaving bubbles in the surface of the metal, so be careful to keep the tape underneath the shapes. You really don't need lots, just enough to hold the pieces in position as you pour the metal.

7 File the second MDF sheet where the sprue is, then place it on top to make the full sandwich. Squeeze together with the two clamps and put this arrangement into the vise, on the old baking sheet, to hold it firm as you pour the metal.

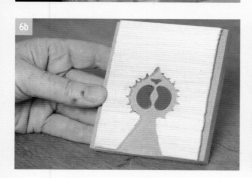

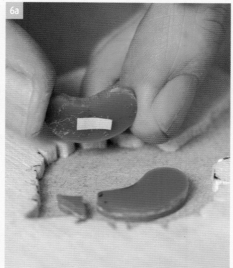

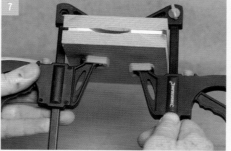

CASTING WITH PEWTER

As an extension to this project you might try other approaches to casting with pewter—its low melting point makes it suitable for pouring into wood, latex, sand, silicone, and cuttlefish. Consider including other materials or objects into your mold to—old beads, buttons, and stones can work well. Whichever materials you use for the mold or for inclusions, they must be moisture free, and you must check that whatever you use will not emit poisonous fumes when heated. As always, work in a well-ventilated area, and wear suitable protective clothing (see page 185). Pay special attention to your feet as they become vulnerable to splashes of hot metal. (See also Step 8, page 112.)

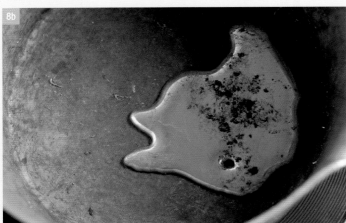

MELTING AND POURING

8 Melt your metal in the pan on the hot plate. You may find as it heats that a crumbly layer of dross gathers on the surface of the molten metal. This is a natural occurrence as heating speeds up the oxidation process. Carefully remove it from the surface—either scoop it out with an old spoon or (this is my preferred method) slowly pour the metal into a second pan—the dross will stay at the back, like an old skin—then tap out this dross and return the pewter to the original pan for a final reheating.

When the metal has returned to liquid form, carefully pour the pewter into the mold. Wait for 10 minutes for the metal to solidify and cool. Go and have a cup of coffee. Oh, the excitement! When you open the mold, it should look something like this (see below).

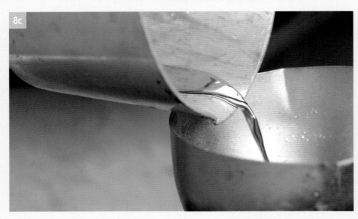

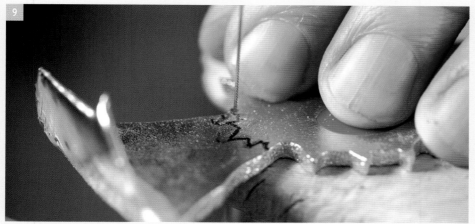

SHAPING AND DRILLING

9 Redraw from the tracing the line you lost when you cut the sprue into the balsa wood. Also mark the drill hole from this tracing. Cut the outline carefully and accurately with a 2/0 blade. File the edges with a needle file.

10 Mark the hole for drilling with a center punch, and use a drill of your choice to drill a hole of suitable size for your leather or cord. I opted for a $\frac{1}{10}$ in (2.5 mm) hole. Use a countersink, or a larger drill, to de-burr the hole on both sides.

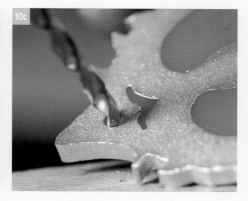

FILING AND POLISHING

11 File all the edges smooth using a needle file, then rub over to remove scratches with 1000-grit wet and dry paper.

12 To smooth the surface, take a 400-grit wet and dry paper, and using it wet, surface the back and front of the pendant, using a figure-eight movement, until there are no inconsistencies across the pewter or the acrylic. (I use a latex stationery thimblet to protect my thumb so that it doesn't wear away with the pewter!)

Work your way down through paper grades to 1000 grit, still using water to assist. Watch out for your fingertips—you can grind them down without even noticing.

Polish to your desired shininess. I used a bench polisher, but a tumbler also works nicely and standard metal polishing compounds tend to work well on acrylic too. Thread as desired.

SAND CAST RINGS

Delft casting, also known as sand casting, is a speedy way to produce small batches of jewelry. This technique involves making a cavity in a two-part mold. Because the mold can be opened, you can use all manner of objects to make impressions into the soft, clay-like sand. The only limitation is that whatever you push into the sand must come out leaving a clean indent.

I made a wax master for my casting because it is quick and easy to form, and I will be able to make numerous variations in metal from this master by slightly altering each mold once the wax impression has been made.

I love the endless possibilities that arise with the sand cast technique. Time is the only thing you can lose here, as all the materials are easily recycled or reused. And it's a perfect opportunity to use up all your scrap silver and unwanted jewelry. (You can also use other metals—for example, gold or pewter—but be sure not to mix metals in the melting pot. See also Tools tips for the Pewter and Acrylic Pendant, page 103).

I incorporated garnets, rubies, and sapphires into the mold before pouring the metal. Heating often changes a stone's color, so don't try anything too precious! Garnets are an inexpensive stone and in fact stand up to high heats fairly well. Rubies and sapphires are hard stones and difficult to damage, even under extreme heat—but there are always the exceptions! Other materials may also work if they can withstand temperatures of 1652°F (900°C) plus. However, you should exercise caution when experimenting.

Once you have made a few attempts at the ring, you will begin to see the endless and exciting possibilities that this technique presents—as ever, play on!

TOOL TIP

ANYTHING GOES It is possible to use any hard material as a tool for pressing into the delft clay to make a mold. Once you have gained some confidence with the basics, try adding textures into the hollowed mold—pepper the surface with spikes by pushing a scribe into the clay; press shells, crab claws, or other found objects into the surface to create a montage of textures; draw into the surface with wooden tools; make reusable formers out of modeling clay.

SAFETY EQUIPMENT

In addition to the usual workshop safety rules (see page 183), when working with molten silver make sure that you are adequately protected from the dangers of spillage or explosion, which can result in burns and scalds. Wear a suede (or similar) apron to protect your front, suede gauntlets to protect hands and arms, shoes that entirely cover the feet (ideally made of leather), and goggles to protect eyes (see also page 185). Fumes are also a potential hazard when using extreme heat, so do make sure that you have good ventilation in your workspace.

MATERIALS

1) Rough sapphires, garnets, or other heat-resistant stones
2) Scrap silver

You will also need:

- Ring wax—I used blue wax in this instance because it maintains some flexibility and is less likely to fracture when pressed into the clay
- Delft clay, a commercially available fine red sand that is mixed with glycerine to make it slightly sticky in consistency
- Talcum powder to separate the master from the mold, and to part the two halves of the mold
- Borax powder to keep the silver clean when molten
- Superglue, as a back-up plan for your stone in case it requires strengthening after casting.

TOOLS

- Piercing saw (see page 178), wax saw blades (see page 184); wax files (see page 184), and scalpel (see page 178) for cutting and shaping the wax
- Wax ring sizer (see page 184)
- 12 in (300 mm) steel rule for chopping "clay"
- Pair of aluminum delft casting rings (see page 184) for containing the clay
- Jobbing hammer (see page 180)
- 2 mm drill bit (see page 182) for making risers for air to escape
- $\frac{1}{6}$ in (4 mm) drill bit (see page 182) and sharp knife for making the sprue for pouring the molten silver
- Crucible and crucible tongues (see page 184) for containing the silver for melting
- Large torch (see page 183)
- Water bucket (metal) for submerging and cooling the hot mold
- Size 1 saw blade (see page 178) for removing the sprue after casting
- Files (see page 179): large files and needle files
- Wet and dry papers (see page 184), 800 to 1200 grit

PREPARING THE WAX SHAPE

1 Cut a slice of ring wax to your required thickness. I've used blue wax here because I like its firm yet flexible qualities, but the harder (and more brittle) green wax will also do. Avoid softer waxes, though, as you won't get a clean impression in the delft clay, which tends to stick to them.

2 Make the ring to your size using a wax ring sizer. The scraping blade on this tool tapers, so work the ring from both sides to get a good fit. When the size has been perfected, consider the overall form and contours of the ring in relation to the stones you want to include in the cast. Work the ring into shape using wax files or a scalpel. A candle flame will soften and smooth rough, jagged surfaces should you want a rounder, more organic form.

PREPARING THE MOLD

3 On a smooth, flat surface, chop the clay into small crumbs. Identify the bottom aluminum ring—the one with an inner lip—and put it lip-side down on the surface. Fill with clay, hammering it into the ring. Using a ruler, scrape the bottom flat, then turn face up. Sprinkle with talc, then gently but firmly press the master into the clay until half buried. Recoat with talc and assemble the second ring onto this filled one, aligning the notches on the rings' outsides. Fill with clay, compressing it into the ring. Scrape the top flat. Carefully (without twisting) pull apart the rings and remove the wax master. You should have two matching, perfect impressions.

4 Position the sprue just to the outside of the ring form, on the top half of the mold, and use the $\frac{1}{6}$ in (4 mm) drill bit to cut a hole through from the ring cavity to the top side of the clay. With a sharp knife, cut a wide funnel through the clay, from the top down to the underside, taking care not to damage the mold. Remove any loose sand. Turn the ring over and break the $\frac{1}{6}$ in (4 mm) sprue hole into your ring cavity, to allow the metal to flow from the sprue into the ring.

Working on the top half of the mold, use the smaller drill bit to make several 2 mm holes around the edges of the mold, working from the inside toward the top. With a blunt pencil, make small grooves from your mold out to these holes; these risers allow air to escape when you pour in the metal.

5 Reassemble the mold, taking care to match up the grooves. Push the drill bits back into all the holes from the top side, just far enough to make a small indent on the bottom half of the mold. Separate the halves again, and gently open these holes into this half of the ring cavity as before. Brush away any loose sand.

6 If you are adding stones to your ring, now is the time to do it. How you place them will depend on your ring design and the size and shape of your stones. Be prepared for spectacular triumph or jaw-dropping failure. Either result will be a great learning experience, and give you a clearer understanding of how to design for success.

MELTING THE SILVER

7 Take the necessary health and safety precautions (see pages 109 and 183) before you begin, and make sure that you are wearing your protective clothing (see page 185). The heating area must be well insulated with firebricks, and any combustible objects or materials should be removed.

Check that recycled and scrap jewelry is made entirely of silver before you try to melt it. Do not allow moisture or other foreign materials to get into the crucible when you are melting the silver.

8 Place your scrap silver into the crucible. You could use casting grain instead, or a mixture of both. Heat until the silver begins to melt. Remove the flame momentarily to sprinkle a little borax powder over the surface, then continue to heat until the metal is entirely molten and can roll fluidly around the crucible.

CASTING IN SAND

9 Keeping the flame on the metal even as you pour, carefully empty the contents of the crucible into the sprue cavity. There will be a little smoke, and perhaps some small flames, as the oily sand of the delft clay burns a little. Move your head back a little to avoid breathing in the fumes.

As soon as you have finished pouring, you can pick up (with a pair of tongs) the entire mold and immerse it into your bucket of water. It will make satisfying gurgling sounds as the cold water and hot metal meet. Keep immersed for a minute or two, to allow the metal to cool and solidify.

RELEASING FROM THE MOLD

10 When there is silence you can remove the mold from the water. Over a table, release the two halves of the mold to see what you have. Ideally, you will see a complete ring, with your stones encapsulated in the silver. Take care with the stone, as it may have fractured through the shock of the extreme heating and cooling process. If it looks delicate, you can try adding some superglue to reinforce it. As you pull away the sand from the metal, separate out and discard the blackened parts—you can reuse the remaining red sand once it has dried (just dab off the moisture with a cloth).

CLEANING AND FINISHING

11 Using a piercing saw (I use a size 1 blade for this job), cut off the sprue as close to the ring as possible without damaging it. Then file and polish, taking care not to lose the textural quality of the casting.

MOOD PENDANT

The mood pendant presents several quite sophisticated approaches to jewelry-making that could be exploited in numerous other ways, so see how you can expand and evolve these concepts.

BEYOND BLACK AND WHITE

When I came across liquid crystal sheet I was instantly transported back to my early teenage years when I first owned a mood ring! I loved the magical way in which the colors changed, and the moods it described were certainly induced, if not faithful representations.

This project is a wry adult take on that teen-angst. In mine, I have kept the heart motif, but it can be a bird, a word, or some other symbol. As the pendant is double-sided, you might use two different motifs for yours.

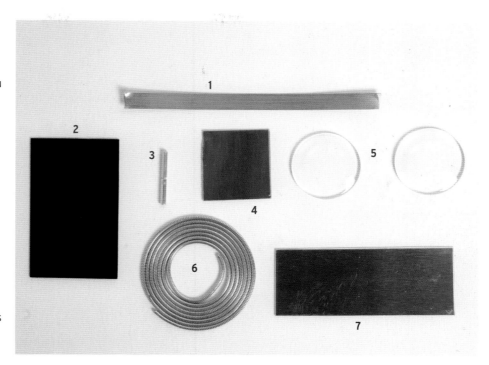

MATERIALS

1) Bezel strip (or fine silver), 0.3 mm thickness, 1$\frac{1}{2}$ x 2$\frac{3}{4}$ in (40 x 70 mm) for the side, or wall, of the pendant
2) 2 x liquid crystal sheet squares, $\frac{3}{4}$ x $\frac{3}{4}$ in (19 x 19 mm), sold in larger sheets of 6 x 6 in (150 x 150 mm)
3) Silver tube for the bail, 2.5 mm external diameter, $\frac{1}{2}$ in (15 mm) long (less is needed, but this gives extra length to let you curve the tube)
4) Sterling silver sheet, 0.3 mm thickness, $\frac{3}{4}$ x $\frac{3}{4}$ in (20 x 20 mm) for sticking the film to
5) 2 x magnifying watch glasses, flat bottomed with curved tops to create a magnifying effect, $\frac{3}{4}$ in (20.5 mm) diameter (see Resources, page 188)
6) Snake chain, 1.2 mm diameter
7) Sterling silver sheet, 0.5 mm thickness, 1$\frac{3}{4}$ x 1 in (45 x 23 mm), for the front and back of the pendant

You will also need:

- Wire, 1.2 mm diameter, to assist in curving the tubing
- Sterling silver finding of choice; for this chain I used a commercially produced bayonet clasp

TOOLS

- Tape for the bezel
- Piercing saw (see page 178), 8/0 blades for the bezel, 4/0 blades for cutting the front and back of the pendant
- Soldering equipment (see page 183): flux (borax), brush, solder paste, torch, tweezers, soldering block, and pickle
- Files (see page 179): half-round file, round file, needle file, and escapement file for getting into the intricate angles of the heart for filing
- Doming block (see page 181) for shaping the silver disks for the front and back
- Punches (see page 181) for curving the back and front
- Fine-line permanent pen
- Bow drill (see page 179), 0.5 mm drill bit, for drilling the back and front for piercing out the hearts
- Wet and dry papers (see page 184)
- Mallet (see page 180)
- Steel block (see page 181)
- Binding wire used for holding the two pieces together for soldering
- Nylon-tipped pliers (see page 180) for gently shaping the tubing for the bail
- Dividers (see page 178)
- Scalpel (see page 178)
- Chamois or suede (see page 185)
- Burnisher (see page 182) for the final rub
- Pusher (see page 182) for setting
- Abrasive polishing block (see page 185) for polishing the final piece
- Two-part epoxy glue for attaching the clasp to the chain

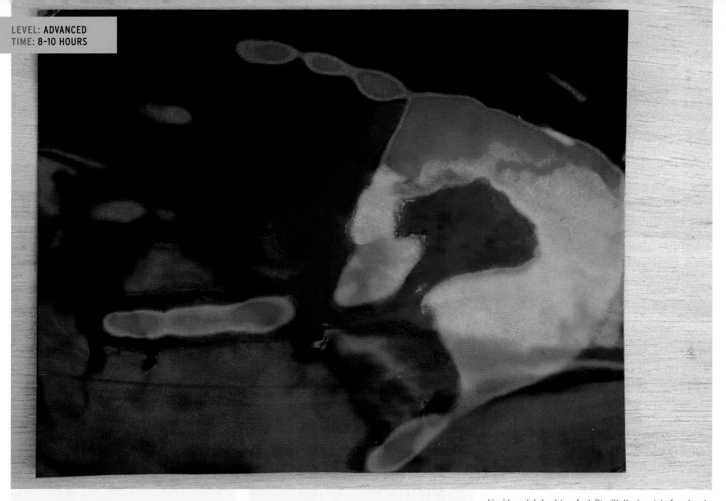

MATERIALS TIPS

Liquid crystal sheet This contains heat-sensitive crystals that change from black through to red, green, and blue as they are heated. The crystals are sensitive: it's unlikely that on flesh you will be anything less than "Amused, Upbeat, Cheerful." If you want the potential for the full range of colors, the film needs to be protected from direct heat sources, as it will go straight to "Excited" and stay there until you get to the refrigerator!

WATCH GLASS This can be made from plastic or glass. Plastic watch glasses tend to be domed, and may easily scratch, whereas mineral watch glasses (i.e. made from glass) are available domed, flat, or magnifying, and less prone to scratching. I have used the magnifying type because I like the weight, the visual impact, and the potential for magnification.

SNAKE CHAIN This has a wonderful fluidity and movement about it, but it has limitations. I don't often advocate the use of glue, but when it comes to attaching findings to snake chain gluing and crimping are the only sensible options, as any kind of heat treatment to it causes it to weaken, kink, and eventually break.

TOOLS TIPS

SAW BLADES Choosing the correct blade for the thickness of metal sheet you are cutting becomes instinctive after time, but if you are still at the stage where your cutting is not a smooth action, try dropping down to a smaller size of tooth. As a rule you should aim for two teeth per thickness of metal. Your eyes are good if you can see this! For the rest of us, here's a guide:

2/0 blade - 1-0.8 mm thickness
3/0 blade - 0.8-0.7 mm thickness
4/0 blade - 0.6-0.5 mm thickness
8/0 blade - 0.4 mm thickness or less

ESCAPEMENT FILES These are beautifully fine, precision files for getting into very small places. If you can afford only one (they are expensive), get a half-round one, as this tackles curves and straight edges.

Liquid crystal sheet (see far left) with the imprint of my hand, indicating that my mood was amused, upbeat, and cheerful.

MOOD RING COLORS

Back to my original ring, I never could remember what each color meant, so the piece of paper that came with the ring was kept preciously screwed up in the bottom of my pocket. Thanks to the internet we no longer need to weep (as I did as a teenager) when instructions go through the washing machine. Here's what the mood ring is all about:

BLACK Stressed, Cold, Uptight, Tense
BROWN Nervous, Anxious, Puzzled
RED Energized, Restless, Distracted
AMBER Hopeful, Mixed Emotions, Unpredictable
GREEN Amused, Upbeat, Cheerful
BLUE Relaxed, Calm, Love, Tranquil
DARK BLUE/PURPLE Passionate, Hot, Excited.

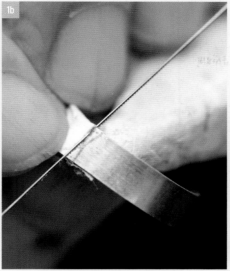

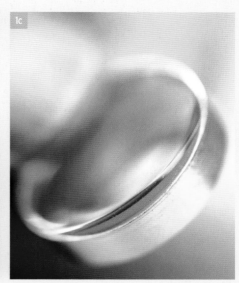

MAKING THE BEZEL

1 Wrap the bezel strip tightly around the glass lens with your finger. Mark a point where the bezel strip overlaps.

Remove the glass, tape the bezel in position with masking tape, and cut through both parts to get a clean and perfect joint. I always use a saw with a fine blade (8/0) for cutting this thin sheet, but you might get away with a sharp pair of snips.

Take the necessary health and safety precautions before you begin soldering (see page 183). Solder (H) and pickle, then check for fit. The lens should sit perfectly inside.

MAKING THE BACK AND FRONT

2 The front circle of the pendant is $^7/_8$ in (22 mm) diameter. The back circle is $^3/_4$ in (20 mm) diameter. Cut out with a piercing saw and file with a half-round file around the two circles.

Curve the circles very gently in the doming block. Don't anneal them—you don't want the metal to stretch very much. I use a wooden block and punches to avoid deformation or stretching of the metal. The aim is to get a perfect fit against your watch glass.

One dome should fit inside the bezel (just like the lens), and the other dome should be slightly bigger than the bezel itself. The larger one will be soldered to the bezel, and will become the front of the pendant.

3 Carefully draw your heart or other motif onto each dome—I use a fine-line permanent pen.

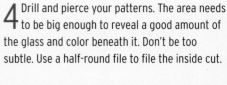

4 Drill and pierce your patterns. The area needs to be big enough to reveal a good amount of the glass and color beneath it. Don't be too subtle. Use a half-round file to file the inside cut.

5 Once the patterns are cut, check each dome against the watch glass to see that the silver sits flush against the curved glass. If necessary, tap gently downward onto the glass with a mallet to bring the surfaces together.

SOLDERING THE FRONT TO THE BEZEL

6 Surface the bottom edge of the circle on coarse wet and dry paper, then position the bezel on this edge for soldering. Use binding wire to hold in position if you must, but don't make it too taut because the bezel is likely to deform under the heat and pressure. Add five or six large pieces of solder to the inside joint and heat from the outside to draw the solder through. Pickle, then file back the edges.

SHAPING AND ATTACHING THE BAIL

7 Anneal the silver tubing for the bail, insert the 1.2 mm wire to support the internal hole, then use finger pressure, or nylon-tipped pliers, to add a gentle curve to the tube. Don't squeeze or grip too hard! When you are happy with the shape, remove the wire and give the outside a quick rub with 1000-grit wet and dry paper in preparation for soldering.

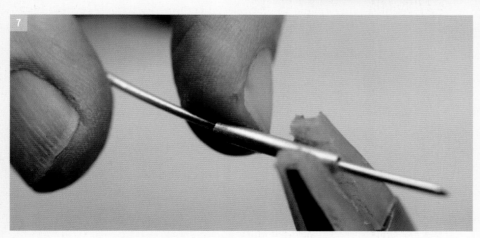

8 Use dividers to mark a light line $\frac{1}{10}$ in (2.5 mm) from the open edge of the bezel. Find the correct position for the tubing so that your motif hangs in the upright position and mark the center point. Use a round file to make a very light groove (remember, it's very thin silver) in the bezel where the lines meet, to provide a location for your tubing.

9 Use small chips of solder block to support the tubing in position against the bezel, and solder (E) into place. Pickle and dry, then trim the curved tube to size. Clean and polish all parts ready for assembly.

10 Cut a $\frac{3}{4}$ in (19 mm) diameter disk from the silver sheet of 0.3 mm thickness. Peel off the backing of one of the thermochromic squares and stick onto the disk. Trim to size with a scalpel. Turn the disk over and repeat so that you end up with a two-sided thermochromic disk.

ASSEMBLING THE PENDANT

11 Here comes the exciting bit! Insert the first watch glass into the bezel so that it fits against the front dome. Insert the liquid crystal disk, making sure to center it to the watch glass. Insert the second watch glass face up, then insert the back dome.

There should be roughly 1 mm of bezel standing proud of this assembly. If not, make sure everything is pressed firmly into the bezel. Place a soft piece of chamois or suede onto your peg to protect the front of your pendant for this next stage. Gently ease the bezel over the dome with a pusher, as you would when setting a stone (north/south/east/west, then all the points in between, always working in opposites). The sides are easily dented, so use very controlled pressure as you push.

12 When you have pushed all the way around, use a burnisher for a final rub over. Check with your fingers that the setting feels comfortable—if it's edgy, continue carefully with the pusher and burnisher until you feel an improvement. Give the piece a final polish. I use an abrasive polishing block for a satin finish.

FINISHING OFF

13 Thread the snake chain through the bail, and position on your chest to decide on your perfect length. Cut to size, then attach your finding of choice by crimping or gluing as appropriate.

At this stage I hope your mood will be deep blue to violet; please wait for the glue to set before declaring your excitement to the world!

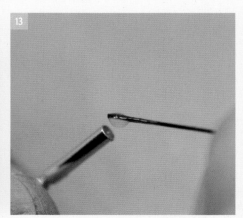

FORGED RAINDROP EARRINGS

The inspiration for these earrings came to me on a rainy day. There's something deeply primal about beating a rhythm with a hammer; it's a multi-sensory experience and the more you tune in the better the result.

The raindrops came easily, but it took some time to work out the most elegant solution of how to join the drops to the ear. In the end the horn-like stud from which the raindrops hang has an almost Viking aesthetic, drawn through time, perhaps, from that mesmeric primal beat.

The stud part of the earrings should sit on, and in line with, the ear. If yours don't, it's likely that you have beaten the silver a little more than I did, or perhaps the pin, which acts as the balancing point, is too close to one or other end of the stud. You can rectify this problem by adding another drop onto one or both of the longest two raindrop chains. Experiment to see what works best for you. Making your own butterflies for earrings is an excellent exercise done once, but more than this is unnecessary torture; I suggest you buy them from your favorite supplier!

MATERIALS

1) Sterling silver wire, 1.5 mm diameter, 3 ft (1 m) long
2) One pair sterling silver butterflies, or other ear-stud backs
3) Sterling silver wire, 0.8 mm diameter, 3/4 in (20 mm) long
4) Sterling silver wire, 1/10 in (2.5 mm) diameter, 2 in (50 mm) long

TOOLS

- Stakes (see page 181): #1 curved stake and #2 curved stake (see below right)
- Hammers (see below and page 180): planishing hammer, large raising hammer, and small raising hammer for shaping and forming the wire
- Vise (see page 181)
- Wire cutters (see page 178)
- Steel rule, dividers, and fine-line permanent pen (see page 178) for measuring and marking
- Drill of choice (see below right and pages 179 and 182), 1.2 mm and 0.8 mm drill bits
- Center punch (see page 179)
- Wedge-shaped block of wood for supporting the raindrops when drilling (see right)
- Graver (see page 178) for cutting a groove into the wooden block, for assisting in holding the raindrops for drilling
- Half-round needle file (see page 179)
- Piercing saw (see page 178), 8/0 blades
- Snipe-nosed pliers (see page 180)
- Steel block and sand bag (see page 181)
- Sprung tweezers (see page 183)
- Soldering equipment (see pages 182 and 183): flux (borax), brush, solder paste (ordinary solder will do too, but this makes life easier), torch, tweezers, soldering block, and pickle
- Tumbler (see page 185) for polishing and surfacing the silver

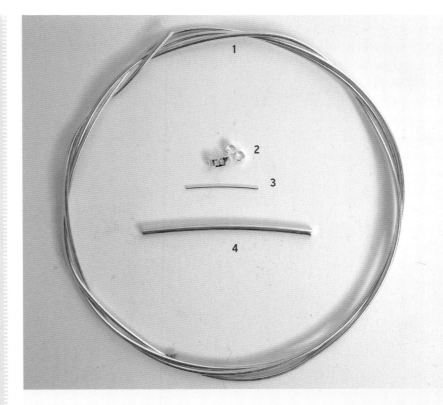

TOOLS TIPS

STAKES AND HAMMERS It's worth taking care of the surfaces of your stakes and hammers. Whacking a raising hammer onto your stake will leave indents on the surface that imprint on any metal you subsequently work with them. Ideally, these tools should have a pristine mirror finish. Imperfections can be removed with files and papers before a final polish. There are some basic stake types, but in the main jewelers do not have standard names for all the stakes they use. In this instance, I use two stakes, which I call #1 curved stake and #2 curved stake.

DRILLING There are lots of holes to drill when making these earrings, and if you have a pillar drill this will make light work of the job. A hand drill will do it too, if you are strong enough. As most of these holes need to be cut through slanting surfaces, it is not uncommon for the drill bit to slide out of position as it cuts. To counter this, use a wedge-shaped piece of scrap wood as a support to even out the slope. This can be shaped and cut as necessary to assist in the drilling process.

SHAPING THE RAINDROPS

1 Using the #1 stake and a planishing hammer, spread the end of the 1.5 mm wire. Be careful not to go too thin on the edges as you need substance for the holes to be drilled, and additional pieces to hang from them. Cut the wire about ³/₈ in (8 mm) from the tip of the spread end with wire cutters. Repeat 30 times, giving you some spares to choose from.

Now work the other ends. Hold the spread end of the wire with the flattened surface at 90 degrees to the stake and hammer flat as before.

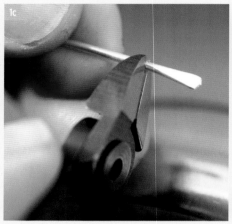

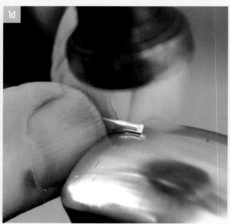

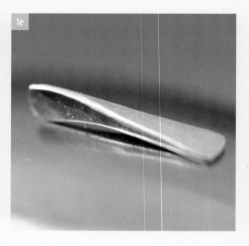

DRILLING THE RAINDROPS

2 Each shaped piece needs to be drilled top and bottom, EXCEPT for the last droplet on each strand. Using the pen, mark the point to drill a 1.2 mm hole. Make it equidistant from the sides and 2 mm from the end of the droplet. Make an indent at each point with a center punch. Check that the indents are where you want them; if the center punch slips out of position, turn over and try again on the back.

3 Cut a groove into the wooden block with a graver to assist in supporting the droplets when drilling. (Push the flattened edge of one end of the droplet into the groove so that the other end sits flat against your wood, ready for drilling.) Drill all the marked holes in this way. Once all the holes have been made, file all the ends round.

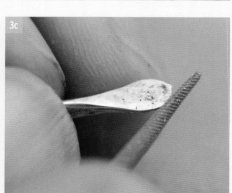

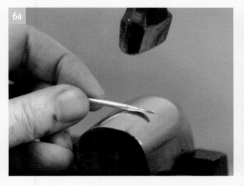

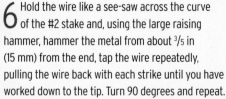

MAKING THE CHAINS

4 The top hole for each raindrop needs to be cut open to connect with the next. Using the finest blade you can handle, ideally 8/0, cut from one edge into the drilled hole to make a hook of sorts. Open this "hook" out and feed it into the hole of the next raindrop before closing with a pair of snipe-nosed pliers. Continue to make two chains each of five, four, and three droplets.

FORGING THE STUD POINTS

5 In order to taper the silver wires to a nice point for the studs, we must first make the ends square. Tap the end of the $1/10$ in (2.5 mm) wire on the steel block with the planishing hammer to flatten the surface slightly, then turn the wire 90 degrees and repeat to get a square section.

6 Hold the wire like a see-saw across the curve of the #2 stake and, using the large raising hammer, hammer the metal from about $3/5$ in (15 mm) from the end, tap the wire repeatedly, pulling the wire back with each strike until you have worked down to the tip. Turn 90 degrees and repeat.

Repeat this raising action, but this time $3/8$ in (10 mm) from the tip, again working down to the end. Flip 90 degrees and repeat. You will begin to get a tapering effect now. Resist the temptation to knock the corners off the square until you are happy with the point. Now use the planishing hammer on the steel block to round off the tapered square section's corners. Repeat for the other end of the wire so that you have two points the same, then curve them slightly over the half-round portion of the stake.

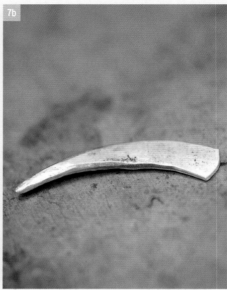

FORGING: SPREADING THE ENDS

7 Cut each end 20 mm (³/₄ in) from the tip. You will have some spare silver from the middle – this extra length is not needed, but it made the piece easier to hold. Flatten the new raw ends on the steel block with the planishing hammer.

8 Using the large raising hammer, work the lower edge over the 180-degree stake, at a 45-degree slant to draw out the flattened, lower edge. When you are happy with the shape, stop, and try to repeat precisely the same action on the next piece. Remember we want mirror images in order to make a pair. Give these bottom edges a rhythmic, linear texture with the smaller raising hammer. Compare both pieces and if necessary file or cut to get a good match.

DRILLING THE STUDS

9 Draw a line with a fine-line permanent pen 1.5 mm from the bottom edge.

Set your dividers to ¹/₁₀ in (2.5 mm), and walk them along the line to get three equidistant points to mark and drill. Mark with the center punch as before, then drill these holes with the 1.2 mm drill bit, using the wedge-shaped block underneath to stop it from sliding out of position as you go.

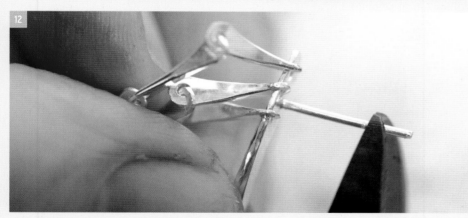

ATTACHING THE EAR WIRES

10 Mark a point on the back of the studs midway between the second and third holes, and slightly above them, where you will attach the wire. I like to part-drill these points so that when I solder the pin into place, it sits in the hole slightly; this makes a much stronger joint. Using a 0.8 mm bit, drill into this point to about halfway through the metal.

11 Cut the 0.8 mm wire into two equal $^3/_8$ in (10 mm) lengths, then use sprung tweezers to position the wire into the partly drilled hole. Take the necessary health and safety precautions before you begin soldering (see page 183). Solder paste works nicely here to join the pieces together; apply a small amount to the joint and then solder. These form the "stud" part of the earring.

12 Pickle the studs, then cut the wires to the desired length for your ears. File the end to a rounded point. I score a line into the wires about $^1/_6$ in (3 mm) from the ends to help the butterflies stay in position. Use wire cutters to make this groove by gently squeezing and turning the wires so that the blades just begin to cut into the surface of the wires.

ASSEMBLING THE EARRINGS

13 Almost done! Take each chain of droplets and attach to the studs using the holes you have drilled. Attach the chain of five droplets to the hole at the wider end of the stud, then the chains of four and three in the next holes. This arrangement makes the chain nearest the face the longest. It's worth soldering these seams shut as they will take more strain than any other joints in the chains (if you are a perfectionist, you will solder shut all the closed hooks on the droplets). I use the paste again as it is easy to apply here and I needn't worry so much about it moving out of position to melt in the wrong place. Pickle the earrings, then barrel polish for an hour or so to bring out a wet shine to your English summer earrings.

CACTUS BOX RING

It's easy to see where the inspiration for this ring came from. "Sharp" is a dynamic and attractive quality for me, but it is often hard to translate into jewelry without making dangerous weapons. In this design, there is a sense of that energy, but somewhat tamed for wear. In keeping with the coarse nature of the subject, I gave my ring a rough, scrubbed final finish, but you may prefer something smoother.

I found a lovely, deep green faceted peridot in my stones box, and in keeping with the spikiness of the form I decided to set this stone with its sharp point facing outward. This does make the tip vulnerable, and for this reason I made sure to place it on a more protected part of the ring. I accept that one day it will probably chip, but between now and then it will give me great satisfaction.

MATERIALS

1, 4, and 5) 3 x sterling silver sheets, 0.8 mm thickness, 7 1/2 x 1/4 in (190 x 5 mm); 0.8 mm thickness, 2 1/4 x 1/4 in (60 x 5 mm), and 0.8 mm thickness, 1 3/4 x 2 1/4 in (45 x 60 mm); you will also need a very small scrap of thin polished silver sheet to make a reflective backing for the stone setting

2) Sterling silver tubing, 2.2 mm diameter, 1/6 in (3 mm) long

3) Peridot, faceted stone

TOOLS

- Ring gauge (see page 178) for measuring your ring size
- Steel rule
- Engineer's square (see page 178) for marking a 90-degree angle
- Fine-line permanent pen
- Piercing saw (see page 178), 2/0, 4/0 blades
- Files (see page 179): half-round file, three-square escapement file, square needle file, three-square (triangular) needle file, flat file, and slotting files
- Soldering equipment (see pages 182 and 183): flux (borax), brush, silver solder (hard solder for the first joints, easy solder for the last joints), torch, tweezers, honeycomb soldering board, and pickle
- Ring mandrel (see page 181)
- Mallet (see page 180)
- Wet and dry papers (see page 184), 600 grit for surfacing, 1000 grit for finishing
- Scribe (see page 178)
- Flat-nosed pliers (see page 180)
- Steel block (see page 181)
- Tube cutting jig (see page 181) for cutting tubing
- Bow drill (see page 179), 0.8 mm drill bit, for the breathing hole
- Tracing paper (see below)
- Steel wool or other polishing material (see page 185)
- 1.75 mm round burr (see page 182) and pin vise (see page 179)
- Pusher (see page 182) for setting
- Burnisher (see page 182) for smoothing around the setting
- Loupe (see page 182)

BOX CONSTRUCTIONS

At first, the box construction of a ring appears quite complex, but once you grasp the principle it is really straightforward, and this experience provides you with scope for further experimentation with other forms. Working with this construction method, you can make large and dramatic forms that are also light and wearable. Combine with forming and folding techniques (see pages 154–69) to make more complex structures.

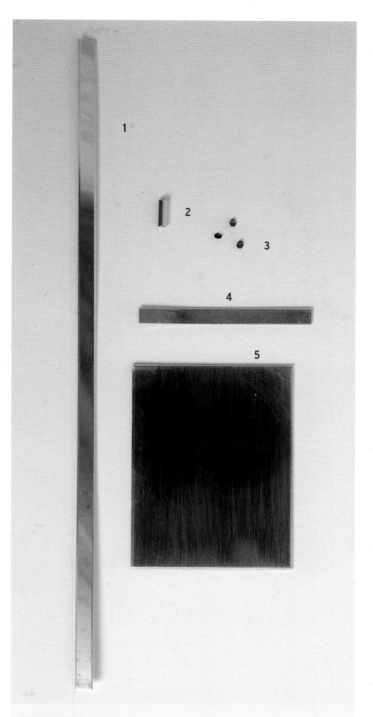

TOOLS TIPS

THIN (SLOTTING) FILES These super-thin slotting files are perfect for getting into sharp angles or difficult places. Take care when using them as slotting files can easily snap if too much pressure is applied.

TRACING PAPER The easiest way to check for fire stain on your silver is by placing tracing paper over the surface. It stops the light and reflections from interfering with the color of the metal so that you can readily identify those nasty dark gray patches where it has stubbornly remained.

MAKING THE INTERNAL RING

1 Measure your ring size with a ring gauge and convert to the circumference length. I use a standard ring conversion chart and add 2.4 mm to this length (0.8 mm x 3). Round your figure down to the nearest 0.5 mm. Mark out this length using the steel rule and the engineer's square, then cut with a piercing saw. File the ends square. Take the necessary health and safety precautions before you begin soldering (see page 183). Solder together using hard solder (H).

2 Make round on a ring mandrel, using a mallet, then rub one edge of the ring flat on coarse wet and dry paper.

MAKING THE CACTUS EXTERIOR

Note: Depending on the size of your ring, you may need to use more or less of your 7 1/2 in (190 mm) strip.

3 Mark your strip with an "A" side and a "B" side. From one end, mark side "A" with a pen at these intervals: 1 3/8 in/2 in/3 in/4 in/5 in/ 6 in (35 mm/53 mm/79 mm/100 mm/126 mm/ 151 mm). Use an engineer's square with a scribe to score across the strip at these points. Turn over and making sure to start from the same end, repeat for side "B" at these intervals: 1 3/4 in/ 2 1/2 in/3 3/4 in/4 1/2 in/5 1/2 in (44 mm/61 mm/ 92 mm/112 mm/142 mm).

Using a three-square escapement file, make grooves into the metal where you have scored the lines. Open them from a tight "v" shape to about 120 degrees using the edge of a square file, then use a flat file. Groove two-thirds of the way through the thickness, and try not to slip out of line.

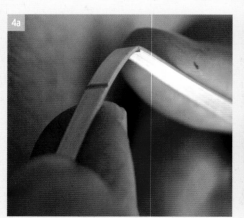

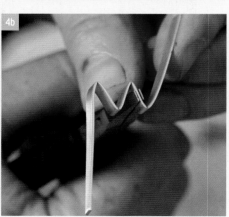

4 This is the fun part. Fold along each of the grooves, using finger pressure at first, to get something of the angular shape. Then, using a pair of small flat-nosed pliers and finger pressure, manipulate the strip into suitable sharp points and curves. Overworking may weaken or break the folds. This is not a total disaster, but it will make your soldering job trickier, so take care. File the outside edges smooth—a half-round file does the job nicely.

5 Curve the remaining flat ends so they overlap, and place around the ring to determine where to cut to size. At a point where they overlap, mark a line with a pen and then cut through the overlap. Tape the ends together beforehand if you like, to give a perfectly matching seam. Solder, and then refine the shape with finger pressure and pliers, making sure the ring fits well inside.

Flatten the bottom edge of the cactus as you did with the ring (see Step 2, opposite), then position the ring and the cactus shape onto the base plate for soldering.

FIRST SOLDERING

6 Brush the surfaces to be jointed with flux. Cut five or six largish pallions of solder (H) and place them inside the ring at the seam. Picking them up with the fluxed brush ensures that they get fluxed too. Cut some additional large pieces to put on the internal points, between them and the ring.

Have several strips of hard solder cut and ready fluxed for feeding into the seam as the metal reaches the correct temperature.

7 Pickle and rinse, then cut out the middle circle from your ring. Drill a hole to thread your blade through to pierce out this inner circle. I use a nice fine 4/0 blade to get me super-close to the vertical sides, but without damaging them. Now cut around the cactus shape too.

File the top edges of the cactus ring flat (I like to use the flat side of the half-round file), and make true on a flat sheet of coarse (600 grit) wet and dry paper as before in Steps 2 and 5 (see opposite and above), in readiness for the next soldering job. Check for complete flatness on a steel block.

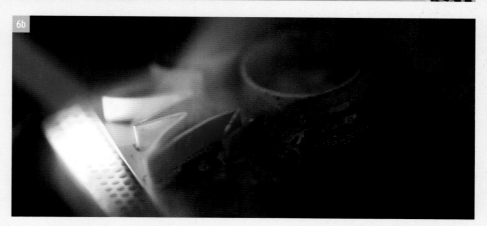

PREPARING FOR THE STONE

8 Cut a ⅙ in (3 mm) length of tubing for the rub-over stone setting, using the tube cutting jig to help hold it and cut straight. File the bottom edge flat and square to the sides.

9 Next, you need to decide where on your cactus you want the stone to go. Take a look at the front face of your soldered cactus ring to find the right spot. Once you have decided its position, drill a 0.8 mm hole through the front at this point. This will provide a breathing hole for the hollow form when completing the next soldering job.

SECOND SOLDERING

10 For the final soldering stage, you can use easy solder (E), without the risk of undoing your previous joints. I use the feeding method here as before, but there are several places with this tricky shape where the flow will be more difficult to control, so I use pallions as well.

Flux all parts to be jointed. Place the ring onto the remainder base plate and position the tubing into place around the drilled hole. Flux these last two parts too, and drop a couple of pieces of easy solder inside the tube at the seam. Cut some more largish pallions of easy solder (I go for long and thin in this instance) and push them into the hard to reach internal points of the cactus. Add some more inside the ring. Prepare some long thin strips of solder for feeding, remembering to flux them.

11 Heat the whole thing very gently to start; you have a lot riding on all the pieces staying in position. Keep the heat general as you build up to temperature, and at the first sign of the pallions melting, focus the heat to draw the molten solder along the seams. Where the solder runs out, touch the tip of your solder strip to the seam to feed more into it. Turn the work as you go, until you get all the way back to where you started, making sure to miss no part of the seams. Finally, turn your attention to the tubing at the top. Check to see if the solder has already gone. If not, give it a few seconds of the flame until you see the solder flow from inside to the outer edges all around.

CLEANING UP

12 Cut away from the base plate and file as before. This is the time to get into those tight inward angles. I use those lovely slotting files to get into these tricky places, but escapement files will do it to some degree, or you can try the wet and dry paper trick with the saw frame (see Tools tips, page 99). Next, remove the inside of the ring as before (see Step 7, page 129) and file all the edges to a smooth box form.

Surface the whole ring with wet and dry papers (from 600 to 800 to 1000 grit) to remove scratches and fire stain. If you can't see any fire stain, check by placing a piece of tracing paper over the surface—this is an effective way to find it.

Polish as you like; I used coarse steel wool in a circular scrubbing motion over the surface to give a rough, scratchy finish.

SETTING THE STONE

For the setting, I have used a faceted peridot, and I set my stone upside-down to add some sharpness to the design of the ring. For this reason, my setting is shallow. Adjust the collet height according to your own stone.

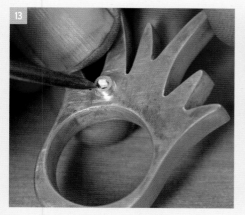

13 File the tube down to 2 mm in height (less if your stone is shallow). Cut a small disk of thin silver (I used 0.3 mm fine silver), polish, and insert this into the tubing to provide a reflective backdrop for the stone. Too small is better than too big in terms of fit.

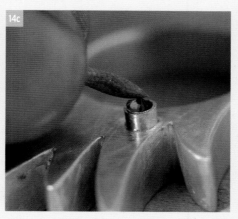

14 Use the 1.75 mm round burr in a pin vise to drill a seat gently into the tube wall. Keep checking your stone for fit; aim to have 0.5 mm of tube wall protruding above the girdle of the stone.

15 Carefully set the stone, first using a pusher with a very controlled action, then smoothing around the setting with a burnisher. When the stone is set as you would like it, check with the loupe to see how well you have done! Rework the texture around the stone to remove the scratches and marks you may have made from the setting.

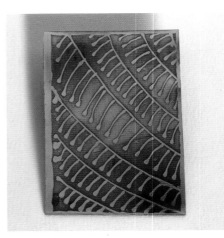

Photo etching from an image created using a QR mobile app.   *The same image reversed; photo etching with enamel.*   *Nail polish etching; hand drawing from a photograph.*

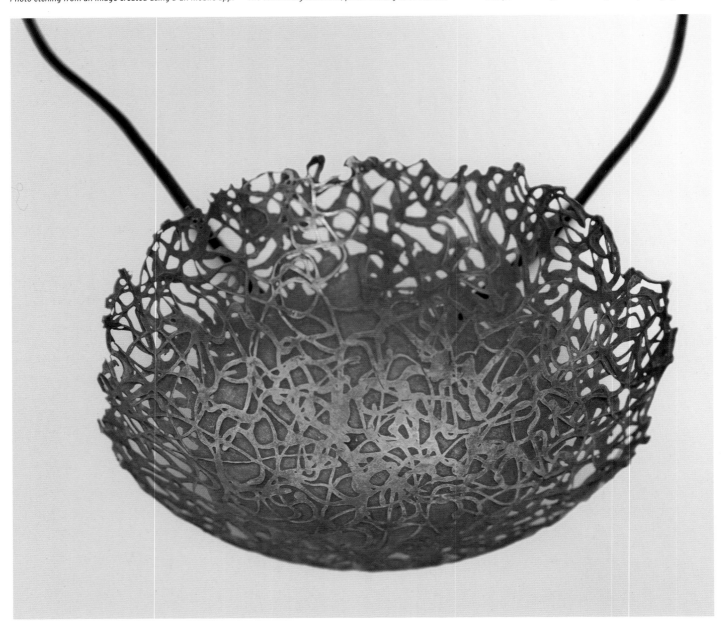

Nail polish etching; hand drawn, freehand pattern.

ETCHING PROCESSES

Etching is a versatile technique for adding texture and contrast to your metal surface. There are a number of approaches to this process, and each imparts its own subtle flavor to the result. The choice of method depends upon the desired quality of line, as well as on the type of metal you are working, its form, and the tools, equipment, chemicals, and technology available to you.

I encourage you to experiment with as many of these approaches as possible to become familiar with their advantages and limitations. Find the methods that suit your style of work best.

DIFFERENT APPROACHES TO ETCHING

The processes described here are intended for application in the standard studio environment. I have used readily available and inexpensive materials or equipment, and the chemicals listed are considered less harmful than those traditionally used for etching.

The quality of the result is not entirely predictable, as etching is subject to so many variables—from the temperature of your iron to the age of the acid. This in itself can add an extra quality to your work, depending on your outlook. If you require precise or complicated cuts into your metal, it is worth exploring commercially available services for photo etching, laser etching, or rapid prototyping.

Once your metal surface has been etched, you can treat it in a number of ways. You can polish it as it is, to accentuate the difference between the lower textured surface and the upper shiny face of the metal. You could oxidize or patinate it—rubbing back with a light abrasive will bring contrast between the patina and the clean metal. You can burnish the upper surface of the etched metal to give a subtle light-changing effect to the piece. Selective silver- or gold-plating is an option too, or you might try enameling into the cuts, either with vitreous or cold enamels. Any of these processes can add a new dimension to your work.

FINDING YOUR IMAGE

To begin with, you must have an image, a pattern, or a texture you want to transfer onto metal. If you like to draw or paint, you can work straight on the prepared metal with nail polish. If you take photographs, or if you enjoy using graphics software, photo etching might be your preferred option. In the following pages, we will look at each of these approaches to reproducing imagery on metal.

WORKING WITH ACIDS

Although we are using safer, more environmentally friendly mordants (acids) than would traditionally be used (i.e. nitric acid), ferric chloride and ferric nitrate still carry serious health risks.

Health and safety

- If you get the solution onto your skin or nails, it will dye this part of you yellow/brown/black. This will last several days at least. It will also permanently stain your clothes.
- Although virtually no fumes are produced by the solution in normal circumstances, burning and agitation can cause the release of some harmful gases. These can irritate your lungs, causing coughing.
- If you ingest the solution, you will irritate your gastrointestinal tract. Repeated large doses can cause excess iron build-up in the body. Symptoms include gastrointestinal irritation, with abdominal cramps, vomiting, diarrhea, and liver damage.
- Ferric nitrate presents more severe dangers through inhalation or ingestion, and may also cause skin irritation after direct contact. Take extra care when using this substance.

Simple rules to follow for safe working practice

- Use in a well-ventilated area
- Keep bowls and other utensils for etching exclusively for this activity; never rinse off chemicals in a basin used for food preparation or dishwashing.
- Do not eat or drink while etching.
- Wear disposable gloves when handling metal/tweezers/acids for etching.
- Wear a disposable apron.
- Wear goggles to protect your eyes from splashes.
- Be alert and be responsible. Look out for drips and spills you may cause, and wipe up immediately with a rag. Wash out the rag after use.
- Always flush/wipe all surfaces with a wet rag after handling the acid/etched metal. Wash out the rag after use.
- Think about others, and how they might be affected by sloppy handling of dangerous substances. Clean up after yourself. Wash out the rag after use.
- Use tweezers to remove work from acid. Wash after use.
- If you choose to heat the acid, use a heatproof glass dish. A tea-light candle beneath the dish will provide sufficient heat. If you see steam is rising, the acid is too hot and you are being poisoned!

In all circumstances, seek medical advice if you are affected by the use of these substances.

Disposal

Neutralize with bicarbonate of soda: add a cupful of powder at a time, slowly, until the liquid stops frothing. Store safely in a sealed, labeled container, and check with your local environmental regulatory agency, or health department for disposal advnice.

MATERIALS

VARNISH RESISTS

- *Stop-out varnish*—a thickish, black liquid that can be painted onto the metal. Good for all-over protection, brush lines, or scratching through. It's sometimes flaky, and I find it too thick to get a really nice brush stroke.
- Nail varnish—a much easier substance to deal with, providing equal resistance to most mordants. It's available in a range of formats that make it beautiful to draw or paint with. Check out the fine brush and the drawing tip you can get for "nail art."

STICK-ON RESISTS

- Brown parcel tape—a brown, thin, waterproof tape for packaging. This provides a fast and effective waterproof seal for the back of your metal; it can also be used to mask off areas for patterns, etc. Once it's positioned, you need to make sure it's firmly pressed onto the metal surface.
- Self-adhesive plastic—as above. May be laser-cut beforehand to give precise and repeatable patterns. Can be awkward to lay out and stick securely onto the metal once cut.

IRON-ON RESISTS

Note: Your final result in metal will be the reverse of your print; lettering should be printed out back to front.

- Laser copy on paper—this most basic approach to photo etching requires only a laser copy of an image, either from a laser copier or a laser printer. The image quality is reasonable, but it's difficult to get density of toner onto the surface and some break-up of the image is usual in the process.
- Press-n-peel Blue (PNP)—this is a type of transfer film used for electronic circuitry. Your image is copied onto the PNP, and in the transfer process an extra layer of "blue" is delivered on top of the toner to give a more complete mask. Inexplicable gaps sometimes appear, though, and it can be an expensive experience with your initial experiments.
- Wax paper/baking parchment/sticker papers—all, in principle, should work, but best used with imagery that is easy to touch up. (Sticker paper is the backing for that self-adhesive plastic you may have tried, above). Try these when you can handle the possibility of mishaps, and feel ready to stretch your repertoire.

MORDANTS

- Ferric chloride—this is effective with copper, brass, and gilding metal.
- Ferric nitrate—used for etching silver.

NOTE: Always follow the manufacturer's guidelines when preparing, using, and disposing of these chemicals.

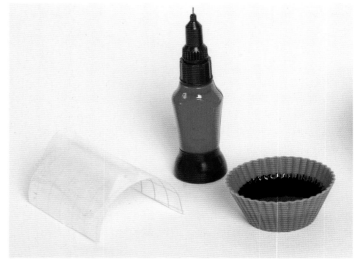

Stop-out materials: from left to right, self-adhesive plastic, nail art polish applicator, and traditional black stop-out,

Ferric chloride (left) comes in pellet form and should be diluted with water to the manufacturer's instructions. Ferric nitrate (right), a purple crystalline powder, turns yellow in contact with water.

MATERIALS TIP

DRY FORM OF CHEMICALS I buy these chemicals (ferric nitrate, ferric chloride) in powder or pellet form as they are easy to post, and safer to store. Be very careful not to inhale the fumes when mixing with water, as gases are released in this phase and they are toxic. Always add the chemical carefully to the water, not the other way around, making sure to avoid splashes. Always follow the manufacturer's safety and product instructions. When mixing, as a guide expect to add 1 lb 2 oz (500 g) to 1³⁄₄ pints (1 liter) water (for ferric nitrate or for ferric chloride). The process of etching causes a sludge build-up in the acid, which sinks to the bottom of the dish. To get the best etch it is advisable to remove the metal and rinse it under cold running water every 20 minutes.

COMMERCIAL ETCHING SERVICES

From a vector-based drawing (a computer-generated artwork that uses lines, or paths, rather than pixels to create the image), your design can be:

- Screen printed with a resist and then etched chemically in a precisely controlled manner to give crisp lines and an even, smooth, etched surface.
- Precision laser-cut to your specified depth.
- Rapid prototyped in wax, ready for casting.

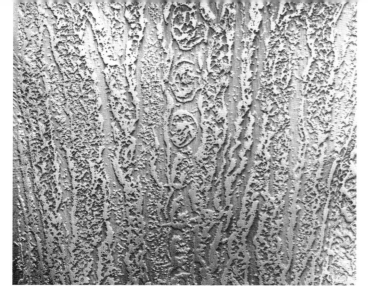

Photo etching from a close-up of a photograph of tree bark.

ETCHING IN THE STUDIO—THE PRINCIPLE

A resist This is a protective coating which is selectively applied to the surface of the metal to create a texture or pattern. The metal is then immersed in a MORDANT (acid, see box opposite) that dissolves any surfaces that are not covered by the resist. The depth of the cut is controlled by the strength and type of chemical used, and by the length of exposure. Suitable metals for your experiments include copper, brass, or gilding metal. When you can anticipate the results better, the same principles can be applied to silver.

Suitable resists Depending on whether you are working on a finished piece of jewelry or a flat sheet of metal, you can choose a resist that best suits your needs. Each resist has its limitations. Photo etching (see opposite and pages 136-7) only works on sheet metal, and self-adhesive plastic (see box opposite) works best on flat planes, having limited use on curved surfaces. All the varnishes (see page 138) work very well on curved and formed surfaces as well as on flat sheet, but they rely on you being able to draw or paint a good line. Of course, you can also use a combination of resists, so you might use tape to mask a flat bottom, and varnish to apply words on the upper curved surface.

The box opposite lists some of the resists to experiment with. Iron-on application approaches (see page 137) rely on the use of a laser copier or printer, where a secondary medium is used to transfer the toner ink (which acts as a resist) from the copied image onto your metal, using an iron to provide heat and pressure. In all "transfer" processes, your image must be reversed before printing, as in the transfer process it goes face down onto the metal.

Suitable mordants Nitric acid is often used as a mordant for etching, though I prefer to use ferric chloride for etching copper, brass, and gilding metal, and I use ferric nitrate for etching silver; these chemicals are considered more environmentally friendly and safer to work with than the acids traditionally used for etching. Please pay attention to health and safety when etching.

Read the Health and safety guidelines on page 133 before commencing.

PHOTO ETCHING IN THE STUDIO

Photo etching is a great way to transfer an image—for example, a photograph or a monotonal graphic—onto metal. The process allows you to repeat the same image again and again, so if you need to make 20 identical pendants—or 200— this is the process for you.

Choosing images Graphic images work well, as do "texture" and "detail" photographs. Ideally you will need to be able to manipulate your image on a computer, ready for output through a laser printer, but at the most basic level you can also just take an image to the copy shop and ask for a straight black and white laser copy of the image.

If you have the facility to work with your chosen photograph or graphic on a computer, the image quality does not need to be great to start with because you can manipulate it in Photoshop or a similar graphics program to reduce it to a black and white image.

It is also possible to use images from other sources, and simple graphics and glyphs can work well. In one of my samples here, I used a QR code (short for Quick Response Code, a type of barcode often seen in advertising and on packaging) that I made using an app on my smartphone. The QR app translated my typed message "The Art of Play" into a readable QR graphic that I was able to save as a jpeg ready for laser printing.

Working in reverse Photo etching is a basic transfer process; much like a child's temporary tattoo, the image is applied face down onto the metal, and after the transfer process the backing paper is removed. Therefore, what you see as a printout on paper is precisely the reverse of what you will get once it has transferred onto your metal for etching. In most instances, this will not matter, but if your image contains writing or another form of legible information, you must reverse the image now so that when you apply it to the metal it will be the correct way around.

Preparing to start To prepare for Part 1 on page 137, print out your image using a laser printer, or photocopy it using a laser copier. If you have one at home, you are at an advantage as you can experiment with numerous different types of paper for the print. A commercial printer may be too precious of their machine to indulge in your experiments with parchment paper, but they should be willing to run PNP blue film through it.

SAMPLE IMAGERY FOR PHOTO ETCHING

Here are some examples of images I have used to photo etch onto pieces of copper sheet. Starting with the source material, each sequence shows how the original image was manipulated before laser printing and applying to the metal.

Dried palm leaves

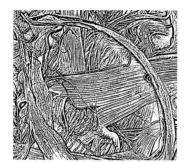

The original photograph; this image has a beautiful, sharp, linear quality.

When the photocopy filter is applied to the image, the lines become stronger.

The resulting photo etching shows how the image is reversed once applied to the metal sheet. This example has been cold enameled to enhance the texture.

Fern frond

The high contrast nature of this image lends itself well to translation to black and white for etching purposes.

Once reduced to black and white, I played with the levels to get a sharp and flat graphic image.

I like the rhythms in this image, and rather than printing the whole thing I took a smaller detail of the image to work with.

This image has translated well onto metal. Again, I applied cold enamel and then polished it back.

Amber

This was a poor-quality image to start with, but this problem is negligible when the "sketch" filter is applied (see right).

Bearing in mind that "black" will remain untouched by the acid, and white will be eaten away, I decided to invert the image.

In the end result, the shadow areas will be textured and oxidized to give a more faithful representation.

The etching has a subtle and abstract quality; note how "light" is shiny metal, and "dark" has a grainy texture.

The art of play

In this sequence, I used a QR application on my smart phone to turn the phrase "The Art of Play" into a readable image format. I've included the phrase here to show how text is affected by the process.

A printout of the original image once transferred would be etched the wrong way around, thus making it unreadable.

Using Photoshop, I was able to reverse the image before printing.

Once the reversed image is applied to the metal, the image and writing are legible.

PART 1

TRANSFERRING THE DESIGN USING PAPER OR PNP FILM

1 Once you have prepared the image you want to etch onto your metal, print it out on white standard paper using the manual feed tray of a laser printer, with the darkest ink setting. Before the paper runs through the machine, mark the top left-hand corner of the page with a small "x" so you know the correct orientation for subsequent feeds. Now set the printer to "transparency" and make sure that it is set to a low heat output. Cut a square of PNP blue large enough to cover the printed area of your image on the copy. Tape the edges down with masking tape, making sure that the blue film is matte side up. You now have two images to transfer and compare, one from the paper and one from the PNP blue film.

2 For the resist to protect the metal adequately, the metal surface must be absolutely grease-free. It also helps to key the surface of the metal for the transfer to stick to the metal in the next stage, so do both jobs in one go with a 1000-grit wet and dry paper under cold running water. When the water forms a film across the surface without pulling away from the edges, the metal is clean. Dry the metal with a tissue. Wear latex gloves to avoid re-greasing the sheet.

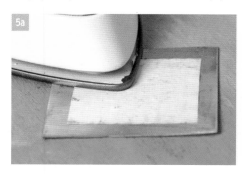

3 To transfer the image, you will need an old iron used only for this purpose (please don't try to iron a white shirt with it afterward), set to high. Make sure that the iron has no water in it so that there is no chance of steam ruining the job. Lay the PNP onto the surface of one piece of copper sheet, and stick two opposite edges down onto the metal with masking tape to help keep the paper in position. Place the iron onto the paper and allow the heat to pass through for a few minutes. Then, using a burnishing action, work over the area with the tip of the iron; a small image should take around 5 minutes. Peel a corner of the PNP back to see if the image has transferred to the metal. If not, rework areas that still need to transfer. When you are happy with the quality of print, peel off the PNP. Inspect the transfer for any defects in the image.

4 PNP has an annoying habit of just not working in some areas, so you may need to touch up any loss of image with some nail polish and a fine brush. If you find that blue has transferred onto the metal where it should not have, this is easily removed by gently dabbing the sticky side of the parcel tape over the metal. It's safe; you won't pull off the toner.

5 With the paper print, you follow the same process. Iron straight onto the back of the paper (see 5a). The toner makes the paper stick quite firmly to the metal, so you won't need to use masking tape. After 5 minutes of ironing, soak the metal in water, and gently rub away the paper. It feels a little risky, but the toner should have adhered well to the metal, so in spite of your action on the paper, the toner should remain. Dry the piece. Your test piece is now ready to etch (see the etching process overleaf).

PART 2

PAINTING, DRAWING, AND STICKING RESISTS

Using these low-tech resist applications, there is room for additional character to come into your designs. In these examples, I have used a section of the fern frond image from page 136 as inspiration when applying the various resists. The subtle differences between each sheet here are entirely caused by the quality of the medium; each approach affects the quality of line that is achievable. Try these four different techniques for applying resist by hand to create the same image:

1 To begin, you need to clean your metal (see Part 1, Step 2, page 137). Make sure that you wear latex gloves to avoid re-greasing the surface–even washed hands will transfer a film of oil to clean metal. As you are not applying heat to the metal, you should also cover the back with parcel tape now.

2 **Method 1:** Use the very fine brush from a "nail art" polish applicator to draw your design.

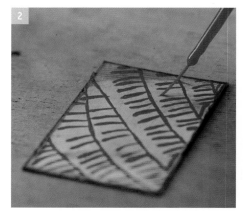

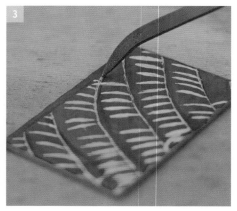

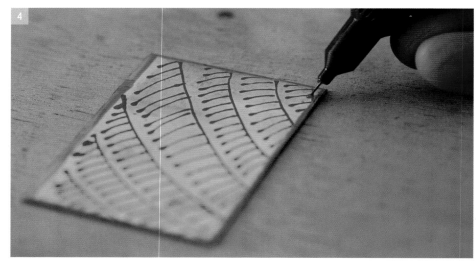

3 **Method 2:** Cover the sheet with nail polish and once dry, scratch through the varnish to expose the metal. I used the end of an old, cheap, chipped rifler file here.

4 **Method 3:** Use the drawing tip from a nail art bottle of nail polish. This tip gives a lovely controlled line; the thickness of line is varied according to squeezing pressure to the bottle.

5 **Method 4:** Apply parcel tape to the metal and cut out your design with a sharp blade. Remove the "waste" tape and press the remaining tape firmly onto the metal, paying special attention to the edges.

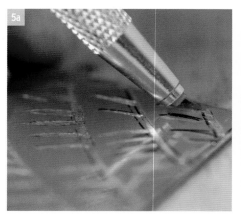

PART 3

THE ETCHING PROCESS

If you haven't done so already, apply brown parcel tape to the back of each sheet of metal to be etched, making sure to exclude air bubbles, especially around the seams and edges (you don't want the acid to creep into the air pockets).

1 Follow the manufacturer's directions on preparing the ferric chloride solution. Wear protective gloves and an apron. Using plastic tongs to avoid splashes, carefully place the metal sheet into the ferric chloride solution. Leave for 20 minutes before checking for depth of etch and for flaking away of the resist. With a fresh mixture this should give a reasonable cut, but if you want a deeper etch, rinse the metal and then return it to the bowl for another 20 minutes.

2 Rinse the metal under running water using soap and a bristle brush to remove all traces of the ferric chloride. To neutralize any remaining acid, mix a few teaspoons of bicarbonate of soda in a small bowl of water to make an alkaline solution, and soak the metal for a few minutes. You will get some fantastic yellows and oranges on copper.

3 Remove the resist from each of your test pieces. Laser ink can be gently scrubbed off the surface with a 1000-grit wet and dry paper, used wet. Nail polish will come off with standard nail polish remover.

Compare your results. If you are organized, you might mount these test pieces in your sketchbook with notes relating to your experiences and observations. It is useful to have a record of the timing of the metals in the acid bath, and depths of etch achieved (see below).

HAVE FUN AND EXPERIMENT!

Experiment with all the variables that present themselves:

- Positioning in the acid bath—what happens if the piece is propped vertically/upside down/upright in the acid bath?
- Temperature—how does this affect the cut of the metal?
- Metal types—is there a significant difference in the behavior of the process when using copper/brass/gilding metal?
- Resists—what other safe substances could provide a mask? What quality might they impart?
- Layers—try applying successive layers of resist on a test to cut away the metal in layers.
- Secondary techniques—what happens if you shape the metal with a mallet/hammer/punch? Can you score and fold the metal? What problems do you anticipate might arise? How could you resolve these issues?
- Patination—which patinas work well? How can you "fix" the colors you achieve? Try polishing/burnishing the metal after patination.
- Color—how else can you add color? Try enameling, plating, or flocking.

Find new and original ways to use etching in your designs. Play on.

1 *The result from my brush effect.*

2 *The result from the parcel tape stencil.*

3 *The result from the fine drawing tip of a nail art pen.*

4 *The result from scratching through the nail polish.*

"The Art of Play" oxidized.

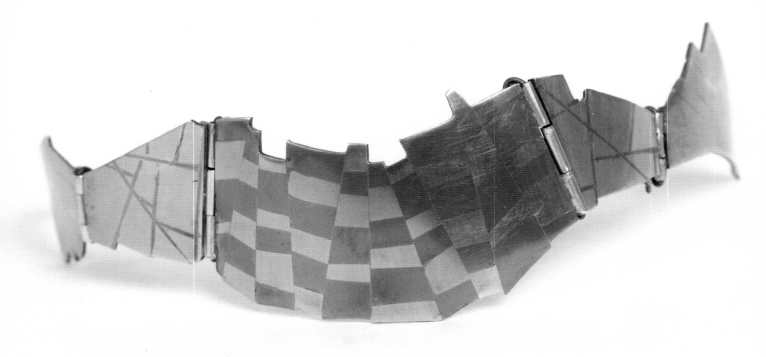

Copper and brass bracelet.

Brass bangle with copper circles.

Pin made from married copper and brass that has then been folded (see pages 164-9).

Simple copper pin with married circles of brass.

MARRIED METALS

I first came across the use of married metals when I was a student of the inspirational jeweler and lecturer Barbara Christie, who used the technique extensively and to beautiful effect in her jewelry at that time. Barbara's work gave me a new appreciation of the notion of "preciousness," and how this can be achieved in a piece of jewelry. Her brilliant combination of colors and textures added a refreshing quality that could not be matched in the traditional treatments of silver and gold.

The technique of married metals, although labor-intensive, makes the most of the range of the metal colors available to you. By cutting and soldering strips of metal together you can make a single, beautifully colored sheet of metal that you can then fold, form, cut, and re-solder to make your desired piece of jewelry. The effect of married metals has similarities with lamination techniques, but carries the advantage of being (potentially) two sided, so the color contrast can be appreciated on the back and the front of the resulting piece. There are similarities, too, with *mokume gane*, the ancient Japanese art of forging metals, but there is a graphic and controlled quality to married metals that sets these techniques apart.

You can experiment with any metals that have a melting point above 800°C (1472°F). I'm not so fond of brass because of its bad behavior (it's an uncompromising, hard metal that tends to warp, and it doesn't like to work with silver), but copper, gilding metal, bronze, steel, silver, and gold all work well. In fact, this is a great way to make your precious metals go further, as little touches among other metals provide a pleasing contrast. Solder in its own right can be enjoyed for its color, too. This process takes a lot of solder, so be prepared, and it is best to use only the highest temperature solder (i.e. hard solder) for all the reassembling. This then gives you an advantage of using easy solder when reworking your married metal sheet into jewelry.

Fluxes need to be chosen to suit your metals. Some fluxes work better than others (see the tips box on page 142 for more details).

EVOLVING YOUR SKILLS

There are two different approaches to making a sheet of married metals here; once your cutting, filing, and soldering skills are honed, you can try more complex patterns in your metals—try cutting more elaborate curved lines, for example, rather than circles and straight lines.

The sheets themselves can be quickly turned into something wearable, and the effect is so lovely that I don't like to over-complicate it with clever designs, so see what you can do with yours.

MATERIALS
- Brass sheet, 0.9 mm thickness, 6 x 1 in (150 x 25 mm)
- Copper sheet, 0.9 mm thickness, 6 x 1 in (150 x 25 mm)
- Gilding metal sheet, 0.9 mm thickness, 2^1/$_2$ x 2 in (65 x 60 mm)
- Silver sheet, 0.9 mm thickness, 1^1/$_4$ x 2^1/$_4$ in (32 x 60 mm)

TOOLS
- Circle punch tool (see page 181) for making holes in the sheets of metal, and making disks
- Hammers (see page 180): jobbing hammer and planishing hammer
- Mallet (see page 180), steel block, and sandbag (for muffling the sound) (see page 181) for flattening the metal sheet and disks
- Large file (see page 179)
- Pumice (see page 185) for cleaning up the punched metal and disks
- Soldering equipment (see pages 182 and 183) : auflux (see box on page 142), brush, solder pallions, hard solder, torch, tweezers, honeycomb soldering board, and pickle
- Arm mandrel (see page 181) for bending the metal strip
- Wet and dry papers (see page 184), 600, 800, 1000, and 1200 grit
- Steel rule
- Fine-line permanent pen
- Piercing saw (see page 178), 4/0 blade
- Pumice (see page 185), or wet and dry paper (see page 184)
- A few panel pins for holding the metal strips in place on the honeycomb soldering board
- Abrasive polishing block or steel wool (see page 185) for the final polish

GETTING THE MOST FROM MARRIED METALS

How can you get the most mileage from your married metals? Consider these options:
- Use for one or more surfaces for a box ring.
- Cut circles to form into gentle curves for rings, earrings, or pendants.
- Use to make a unique hollow bead.
- Use folding techniques to create an architectural form.

When you have reached a conclusion with your married metal pieces, the contrasting colors can be heightened through the application of very gentle heat to the surface. Use a good wax, such as Renaissance wax (a fine wax polish widely used by restorers and museums) to seal the surface when you are satisfied with the results.

EXERCISE 1

MARRYING BRASS AND COPPER

To make a sheet of married metal, two or more sheets of contrasting metals of identical thickness are cut into pieces. The pieces are reassembled to create the desired pattern of color contrast. All meeting edges are filed to fit perfectly, then they are laid in position and soldered to make one new multicolored sheet. This sheet may be re-cut, rearranged, and re-soldered, or new metals of another color can be added to make even more complex color patterns in the final sheet.

1 Take a piece each of 0.9 mm thickness brass and copper sheet, 6 x 1 in (150 x 25 mm), and anneal both sheets. Using a circle punch tool, cut five random-sized holes in a scattered pattern toward the middle of each strip.

2 You will end up with five circles each of brass and copper, and two strips of metal with holes in them. Tap the strips back to flat on a steel block, and carefully work down the raised edges of the circle that were caused by the shearing action of the punch. You can use a planishing hammer for this, but avoid denting or overly spreading the metal.

3 Next, fit the circles of opposite colors into these holes—brass circles to copper strip and vice versa. File around the edges of the circles, keeping a rounded action so you are continuing to make the circles round, testing for fit after each swipe. You want a perfect fit. Clean up the pieces with pumice. Focus on one strip at a time for the soldering.

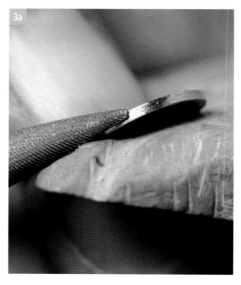

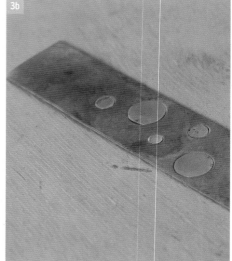

HOT TIPS—FLUXES FOR MARRIED METALS

AUFLUX This is a high temperature, green-colored solution, intended for gold soldering, but also useful for silver and base metals. This is the best flux to use for married metals because there is very little disturbance to your soldering arrangements in the initial heating phase, making it a first choice for when you have numerous pieces of metal laid in position for soldering at once.

The downside is that, because the flux is a liquid rather than a paste, when it is applied to your metal it pulls away from the surface if there is any grease or dirt, so you need to make sure your metal is super-clean before you start.

BORAX Although this is my preferred flux for most soldering jobs, borax for married metals has limited use; the bubbling up and subsequent expansion in the early heating stages can throw things out of place. Usually everything gets sucked back into position for straight soldering jobs, but with married metals this bubbling is a

real problem, as you are often not in a position to push your jigsaw pieces back into place. You can use it for patching holes in your seams, though (see Soldering Married Metals, page 145).

TENACITY™ NO. 5 FLUX POWDER This does what it says— Tenacity™ No. 5 flux powder's tenacious behavior makes it the only flux to use if you are soldering steel with other metals. The powder is mixed with water to make a creamy paste, which becomes sticky when you begin the heating process. This sticky pool remains on the surface of the metal, providing a complete mask. This prevents steel from oxidizing as you heat it, thus your solder will flow and adhere. But take care, the fumes are sharp and can damage your eyes, nasal passages, and respiratory system when heating (see tips on Safety, page 185). Also, any spilt flux will remain on your solder blocks, sticking to everything else and generally ruining your soldering area. Keep a block specially designated for use with this flux.

4 Lay one strip onto a honeycomb soldering board with the circles in position. Paint with auflux and add one or two solder pallions to the seam of each circle. These will act as gauges to show when the joint is hot enough to feed a strip of solder in.

Take the necessary health and safety precautions before you begin soldering (see page 183). Give the strip some general heat to start with and as it builds up in the piece, focus on one circle at a time, feeding solder to the joint (4b) when the pallions melt. Continue in this way with the remaining circles. Leave the strip to cool, then pickle, rinse, and dry. While it's cooling, complete the second strip in the same way.

5 File the edges and the corners of the strip so that they look tidy, and not too sharp.

6 Bend the strip around an arm mandrel with the cleanest side showing outward. File the surface until you are happy with the interchange of colors between brass and copper. You might like crisp lines, or there may be some room for your moons to be shrouded in a solder "haze."

7 To remove all file marks and inconsistencies from the surface, you need to work through the range of wet and dry papers, from 600 to 1200 grit, then polish as before. Hey presto, you have made two bangles, which are similar, but not the same. The example shown here is a sample piece, showing the final effect in close up.

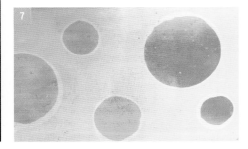

EXERCISE 2

GILDING METAL AND SILVER

Choose two pieces of contrasting metals for this exercise. They don't have to be the same size, but it is important that they are of equal thickness. I used 0.9 mm thickness gilding metal, 2^{1}/$_{2}$ x 2^{1}/$_{4}$ in (65 x 60 mm), and 0.9 mm thickness silver sheet, 1^{1}/$_{4}$ x 2^{1}/$_{4}$ in (32 x 60 mm).

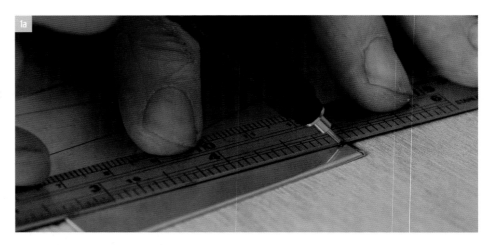

1 Draw a series of lines across the gilding metal with a steel rule and a fine-line permanent pen, and make a few more on the silver sheet.

In my example, I made four lines on the gilding metal and three on the silver, also making my lines angular and irregular to the bottom of each sheet.

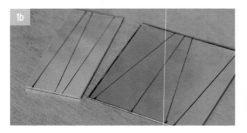

2 Using a piercing saw with a 4/0 blade, cut along the first of the lines. Make sure that your cut is absolutely straight and clean.

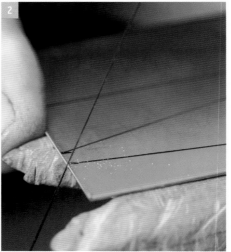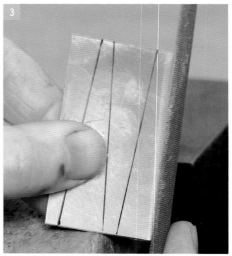

3 File both of these cut edges true. These edges must be perfectly straight in order to have good contact for soldering in the next stage of making, so spend time getting it right. Remember to collect the silver dust.

I find it easier to cut a line then file, cut then file, and so on, until I have all my pieces cut and ready to reassemble. Play with the arrangement of the strips until you are happy with the order, then check that all the strips are lying flat. Do this on a steel block, using gentle persuasion with a mallet where necessary.

4 Next, clean all the strips with pumice or wet and dry paper, then place in order onto the flat side of a honeycomb soldering board. Put a few pins at one end to give you something to push against if necessary, when you start to solder. You might also add a pin at one end of each strip, for the same reason, but DON'T pin all the way around the work because you need to allow for expansion when the metal is heated and if it can't go sideways it will buckle up.

5 Coat the work with auflux. If there is significant pulling away from the metal, try gently heating the metal, and reapplying the auflux. Cut up five or six strips of hard solder (H) and flux these, too, in readiness for the soldering. Heat the whole assembly to start, to get the auflux sticky, then concentrating on the first of the seams, begin to solder. Keep both sides of the seam equally hot so that the solder will flow between them. When the first seam is complete, move to the next, and so on until all joints have been made, then pickle.

6 Draw a new series of straight cut lines across this sheet of metal. Cut, file, and make an arrangement as before, making sure that you have the soldered side of each strip facing upward.

7 As you will be using hard solder again for this job, there is a risk that all the solder in the previously jointed seams will re-melt and shift. For this reason, I use pallions, carefully laid along each seam, which helps to avoid any unnecessary contact with the pieces that might push them out of position at the crucial moment. Place pins, as before, along one edge of the work, but try not to use them.

Once soldered, pickle, clean, and dry. As you have soldered all from the same side you should have a clean side, and a side that is fairly covered in solder. If you want both sides to be beautiful, file both of them back to the metal. I focus on just one side; the cleanest of them. Curve the sheet gently to make the filing of this side a little easier to manage. File away at the surface until the solder has become a fine line between each of the pieces of metal, and the surface is smooth.

8 Unbend the sheet with your hands, then tap flat with a mallet, making sure that the filed surface is against the steel block. Remove the file marks with wet and dry paper, starting with 600 or 800 and working to 1200 grit, and polish to the desired effect. The colors show best when the surface is given a satin treatment; try using an abrasive polishing block or steel wool for your final finish. Beautiful as it is, this sheet is intended as a beginning for a piece of jewelry, so more work will be done with it.

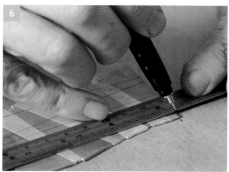

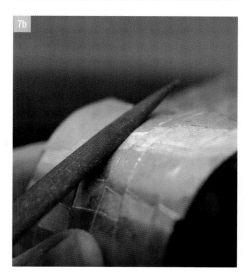

SOLDERING MARRIED METALS

With all future soldering jobs that incorporate a piece of your married metal, easy solder (E) should be used. Any unfilled seams in your sheet of married metal can also be filled with small pallions of easy solder using borax as a flux, but remember that the sheet is vulnerable when hot enough for solder to melt. All good seams should be protected with a layer of correction fluid (work in a well-ventilated area as the fumes from the heated fluid are toxic) to avoid the piece collapsing if overheated.

Silver pin made from a fusion of scrap parts to create texture and movement.

Silver ring fused with gold dust and etched.

Silver pin fused with randomly placed silver nuggets.

FUSION

This project explores a number of ways to enhance the surface quality of silver through the application of heat-related processes. Technically, fusion describes the way in which metal pieces are joined together permanently by carefully heating all the parts until the surfaces just begin to melt, thus allowing the parts to fuse together. No solder is required. Reticulation and gold dusting require similar heat application to the surface of the metals, and they are also included here.

All these processes described in this project are specific to silver, so you need to be prepared for the expense of potential failure—or astonishing success.

I use sterling silver—these next exercises are a great way to make use of all your scrap and sweepings, so the cost for fresh sheet is minimal. Ultimately, if you feel that your results don't merit inclusion in your jewelry, you can put them all in the melting pot for recycling into the sand cast ring (see pages 108-113).

One of the elements I most enjoy about fusing with off-cuts and scrap is that the resulting pieces also carry a record of your working history; if you frequently cut circles from silver sheet, for example, your scrap is going to have that negative shape from in-between the circles, or if you weave a lot and have sections of woven silver wires that didn't work out, here is a place for them to re-emerge.

I am very fond of using oxide when I am working with fusion; I suppose there is validity in giving old scrap that "antiqued" look—it has that history, and the gray to black shades produced by the oxide throw up the textures and the three-dimensionality of the resulting pieces. The effect is particularly stunning when combined with gold dust on silver, as the higher-karat golds will not oxidize and the contrasting black of the silver enhances the rich color of the gold.

If you keep your test pieces to a specified size, you will end up with a series of panels that can be linked together to make a wearable and attractive reference for the techniques you have explored (see for example the pendant in Linkages, pages 176-7). With this in mind, it is worth considering the aesthetics for each panel so that at the finish you have a series that present a sense of accord. I suggest that you aim to make six panels to start with, but add more panels if you like what transpires. As you add layers of scrap to the silver panel, the result can be quite bulky, so it's a good idea to start with thin sheet as your base.

THE PRINCIPLES OF HEAT-RELATED PROCESSES

FUSION Pieces of metal (in this case sterling silver) are carefully heated to the point where their surfaces become molten; the surfaces flow into each other to create a permanent bond.

RETICULATION Metal is heated to the point where the surface becomes liquid; in this state the liquid metal surface is manipulated by movement of the flame.

GOLD DUSTING 18 karat or 22 karat gold dust (i.e. filings from previous gold work) is sprinkled over a fluxed panel of silver; the metal is heated to the point of fusion so that the gold dust bonds permanently with the silver.

Although all these processes can be achieved to some degree without it, flux is helpful in getting the metal parts to flow into each other once they reach melting point. Flux also assists in protecting the metals from oxidizing. I like to use auflux when working with all of these heat treatments, as arrangements of parts to be fused are less likely to be jiggled out of position in the early heating stages.

MATERIALS
- 6 x sterling silver sheet, 0.5 mm thickness, 1¹/₄ x 1 in (30 x 25 mm)
- Additional scrap materials
- 0.5 mm diameter wire for creating texture on the silver sheet
- Unwanted silver snake chain for adding an interesting pattern on the silver sheet
- Any small sheet scraps for combining fusion with reticulation and for making some interesting shapes
- 18 karat gold dust (filings from another project are ideal for this one), for fusing to silver

TOOLS
- Pumice (see page 185), for cleaning your metal sheets
- Soldering equipment (see pages 182 and 183): flux, auflux or a similar liquid flux, brush, torch, tweezers, soldering pick, soldering block, honeycomb soldering board, wire mesh, and pickle
- Burnisher (see page 182), for bringing up the gold after soldering

EXERCISE 1

MAKING A NUGGET OF SILVER

This exercise explores heat control: recognizing the transition from solid sheet to fusion, reticulation, and melting points. For reticulation, ideally, you want a hot, sharp-tipped flame, but as you will be experiencing a number of stages in one exercise, keep with the bushy flame throughout.

1 Take a rectangle of 0.5 mm silver sheet and, using a bushy flame, begin to heat the piece with the flame, constantly moving across the whole surface of the silver.

Watch the surface of the metal for changes in color and texture; rising above annealing temperature the metal glows red and then orange. Keep the flame moving. At this point the surface will begin to look wet. This is the temperature at which fusion can take place, as surface metal melts and fuses together. Try to maintain this temperature for a whole minute, without losing that shiny wet look—pull the flame backward or forward to achieve this.

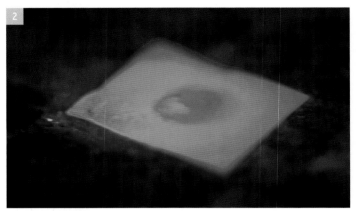

2 Heating the silver sheet above the point of fusion, as you continue to apply the flame you will notice the surface changing from wet to gritty in texture. The sheet will sag onto the firebrick; if this is rough and textured, your silver will take on this quality. Applying more heat, as you move the flame you will notice how the molten surface of the silver also moves with the hot tip. Maintain this temperature, and try to move the molten silver in an interesting pattern. At this point you are reticulating the surface of your silver.

3 With more heat, the edges start to reduce and thicken. See how much control you can exert over the fluidity of those edges by moving the flame. Take the flame away momentarily to sprinkle a pinch of flux powder (I use borax) onto the hot metal. This will help to protect the metal from further oxidation, also resulting in a smoother final surface of the nugget you are making.

4 Continue to heat until the silver has pulled into a rounded puddle. This is your nugget. If you want to play on, you can manipulate the molten puddle using tweezers or a soldering pick. Try with and without the presence of additional flame contact. The nugget can be used as it is—a precious nugget of silver. Make a superb claw setting to show off this object of beauty in a ring, pendant, or pin.

EXERCISE 2

FUSION WITH WIRES

1 Now that you have a handle on precision heat control, try fusing wires onto the next rectangle of 0.5 mm silver sheet.

Clean the surface of the silver panel with pumice and paint all over with auflux or a similar liquid flux (borax would do too, but I like to be able to see what's going on throughout the heating process without the presence of bubbling and crusting).

2 Place the panel on a honeycomb soldering board. This gives extra control over the temperature of the sheet when heating. Cut small lengths of 0.5 mm wire and scatter them across the fluxed surface.

3 Heat the panel carefully with a bushy flame, watching for that telltale wetness on the surface of the silver. When you reach this point, pull the flame back slightly to maintain this fusing temperature for 30 seconds to ensure a good bond between all the elements. Allow the metal to cool to black hot (i.e. not glowing red) before quenching and pickling.

4 The end result reminds me of Japanese tea leaves–a story waiting to be told.

EXERCISE 3

FUSION WITH OLD CHAIN PARTS

1 Prepare the silver sheet as before (see Step 1, page 149). Lay your chain in an interesting pattern onto the panel, also fluxing the chain. Using a more direct flame, heat the arrangement, making sure to keep the flame moving, and concentrating more heat on the silver panel than on the chain (this will quickly melt if it gets too much heat). As before, when you reach the fusion point, hold the temperature for a few moments, then cool, quench, and pickle.

2 The finished panel has a fossil-like quality that could be developed in future work.

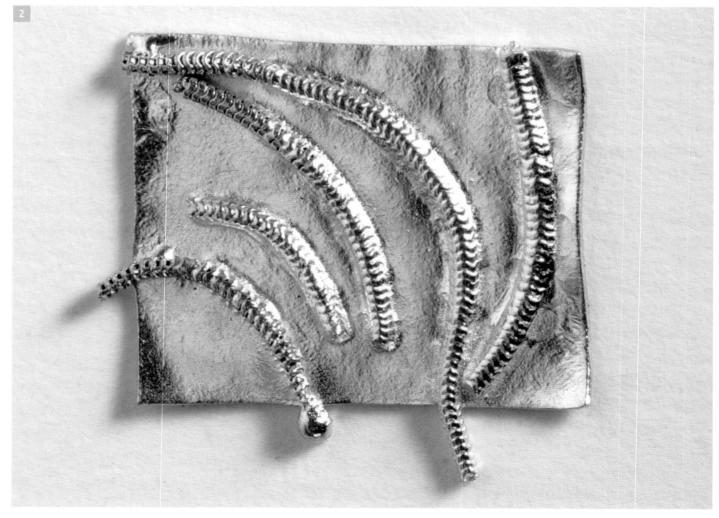

EXERCISE 4

FUSION WITH SHEET SCRAPS

1 Here, I like to combine fusion with reticulation, so I prepare the silver panel as before (see Step 1, page 149), also fluxing the scrap sheets once they are positioned.

2 Using a bushy flame, heat the whole surface, taking care not to let any edges shrink away. Once the surfaces sag together and fuse, continue to heat the surface to give it reticulated character.

3 I am reminded of the Greek myth of Icarus, whose father made him a pair of wings fashioned from feathers and wax. When the airborne Icarus flew too close to the sun, it melted the wax and destroyed his wings.

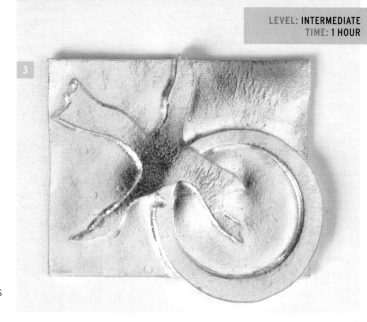

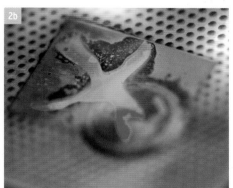

EXERCISE 5

RETICULATION

1 With a sharp flame, begin to heat the next piece of silver sheet. Watch carefully for those visual clues as you go through the stages of annealing— from brighter red to orange, then shiny and wet. Keeping the torch moving, swirl this surface of molten silver with the hot tip of the flame.

2 Now hold it so that it points directly into the center of the panel; see if you can blow a hole into the middle of the panel. Stop when you are happy with the way it's looking.

3 I love this texture, it suggests all sorts of jewelry-making possibilities.

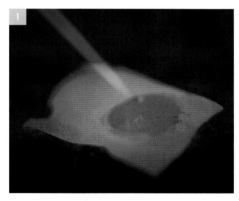

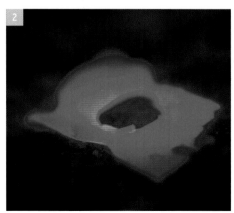

EXERCISE 6

GOLD DUSTING

Building up to the more challenging process on the last piece of silver sheet, the aim here is to fuse a scattering of 18 karat gold dust (filings generated when I made a wedding band) onto the surface.

1 This is quite a precise process requiring heat application from the underside of the silver as well as from the top, so position the prepared panel (cleaned, fluxed with auflux, see Step 1, page 149) onto a wire mesh to allow all-round access.

2 Now sprinkle some gold filings onto the surface. I use the square end of the tweezers, gently tapping the side to spread the dust finely. For contrast, I leave some areas without the gold dust.

3 Begin the heating process from the underside of the silver, bringing the color up to a dull red before switching to the upper surface (I use a sharp, hot flame).

Now work the top surface with the flame, keeping it moving all the time and pointing more at the areas without any gold. Bring the piece up to the fusing temperature (look for the "wet" sign), then hold at this heat, using the tip of the flame to work over the gold dust. You need to see this become "wet," too, so that its surface can fuse into the silver surface.

Bear in mind that gold is denser and thus heavier than silver, so if the silver gets too hot while the gold is still solid, it can sink down into the silver, which is a waste. (However, you can reveal it by etching the silver away, if necessary, so all is not lost. See Etching Processes, pages 132–9.) You will also need to take into account that the melting temperature of gold is higher than that of silver, so it needs more heat, but as the dust grains are very small they do pick up the heat quickly, so this equation works itself out.

The process takes longer than you might expect. Be patient, and make sure that the temperature is controlled. Once it appears to have made a bond, quench, and gently rub the surface with your thumb. If the gold starts to come off, wick off water with a tissue, reapply auflux to the panel, and reheat as before. When you have success, pickle, then rub with a burnisher to sparkle up the gold.

4 The sparkle of gold remains subtle against the whiteness of the silver; I especially like to bring extra contrast to the gold by oxidizing the silver.

3b

Lay out all your tests and decide how to proceed. Do you want to join them together? How best to do this so the links remain in harmony with the quality of the pieces? You might try out one of the techniques described in the Linkages projects (see pages 170-7). Consider also how you might further enhance the colors and textures of the panels. As mentioned previously, oxidization always works for me, but I can imagine how well a translucent enamel would work if the surface was polished beforehand (see Sweet pea pendant, pages 68-73).

WORKING WITH FUSED METAL

SOLDERING If you intend to solder additional items to the panels, it is worth noting that fused or reticulated surfaces are quite porous and so you will need to use more solder than usual. In addition, you will need a very good contact area to improve the likelihood of the joint being strong. Try burnishing the surfaces to be soldered to reduce the porosity. If you intend to bend or shape the sheet, gentle annealing beforehand will reduce the brittleness of the metal.

OXIDIZATION This is an easy way to enhance fused metals. There are several commercial oxidizing solutions available on the market. Generally, application of oxide is the last process in finishing your jewelry.

Copper bird and branches formed using the two-part die process (see pages 160-1), and further embellished using wooden punches to highlight detail and to add texture.

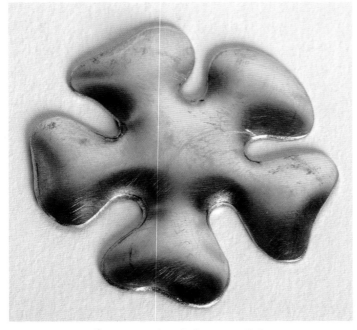

Flower formed from a (¹/₄ in (5 mm) sheet acrylic die (see page 158-9).

Conch formed using the two-part die process (wood and polymorph, see pages 160-1).

LOW-TECH BATCH FORMING

Stamping, pressing, and punching processes provide the lightweight alternative to casting when batch producing three-dimensional forms. These forming techniques can transform thin (light, cheap) sheet metal into hollow forms (structurally strong), and if you have some tool-making skills, it's possible to create multiples of quite complex forms relatively quickly. If you've ever had the chance to work with a hydraulic press or a fly press, you will appreciate how access to this kind of equipment can change the way you think about making jewelry; where previously you might have been preoccupied making time-consuming one-off forms, instantly you can make beautiful, soft forms quickly, repeatedly, and precisely.

MAKING BEST USE OF THE HOME STUDIO

Not many home jewelry studios can afford the expense of (or space for) specialist equipment such as the hydraulic press or the fly press, but with a little ingenuity similar benefits can be gained using tools and equipment that any home studio can muster. Ultimately, you are looking for ways to squeeze your metal sheet into form, and while it is an easy action for the fly press, this force can also be exerted using a vice, a C-cramp, a mallet—or even well-placed body weight! So as much as this section is about forming, it also explores cheap work-arounds and problem-solving for the process of making repeatable three-dimensional forms.

Borrowing from traditional approaches to die forming, I also combine punching and repoussé processes that offer an effective pastiche of forming techniques. Given practice, these can be skilfully applied to your work.

MAKING TOOLS

I love the concept of tool making. Where commercially available tools are made for a generic audience to do a specific job, a hand-made tool carries a greater sense of purpose and a higher degree of precision. It is made for the hand that holds it, to do a particular job that relates to the maker's aesthetic technical repertoire.

The following exercises explore how to make your own dies from a range of available and inexpensive materials, and how to give new purpose to old and unwanted tools, to provide you with customized chasing tools and punches.

MATERIALS
- Acrylic sheet, 1/4 in (5 mm) thickness; if you don't have acrylic sheet to hand, try a 1.2 mm brass sheet, with 1/4 in (5 mm) plywood to allow extra depth to the form
- 2 x copper sheet, 0.5 mm thickness
- Latex sheet (1/4 in/5 mm thickness is ideal) for protecting the acrylic/copper from the steel plate (if you don't have latex sheet to hand, an old flip-flop/thong or multiple layers of silicone sheet will also work)
- Hardwood block (an old kitchen chopping board would do if you can't find anything else)
- Polymorph (moldable plastic, see box on page 157)

TOOLS
- Tracing paper
- Pen or pencil
- Bow drill (see page 179), 1/2 in (12 mm) drill bit
- Files (see page 179): raspy file, large file, and needle files
- Gaffer tape or similar
- 2 x steel plates for pressing; you can also use a steel block
- Bench vise (see page 181)—alternatively try a C-cramp, punches, and a mallet, or try one-footed jumping or bouncing on the sandwich (on the floor!)
- Piercing saw (see page 178), wax blades (page 184) for cutting the acrylic sheet
- Traditional hand-carving tools such as chisels, lino-cutting tools (see pages 162 and 178)
- Pendant drill (see page 182) with raspy grinding tools if you prefer this to the hand-carving method
- Wall putty
- Heatproof dish for the polymorph grains
- Petroleum jelly to rub on the hardwood block
- Wooden punches (see page 162) and a mallet (see page 180) to add extra detail to the final form

DIE FORMING: THE PRINCIPLE

Sheet metal is pressed into a die with the use of force resulting in a hollow, 3-D form. From this die numerous hollow 3-D forms can be produced. The die may be made from one or two parts, with the one-part die producing a soft form and the two-part die resulting in a more crisp and detailed form.

DIE FORMING: THE PROCESS

For a one-part die, you need a resistant material into which you can form a cavity that thin metal sheet will be pressed into. Industrially produced dies may be made from precision-cut steel, but more manageable materials are acrylic sheet, brass, wood, polymorph, or a combination of all these materials.

Sheet materials To make a die from acrylic or brass, you simply cut out the outline of the shape you want to make, and press into it to produce a soft, pillow-like form of that shape (see opposite). Acrylic sheet should ideally be ¼ in (5 mm) thick; brass can be thinner (2 mm), but should be used in conjunction with MDF to give potential for extra depth. This type of die has the added advantage of having perfectly matched outlines on both sides of the sheet (if you're good at cutting), so from the one die you are able to produce left and right for earrings, or the back and front for a locket or bead form (see right center and bottom).

Hardwood block With a block of hardwood and carving tools, you can carve more complex forms, and with the assistance of punches much more detail can be impressed into the sheet you are forming (see top left).

Second die This can be used to work with your original "negative" die (see top right and pages 160–1). A second die can assist in pressing your sheet into the detailed form you have made, and additionally a two-part die provides a positive against which you can also use punches to get even tighter definition into your detailed 3-D form.

A one-die process where a form is carved in hardwood, then a thin copper sheet is pressed into the form to create a 3-D shape.

A two-part die process; polymorph is pressed into the carved shape to create a mold. This is then pressed in a bench vise with a thin copper sheet.

Polymorph can also be used with acrylic to increase the depth of the resulting metal form.

Polymorph (moldable plastic) This plastic, which is a type of biodegradable polymer (polycaprolactone, or PCL), provides a fast and effective material for making this second, positive die (see also box opposite). You can also use polymorph to make a die from an object you already have—for example, a shell or a pebble. Once you have made one die by pressing the object into it, you can make a second die from the same material, as in the example of the scallop shell opposite.

A great advantage with the acrylic die is that mirror forms can be made from the same tool to make a matching pair–perhaps to make earrings, or to be soldered together to make a 3-D hollow form.

USING ACRYLIC AS A DIE

Acrylic is an ideal material for making a die in that it is incredibly resistant to pressure, and as long as it is kept flat when the pressure is applied, it is unlikely to break. Keeping acrylic flat when working with it is important, as acrylic does not take kindly to bending, tending towards brittleness and chipping under this influence.

Both sides of the die can be used, so it is possible to make symmetrical, mirror forms that can also be joined along the edges to make hollow bead forms.

CUTTING ACRYLIC Drill and cut at low speeds to avoid the swarf (the material that is removed) fusing the cut back together. When piercing the sheet, it's best to use wax blades. These large-toothed, twisted blades can cut in any direction without having to spin the saw frame around, and they can also cut swiftly through the material without clogging.

Try to keep your cutting as vertical as possible so that forms taken from either side of the die will match exactly.

You can use ready-made objects and polymorph to create suitable dies, here shells provide the form. If you try this method, allow the first die to harden, then coat the first polymorph die in petroleum jelly before making the second die from it, or it will stick to itself.

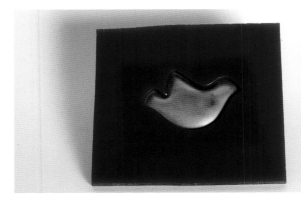

The simplest die form can be made from ¹/₄ in (5 mm) thick acrylic sheet.

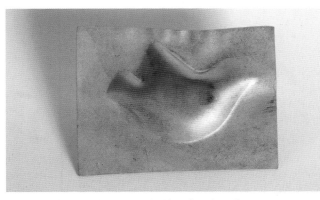

The resulting form made from copper sheet is "soft" and graphic in appearance. Compare this to the two-part die result on page 161.

POLYMORPH

This is a very useful material to have in the workshop, and once you have tried polymorph you will find endless uses for it. A form of plastic, it becomes transparent, gummy, and pliable when it is heated in hot water, returning to a white, tough, nylon-like consistency at normal room temperature. Polymorph comes in granular form for ease of use. Once formed, it can be endlessly reshaped by immersing again in hot water, although a solid block takes much longer than small granules to become pliable. It can be used to make formers or temporary holding devices, or to replace missing or broken handles for tools. Polymorph can also be used to make protective linings for pliers or for your vise. Use grease such as petroleum jelly to stop it from sticking to itself and other objects.

ONE-PART DIE FORMING

This project focuses on the sheet method, which is cutting a die from acrylic or brass sheet. I will focus on the use of acrylic in the description below as I find it easier to use, but a 1.2 mm thick brass sheet will also work in the same way. You will need to have a supporting piece of plywood (with the same shaped hole cut into it) to provide depth for your form if using brass.

1 Take a sheet of ¼ in (5 mm) thick acrylic and trace your simplified shape onto it (see Templates, page 186). In this instance I used a flower and drew three different sizes of the flower, but I suggest starting with one shape, and learning from your experience of working with it.

2 Drill a hole into the middle of the shape to be removed, and cut away the shape to leave a negative space. Be sure to cut on the inside ("waste" side) of the line, as any deviance with your saw from perfectly vertical will mean that the underside of the cut will not match the front; cutting with this tolerance will allow you to rectify the edges with a file afterward.

3 File the edges with a raspy file. I use wax files for this too, paying attention to making all the cut lines vertical. Tidy up the very top edge with a standard needle file. This edge will define the precise limit of the form in metal, so get a nice flowing line, back and front. Your first tool is ready for use.

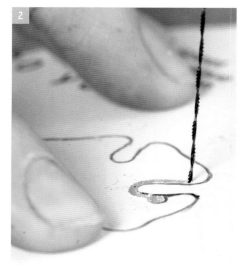

4 Anneal a sheet of 0.5 mm thick copper. It needs to be ¼ in (5 mm) wider in all directions than the shape cut in the die. Stick it over the hole in the acrylic using gaffer tape or a similar strong tape.

5 Make a sandwich like this: steel plate, acrylic with copper, latex sheet, steel plate. Place this sandwich into the vise and crank up the pressure as far as you can go, making sure that the copper sheet is centrally placed between the pressure points of the jaws. Release the sandwich from the jaws and see what you have.

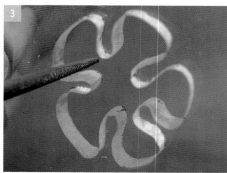

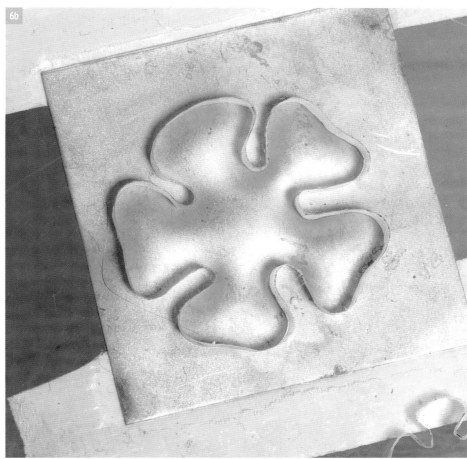

6 Extra depth can now be achieved by cutting a small latex insert to fit inside this indent. Anneal the metal again and remake the sandwich with the insert nestled into the partial form. Squeeze as before. Release the sandwich from the jaws, then remove the latex insert to reveal the finished model.

7 When you are happy with the result, cut away the form, allowing 1 mm distance from the defined edge. Try making the model from the other side; check to see how well they fit (how good is your cutting?), and if possible, join the trimmed forms to make a complete, two-sided hollow shape.

8 The finished piece. The item can work as earrings or as a pendant, or you could make several more to use as a repeated motif interspersed with beads on a chain.

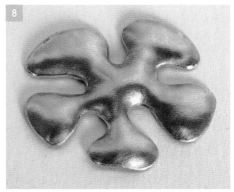

TWO-PART DIE FORMING

This is a hardwood and polymorph method. You will need a block of (relatively) hardwood for this die. I have slices from a birch tree, which were donated by my lovely neighbor, and though I'm told this is not the hardest of woods, it will suffice for my needs. If trees are distant from your daily experience, you could get a chopping board from the hardware store.

1 Trace your pattern onto the wood in readiness for carving. Remember that you are working in reverse as you carve, so you need to think inside out and back to front. You need to make a few locators in the wood, using the corner of a large file, for the polymorph to know where to sit in the die once cut. Mark some triangles on the side and make deep grooves with a file. Alternatively, drill holes about $3/5$ in (15 mm) away from the outline of the shape to be carved.

2 To make the carving, you can use traditional hand-carving tools (chisels, lino-cutting tools, etc.), or you can use raspy grinding tools with a pendant drill.

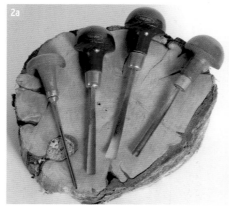

3 Although the drill removes material quickly, it may feel jumpy and out of control, so I prefer the slow method. Try using both, if you have all these tools. Carving into wood is not something I do with great regularity, so my skills are limited and I stick to quite simple forms. I have my father's woodcarving tools, and as I work with them I think of his woodcuts and how each stroke conveys purpose and energy. I begin to remember how he taught me to handle the tools, with every part of both hands doing a job to exert controlled pressure, always ensuring that no flesh is in front of the cutting blade as I work.

If you have not used chisels with wood before, I suggest you take them for a test run before starting on your proposed hardwood die.

4 When you are happy with your carving, press some wall putty into the die to see what the positive form will look like, then resolve any issues that are apparent. You have made your second tool; now for your third tool.

5 Put a handful of the polymorph grains into a heatproof dish and pour boiling water over them. They should start to look like frogspawn as they become transparent and soft. While you wait for them to soften completely, rub petroleum jelly all over the wooden block. Pour the water away and leave the polymorph in the bowl to cool for 1 minute. It should be cool enough to work it with your bare hands now.

6 Take the translucent polymorph out of the bowl and squeeze into a ball, squeezing out any remaining water. This will help to bond the individual beads. Press the ball into the die, making sure to force the plastic into the recesses of your carved form. Use a steel plate to make the back surface flat and pretty much parallel to the surface of the wood. Allow the plastic to cool and harden in the wooden mold. The plastic must be entirely white. This should take an hour or two. Don't rush it.

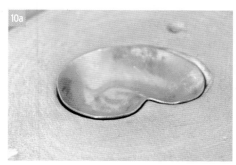

7 Once ready, anneal a 0.5 mm thick copper sheet and make a sandwich with a latex sheet and a steel plate, as before (see Step 5, page 158). Squeeze in the vise to get an indent, then make a second insert of latex, just as you did with the previous method (see Step 6, page 159). Your shell will have taken the majority of available depth by now, though surface detail may still be absent. Remove the copper model and draw a line along the edge where the metal starts to take form.

8 Cut right along the line you have drawn, and anneal the shape.

9 Replace in the die and put the polymorph on top, locating the grooves so that you know it will fit in place. Put the sandwich into the vise, slipping a steel plate between the polymorph and the vise to ensure even pressure when it is tightened. Much more detail should now be evident on the form.

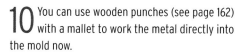

10 You can use wooden punches (see page 162) with a mallet to work the metal directly into the mold now.

11 The finished piece can be soldered to a flat sheet of copper or other metal to make a contained, hollow form. Take care to file and grind the surface edge completely flat before you start soldering.

MAKING WOODEN PUNCHES

What can you use to punch the metal back to reveal crisp detail? A metal chasing tool might do the trick, but this will also, to some extent, cut into the metal. To retain the softness of form you might want to stay with wood. Hardwood is the best material from which to make wooden punches. Holly, cherry, plum, or other dense wood, all make for excellent punches as they hold their shape without splitting.

Alternatively, you can use old wooden spoons or the wooden handle of a dead paintbrush to make perfectly adequate (if short-lived) punches.

Cut your sticks to a comfortable length–3 in (80 mm) seems about right for me. Use a file to shave the tip to a useful shape–fine point, thin flat edge, triangular, and teardrop shapes all find use. With rough sticks, I let the shape of the stick itself dictate the final tip. The hitting end should be entirely flat.

Once you have the shape honed, rub the whole thing down with very fine emery paper–you want it to be lovely to hold. Take them for a test run on your form. With use, the ends begin to fray from impact. Just file them back to the shape you require.

MATERIALS
- Pieces of hardwood such as holly, cherry, plum, or other dense wood; old wooden spoons or the handles of old paintbrushes are other options
- Old tools–any old tools are suitable for adapting to make punches

TOOLS
- Piercing saw (see page 178), for cutting the pieces of hardwood into shape
- Files (see page 179): large wood files for filing the punches to your desired shape; large files for shaping the tips of the steel to your desired shape
- Fine emery paper for polishing the wooden punches
- Bench vise (see page 181), for holding the tool while shaping
- Hacksaw for cutting the old tools to appropriate lengths for punches
- Wet and dry papers (see page 184), 240, 1000, and 1200 grit

If you are tempering your tool:
- Protective gauntlets, apron, and good boots for your health and safety
- Torch (see page 183) for tempering the steel
- Tongs to hold the tool safely while heating

TEMPERING

Tempering is a process of hardening steel by heating and quenching the metal at specific temperatures. Quality tool steel has a high carbon content and can be made tough through this process of tempering. Stamping tools are intended to impress cleanly into annealed metal, so you want to keep the stamping face details sharp (and therefore hard) for long-term use. If you are using steel from an old tool, it is likely that it will be tempered and therefore difficult to modify; to shape it with files, you will first need to anneal it by heating it to red hot, then allowing it to cool very slowly (bury it in charcoal crumbs, perhaps). Once cool, you can then grind and file the tool to your desired shape. Complex curves can be ground away using grinding wheels or burrs in the pendant drill.

THE PROCESS To temper, once shaped, polish one whole side of the tool with 800-grit wet and dry paper so that you can see the silver color of the metal, then heat to red hot. Quench the shaped tip in water until the redness has gone, then remove it from the water; the other end will still be hot even though the redness has gone. The heat will transfer back down to the cold tip now it is in the air; observe the rainbow of colors as they roll down the shaft of the tool to the shaped tip. When the blue band reaches the tip, plunge and completely submerge the tool in the water, stirring it around until the tool is completely cold.

CAUTION Red-hot steel can brand you. Good boots, leather gauntlets, and tongs (in addition to the usual health and safety precautions, see pages 183) are required for this process.

MAKING STEEL PUNCHES AND CHASING TOOLS

Rather than purchasing punches and chasing tools, I much prefer to make my own from old tools that can no longer do their intended job (see top left). Garage sales and flea markets are a great place to pick up such treasures. Old tools like this should be cheap, so don't let anyone suggest to you a screwdriver past its best is a vintage tool. As steel is a much harder metal than our usual non-ferrous metals, working it will blunt your files, so it is a good idea to keep a separate set for use on steel and other hard materials.

1 In this instance, I am using a screwdriver to make a chasing tool. First, cut the posi-drive tip from the tool with a hacksaw. File this cut surface nicely flat, then cut the next 3 in (80 mm) from the tool to make a punch.

2 Put this cut section into the vise, then file the end to a sloping flat plane, as if trying to make a flat-head screwdriver. Work these surfaces smooth using 240-grit wet and dry paper (used with a drop of water), and then 1000-grit wet and dry paper, until the tool begins to shine.

3 Now paying attention to the actual shape of the working end, soften all the corners of the flat, thin tip using the large file, so when using your finished tool it will glide over the metal as you hammer it, thus leaving as little trace of its movements as possible.

4 Further softening of these edges is achieved by reworking the surfaces with 240-, progressing to 1200-, grit wet and dry papers.

It is not necessary to temper chasing tools for your purposes, but if you go on to design and make stamping tools, you will need to use quality tool steel and you will need to temper them (see box, opposite).

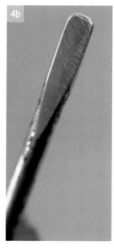

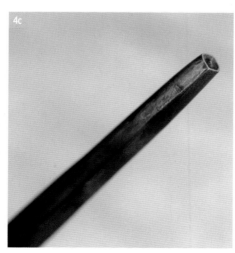

A pair of fan-shaped earrings made from copper (see page 167) .

A series of quick 3-D experiments made from thick metal foil to see how shapes are affected by folding.

FOLDING METALS

One of the qualities I most enjoy about metal is its ability in sheet form to behave (to some degree) like cardstock. Scoring and folding will produce beautiful architectural forms with crisp lines, flat planes, and unexpectedly sensuous curves.

In this project, there are four approaches to scoring and folding. Although the technique is the same, you will see that the results vary quite dramatically according to the position, direction, and quality of the scored lines. These shapes just hint at the potential offered by scoring and folding; a day playing with cardstock or metal foil will be well rewarded as your own distinct forms evolve.

Don't forget to look at the back as well as the front of your forms—both have unique qualities that are likely to present quite different aesthetics. For example, the pyramid from the outside appears soft, tactile, and immediate, while from the reverse side it is more complex, as each curved plane mirrors light from the other sides. There is a greater sense of mystery as the eye tries to understand the form.

In your initial experiments, I suggest you use sheets of copper or brass, but as you get used to scoring, and as you begin to understand how to manipulate the metal to create great shapes, consider how spectacular your results would be if you were to combine this technique with a sheet of married metal (see pages 140-5). What happens to the lines, curves, and squares of color when they are interrupted by sharp bends? How else could you enhance your folded forms? I love the idea of gold leaf or gold plate on those delicious inward planes.

As you make the shapes, plenty of uses for them should come to you, and with little effort any one of them could become a beautiful pendant, a pair of earrings, or a pin. Try to think beyond the obvious.

TOOLS TIPS FOR SCORING

SEPARATING DISKS Used more often for removing sprues from castings, these silicone carbide disks (used with a screw-top mandrel on a pendant motor) have a very thin cutting edge, which is perfect for scoring into metal to create a "u"-shaped groove. These disks provide the best means for cutting curved score lines, but they are great for straight lines too. Practise on scrap metal before working on a special piece of metal—you have to learn to control its wild, marching manner. Wear a full face mask when using this tool as it spits ground metal and silicone carbide straight at your nose.

DIAMOND-TIPPED BURRS In a cheap set from your local hardware store, you will find a burr with the right kind of profile to open up the "u" of the separating disk to the "v" you need to create any degree of angle for your final bend. Once again, practise on a piece of scrap metal to get used to it, and wear a face mask.

HAND TOOLS It's possible to make a scoring tool from the tang of an old file, but I have found limited use for the tool, which you pull along your line toward you. In preference, I use a square needle file or a three-square (triangular) file, depending on the angle. Purists might be upset by this next suggestion, but I found a particularly good scoring edge was made when I snapped the tip off an old, square needle file (clamp all but the tip in a vise, then swipe off the end with one weighty sideways blow from a hammer). This tool can be further refined to carve and file at the same time by grinding the broken tip to 40 degrees from one corner on a whetstone.

MATERIALS
- 2 x copper sheets, 0.9 mm thickness, $1\frac{3}{8}$ x $1\frac{3}{8}$ in (35 x 35 mm)
- 1 x copper sheet, annealed, 0.9 mm thickness, $2\frac{1}{4}$ x 1 in (60 x 25 mm)

TOOLS
- Steel rule and dividers (see page 178) for measuring and marking
- Circle template for marking out arcs
- Fine-line permanent pen
- Pendant drill (see page 182), separating disk with a screw-top mandrel (see left), diamond-tipped burr to widen grooves
- Full protection face mask (see page 185)
- Square file (see page 179)
- Burnisher (see page 182) in case you cut too far through the metal when grooving
- Wet and dry papers (see page 184), 600, 800, 1000, and 1200 grit for polishing
- Pliers (see page 180): parallel pliers, nylon-tipped pliers
- Soldering equipment (see pages 182 and 183): flux (borax), brush, hard solder, torch, tweezers, soldering block, and pickle
- Piercing saw (see page 178), 2/0 blades

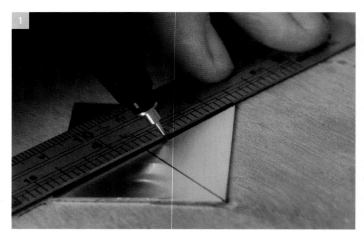

EXERCISE 1

THE SOFT PYRAMID

The process of scoring and folding involves cutting a "v"-shaped groove into the sheet of metal to a depth of about two-thirds of the thickness of the sheet. The sheet is then folded along the groove until the sides of the "v" meet, and solder is run along the seam to make the fold permanent.

1 Anneal a square of 0.9 mm thick copper sheet, 1³⁄₈ x 1³⁄₈ in (35 x 35 mm), and use a pen and ruler to draw two lines joining opposite corners to make a cross.

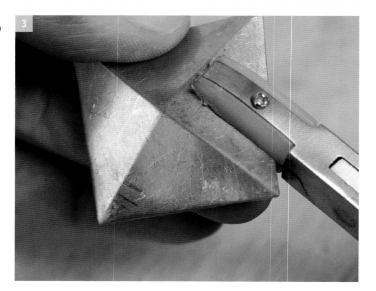

2 Wearing a face mask, use a separating disk to grind carefully along the full extent of one line, making sure not to let the tool wander. I prop mine on a piece of wood to make the action comfortable for my hand, and I keep my eye in line with the line to be cut.

When you are about two-thirds of the way through the metal, you will begin to see a slight hint of an indent where the score mark is, on the opposite side. This indicates that you have cut deeply enough. If you go too far, you will either cut through the metal or you may cause a raised line, indicating that you are nearly through. Burnish down this raised line, and take care with all subsequent processes to avoid the line snapping off. Repeat this process with the second line.

These "u"-shaped grooves need to be opened to 45 degrees; use the tip of a broken square file (see page 165) to scrape out this angle. Now surface with wet and dry paper to remove any scratches from both sides of the metal.

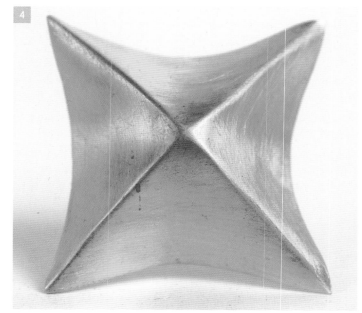

3 When you are happy with the surface appearance, you can bend your form (you will be able to use either side when it is folded). Using only finger pressure to start, begin to manipulate the metal to cause a bend along one axis. Now work the other fold with the same pressure. Start to curve the edges of the square inward, and if necessary use nylon-tipped pliers to give additional leverage.

4 Take the necessary health and safety precautions before you begin soldering (see page 183). Once you have achieved a good shape, flux the inside bends and run solder into the seams. I use the feeding system for this (see Step 15, page 25). Admire your form.

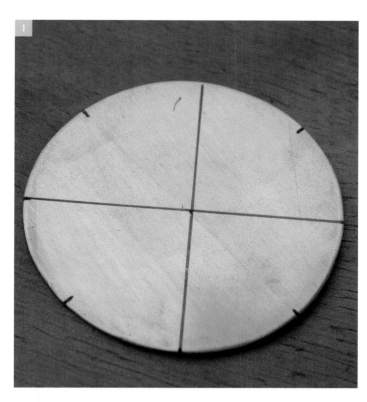

EXERCISE 2

FANS

1 Cut out a 2-in (50-mm) diameter circle from a square of non-annealed 0.9 mm thick copper sheet, 1³/₈ x 1³/₈ in (35 x 35 mm). Mark a cross on one side of the circle and groove (see Step 2, opposite) with the separating disks, then with the square file.

Mark halfway points between each quarter you have made, and transfer this mark to the other side (front) of the circle. Join these points to make an intersecting cross on the front.

2 Groove just one of these lines as before (see Step 2, opposite), then with your saw, cut along the other to make two semicircles. Surface the two sides as before.

3 Using parallel pliers and hand pressure, bend along the grooves to make two pleasing fan shapes.

4 Run solder along the insides of three folds (see Step 4, opposite). The resulting fan shapes could be made into earrings (see page 164); how else could you adapt these forms to make them wearable?

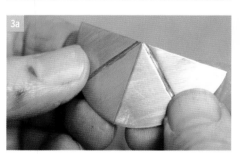

EXERCISE 3

CURVING CONCERTINA

1 This exercise combines rhythmic curves with two-way folding. Take a rectangle of annealed 0.9 mm thick copper sheet, 2¼ x 1 in (60 x 25 mm), and mark both edges at ⅜ in (10 mm) intervals. Every second score will be made on the back of the sheet, so you will have three arcs on one side and two in the spaces between them on the other. Use a circle template to join the points in five identical arcs (three on the front of the sheet, two on the back).

2 Now you have begun to master the behavior of separating disks, gentle curves will be less challenging to you. Get your pendant drill hand in a comfortable position so that it naturally swings around the curves.

3 Opening up the "u" channels into 90-degree "v" grooves is far more difficult with a file, so I use a diamond-tipped burr. (A drop of water on the work will lubricate as you cut, making the burr last longer.)

Draw a center line down the front of the boat-like curve, and once again groove with the separating disk (see Step 2, page 166) until you can see a shadow of the line on the reverse.

4 Once all the arcs on both sides have been cut and burred, clean up the metal surface as before with wet and dry papers (see Step 2, page 166), and then bend them with a pair of nylon-tipped pliers, one step at a time. The angles can then be sharpened with a pair of flat-nosed pliers and finger pressure.

5 Flush with a little solder and polish. I hope this result is a stairway to heaven?

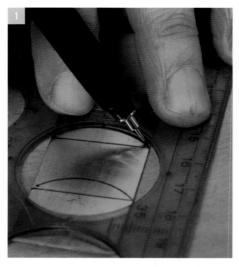

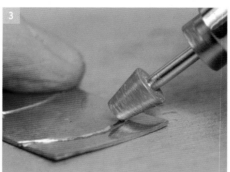

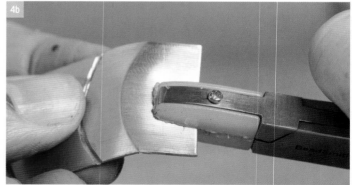

METAL HARDNESS AND FOLDING

When working with straight score lines for folding, the resulting planes should be flat, as in the square and flat sides of a box.

I always begin with a hardened sheet of metal for these forms as the metal will be more resistant and I find it easier to make clean bends and sharp folds with my pliers.

Conversely, when folding up curved score lines, the metal gives into soft curves a little more consistently if it is pre-annealed. If your metal needs annealing before bending, do so before you score the metal.

EXERCISE 4

ENCAPSULATED LEAF

Here's an exception to the rule—although you are working to produce curves, this time start with a hard sheet of 0.9 mm thick copper, 2 x 1 3/8 in (50 x 35 mm).

1 Draw a center line down the length of the metal, on one side of the sheet. Find something large and round to use as a template to make two nice arcs that start and end at the center line.

2 On the back, groove ONLY the curved lines. No need to open them out more than the disks will cut, as the folds are fairly shallow.

3 Using nylon-tipped pliers, firmly grip the outside edge to give enough leverage to bend the sheet along the two curved grooves. You will notice a delightfully tactile, boat-like curve emerging as you bend into these grooves. Run solder into these folded lines to make them solid. Don't scrimp on the solder—you want it to fill up any remaining gaps in the folded grooves because the next steps will put a lot of strain on them.

4 Draw a center line down the front of the boat-like curve, and again groove with the separating disk until you can see a shadow of the line on the reverse.

5 Using a pair of nylon-tipped pliers in each hand, grip the sides of the sheet and push into the form to cause the sheet to bend along that groove. It won't want to do it at first; try gently coaxing, a little at a time, from the middle, then the top and bottom until the form begins to resemble more of a leaf than a boat. Stop when you dare go no further. Flush with solder as before (see Step 4, page 166), and admire the finished item.

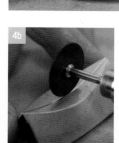

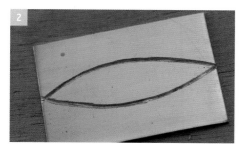

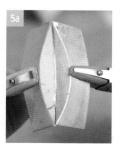

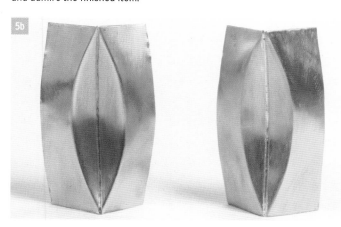

EXPLORING FOLDING

These four experiments have produced forms that range from simple to quite complex shapes. Look at each of them carefully; take a minute to understand how the cut of the groove, and the relationship between each groove you have cut, affects the end result. Consider how the sheet is forced into unexpected changes in surface direction according to the folds you have imposed on it. Appreciate how the grooving and folding on the front and the back of the sheet can add another dimension to the end result. How much more can the metal take? What impact do you think it will have to work in thinner or thicker sheet metal? There are so many avenues to explore.

CONTROLLING THE DEGREE OF THE FOLD

- The final angle of the folded metal can be controlled by the angle of the groove cut. The wider you make the angle of the groove, the sharper the bend will be. A groove cut with a triangular file removes a 60-degree "v" shape, so when it's folded the result will be a shallow 120-degree bend. A groove cut with a square file removes 90 degrees, and the resulting bend will be a 90-degree right angle.

- A scored line can be folded only once. If you open it up again you are likely to weaken and even crack the piece along the groove, so it's important to get the degree of the "v" shape correct the first time. If it's critical to get a specific angle and you are struggling to work out what to remove, try an enlarged test on a strip of wood. Cut the "v" shape wider and wider until you get the angle you want. The wood will snap in two, but you will be able to see when you lay it open, the relationship between what you remove and the angle of bend you end up with.

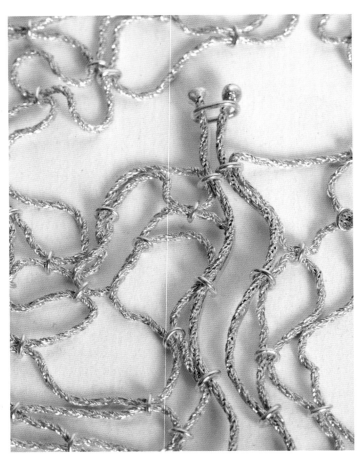

The siren necklace (see also page 11) has a closure that echoes the oval links used elsewhere in the necklace (Precious Collection).

A tiny piece of tubing soldered into place inside the gold wires enables this pendant to "float" inside its connecting neck wire (Astral Collection).

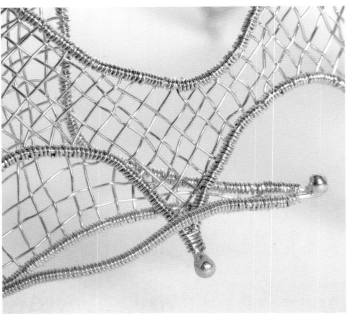

The rose neckpiece (see also page 40) has a flexible wrap, a versatile closure that exploits the flexibility provided by the material and construction method, making the piece pleasingly adjustable (Venus Collection).

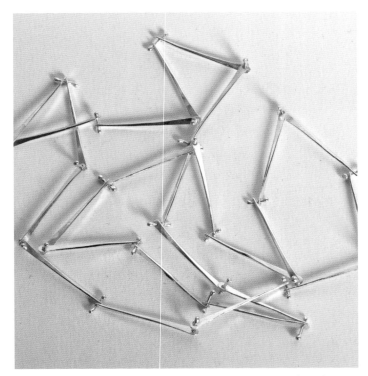

Loose rivets hold the links in this chain together; the rivets have been made from wires that are balled at each end to give a bony appearance and movement.

A hand-made clasp will always improve the aesthetic and quality of a piece of jewelry (hand-made bayonet clasp for a snake chain, Totem Collection).

LINKAGES

In my own jewelry, I am always looking to find ways to integrate aesthetic with technique, and this is evident in the way I look to join elements together.

Linkages—the solutions we find to join two or more elements together—are a subtle indicator of the quality of a piece of jewelry. Commercially available jump rings and clasps provide valid solutions for simple or commercial designs, but hand-made, one-off jewelry pieces demand a more considered conclusion.

To design a perfect linkage solution, you need to understand the complexities of movement and gravity, weight and strength, and rigidity and flexibility. This also requires a good working knowledge of your materials, and so the following exercises look at diverse approaches to linkages with a view to stimulating original solutions for your own jewelry designs. The four exercises are:

1 LATERAL THINKING

Take three pieces of $1\frac{1}{4}$ x $1\frac{1}{2}$ in (30 x 40 mm) foil, paper, or cardstock, and find a way to join them together without using any other material. You can change the shape of each element; scissors (or a knife) are allowed. Find another five methods (think slots, grooves, hooks, tabs; think three-dimensional).

2 PLAYTIME

Spend a day in a toy store. Hang out and play—all in the name of research, of course. There are lots of exciting modular and building systems on the shelves, but examine everything that moves—wheels, magnets, building blocks, clockwork toys—here is an expansive manifestation of linkages in all materials and contexts.

3 EVOLUTION

Find a form in nature that utilizes movement and develop a linkage design that is suggested by this form. Consider how we move, what our joints look like, and the different types of joint/movement. Consider other creatures and their articulations.

4 ELEMENTAL CONNECTIONS

Take a series of elements from your experiments box and develop a way of joining them together that maintains the aesthetic integrity of the pieces. (If you have made a series of fused panels, see pages 146-53, you could use these now.)

Note: As there is no limit as to how you might interpret the experiments that follow, equally there is no limit to the tools or materials you might use to achieve your results. Here is a general list of items you might find helpful.

MATERIALS
- Metal foil, cardstock
- Sheet metal of your choice, 0.9 mm thickness, 0.5 to 3 mm diameter, in copper/brass/gilding metal wire
- Silver tubing
- Test pieces from your play box

TOOLS
- Fine-line permanent pen
- Scissors and scalpel
- Steel rule and dividers (see page 178)
- Glue, duct tape, and wall putty
- Piercing saw (see page 178) and your favored blade sizes
- Files (see page 179): large files, needle files
- Selection of pliers (see page 180), including nylon-tipped pliers
- Mallet and hammers (see page 180)
- Bow drill (see page 179), selection of drill bits
- Fine emery buffing stick (see page 184)
- Doming punch (see page 181)
- Wire cutters (see page 178)
- Steel block and sandbag (see page 181)
- Soldering equipment (see pages 182 and 183): flux (borax), brush, torch, tweezers, soldering block, and pickle
- Vise (see page 181)

The materials I used in the following exercises are listed with the project.

EXERCISE 1

LATERAL THINKING

I am endlessly delighted by the variety of approaches that students present for this exercise. I imagine your ideas are very different to my own quick sketches, so add these to your repertoire. For this exercise, you will need some small pieces of metal foil.

1 My first experiment is a series of links made from the three pieces of foil, with one of them cut into strips to make wide "jump rings." This is quite a literal application and I want to move on, but then I find myself challenged to make a range of shapes for the interlocking units. I realize too late (they are lost on my floor) that I could make use of every last scrap from my initial rectangles of foil.

2 My second experiment takes me in an architectural direction. Cutting slots into each sheet of foil facilitates an interlocking that feels minimal and bold. I'm unsure where this is going, but now those forms are lodged in the back of my mind as a potential solution for a future conundrum.

3 My third is a quick experiment with internal slotting. I try to think how a shape might slot and locate to make an interesting pattern, also allowing movement, perhaps even a clasp for something. Cutting one end into an arrow form and then making a horizontal cut into each unit, I try to work these forms together. Although my model is scrappy I can see the potential here.

4 My fourth experiment moves on from the last idea of internal slotting and linking. I cut a series of tongues into each unit and bend each one out slightly, then link them together. This is working nicely.

5 In my fifth experiment, I try to break away from everything I have explored so far. Curving one unit into a tight roll presents new opportunities. I cut two slots to make a housing for the roll, and I almost have a hinge. In addition to this hinge connection, there is also potential in this slotting and pulling out. I think of those paper lanterns I made at school, and wonder how this might translate into metal. As this is a lateral challenge, I discard the third piece.

6 This experiment begins again with this roll; the remaining two sheets are slightly curved after cutting crosses into their centers. I feed them onto the roll and then squash the ends so that the pieces are captured and yet able to move. The resulting piece has a 1960s aesthetic, and I find interest in the contrasting curves—more so than in the movement within the construction.

7 My seventh experiment also explores encapsulation. Cutting pointed slots into the first sheet is almost like raising a grain in metal. The second sheet is curved slightly and sprung into a pleasing lock with my points. I have no need for the third piece. I think of settings and how similar techniques might be used to hold the thinnest sliver of gold into a silver setting.

Ideas keep on flowing once that door has been opened. This lateral brief has achieved its objective.

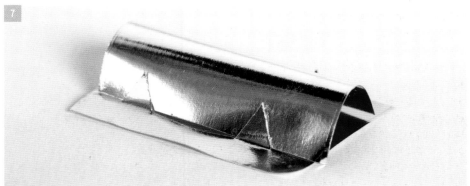

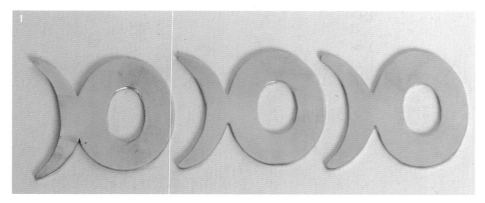

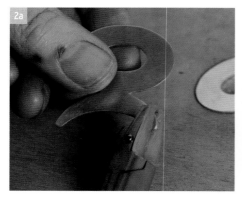

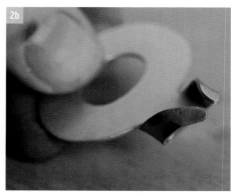

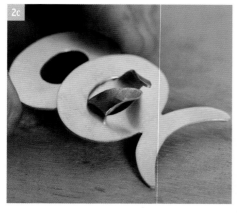

EXERCISE 2

PLAYTIME

After a visit to a toy store I returned with a plastic construction set consisting of flexible components that can be linked together with it's popper-like connections. How does this research impact on my thinking about linkages? Playing with the pieces, I find they offer a fast and effective way to explore repeated forms and how to join them. Owing to the flexibility of the material and the simple "rivet"-style attachment, they quickly manipulate into surprising shapes that are also applicable to metal, which I have not considered before. For this project, you will need a gilding metal sheet 3 x 1 3/8 in (80 x 35 mm) of 0.8 mm thickness.

1 I particularly like the spinal form and the movement the toy pieces provide, and my experiments borrow from this slightly restricted movement and the repetition of a single shape. Rather than working with rivets, I have found a way to link the pieces by exploiting the malleability and rigidity that metal can provide. I find that my ideas are influenced by the experiments with foil from the Lateral thinking brief (see pages 172-3).

2 Starting with a simple base unit—the Taurean in me enjoys this form—transfer the design (see template on page 186) onto your metal sheet and cut out a minimum of three shapes. To link the pieces, bend the horns inward with nylon-tipped pliers so that they can slip into the hole of the next unit.

3 Once opened out and tapped flat(ish) with a mallet, the units are permanently locked together, but some movement is possible. Continue with the next unit to make a longer section.

4 After three units you should sense the potential of this emerging form. I like the way it sharpens when draped over a 3-D model—it might make a good cuff. There are a few issues with the reshaping of the horns after bending. I could continue to refine my technique to get a smooth surface, or consider texturing the pieces so these inconsistencies are disguised by the overall pattern on the metal.

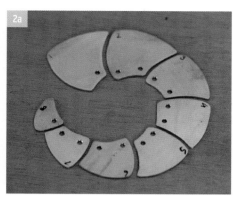

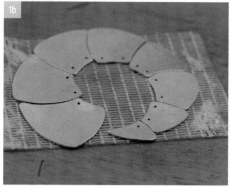

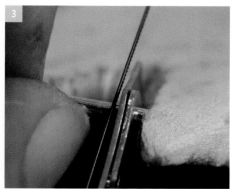

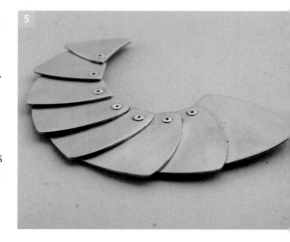

EXERCISE 3

EVOLUTION

A curvaceous motion can be mimicked in other materials by using a series of rivets around which units can swing. Where else in nature is this principle evident? Consider the armadillo shell: what happens if the pivot is de-centralized? For this exercise you will need a gilding metal sheet 2 ¼ x 2 ¼ in (60 x 60 mm) and 0.8 mm thickness, and 1 in (25 mm) of silver tubing, 1.6 mm external diameter.

1 My experiment is based on the armadillo shell. I made cardstock models to devise the shapes that will work best in metal (see page 186 for the template). Use the cardstock templates to transfer the patterns onto the metal sheet. Then cut the metal parts out with a piercing saw. To help identify each piece the correct way around and in the right order, number them and stick them into their correct position on duct tape. Use a center punch to mark the position for drilling (i.e. for the rivet) at a point ¹/₁₀ in (2.5 mm) from the inside corners.

2 Still leaving the pieces in position on the duct tape, drill these marked points using a bow drill with a 1.6 mm drill bit. Drilling inevitably raises a burr, which can you remove by hand by simply twisting a slightly larger drill bit (e.g. ¹/₁₀ in/2.5 mm diameter) into each hole. Just a couple of twists is enough–you don't want to countersink the holes too much. Surface the pieces using a fine emery buffing stick.

3 Now for the rivet: overlap the first two sections of the armadillo so that the holes to be riveted are aligned. Push a section of 1.6 mm external diameter silver tubing through these holes. Cut the tubing with a piercing saw and 4/0 blade, allowing 0.5 mm to stick out at either end. If necessary, file the ends with a flat file so that they are square.

4 Put a small doming punch upright into a vise and rest the underside of the tubing on this punch. This supports the tube and causes it to spread when the tubing on the top side is tapped with a riveting hammer. Flip over to work the top and bottom evenly, and continue until the tubing has spread enough and can't fall out of the holes. Work on a steel block with first the riveting hammer and then a smooth-ended punch to neaten the rivet.

5 Continue this process with successive pieces until all the sections are joined together. I'm delighted with the movement of this piece and I can see that it could be utilized in many different contexts.

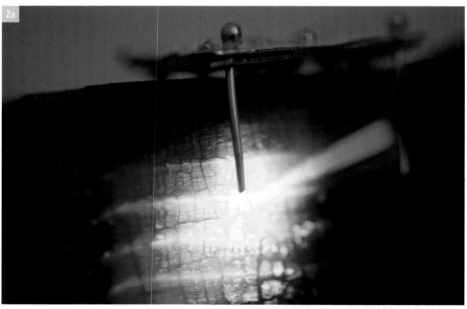

EXERCISE 4

ELEMENTAL CONNECTIONS

Taking a series of units and developing a joining system that is integral to the aesthetic of the piece, I look at my fusing test pieces and consider how I might join these elements together. They could make an impressive long pendant, but they lend themselves equally well to the bracelet format. For this project, you will need six test pieces, for example from the Fusion exercises (see pages 146–53), 20 in (500 mm) length of 0.8 mm diameter silver wire, and a length of 1.2 mm diameter snake chain, with your favorite finding to finish the necklace.

1 The linking system needs to allow movement in numerous directions; a jump ring would do the job in terms of this motion, but would be aesthetically disappointing. Looking at the panels, there is much texture and melting and a balled wire would fit well with the existing textures. Using a bow drill, drill equidistant 1 mm holes in each corner of the panels to provide a means to attach them together.

2 Take the necessary health and safety precautions before you begin soldering (see page 183). Cut 12 pieces of 0.8 mm diameter wire, roughly $^3/_5$ in (15 mm) in length and heat the tip of each pin until they ball up to an equal size so that they look like pin heads. Take the first two panels and match up the holes. Thread through the balled pins, then position the panels so that the straight ends of the pins hang down from a soldering board. Heat the ends until they ball up to an equal size.

3 After quenching, try to stretch out the double-headed pins so that the panels hang down from the other. This movement is good, and the balled wire becomes a punctuation for the panels. When you are happy with the test, complete the row of panels in this same way.

4 Oxidize the panels using a commercial oxidizing solution and complete the necklace with snake chain, thinking about how you can create a simple closure system without having to make a beautiful bayonet clasp.

CHAIN CHOICES

I made my column of panels into a pendant by attaching it to a length of snake chain, which I felt complemented the fused textures of the panels.

When choosing chain for your jewelry there are several issues you need to consider. The chain must be strong enough to support the item you want to hang from it, but there is also the technical issue of how the piece will attach. The aesthetic impact is important, too. You will need to determine how to satisfy each of these requirements when finishing off your designs.

TOOLS

Jewelry tools can be expensive to buy, but it's worth purchasing the best quality you can afford. A well-made hand tool, well looked after, should last a lifetime. It's also worth looking out for second-hand tools in markets (check that they have been loved and cared for by the previous owner). To care for your tools, treat those made from steel, which are prone to rusting, with a proprietary rust inhibitor from time to time. Check your tools periodically for rough edges or nicks (on pliers, for example, these can damage fine silver wires). Smooth sharp or jagged edges with fine wet and dry paper.

Here are some of the most useful tools for the intermediate to advanced jewelry-making workshop.

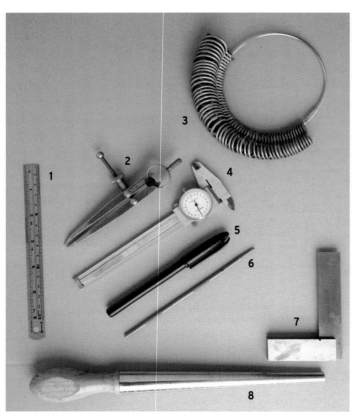

MEASURING AND MARKING

Accuracy is vital when preparing and planning jewelry projects. Here are the most used measuring and marking tools in my box.

1 Steel rule
2 Dividers
3 Ring gauge (also known as a ring sizer)
4 Vernier gauge
5 Fine-line permanent pen
6 Scribe
7 Engineer's square
8 Ring stick

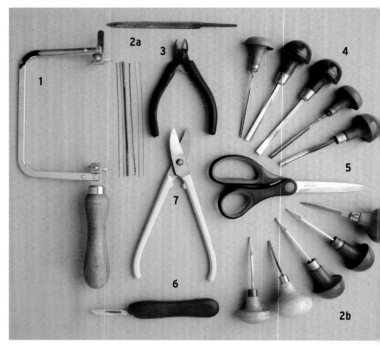

CUTTING, CARVING, AND SCRAPING

We use an array of cutting tools in jewelry making. Whether you are cutting cardstock, metal, or wood, these tools must be kept sharp to provide the cleanest of cuts.

1 Piercing saw and piercing blades; keep a wide selection of blades: size 3 , 2, or 1 for cutting sprues from a casting, sizes 0, 2/0, and 3/0 for 0.8 to 1.2 mm thickness sheet, and 4/0, 6/0, and 8/0 for thinner sheet metal
2 Selection of scorpers and gravers for scraping and engraving metal, and for raising a grain for stone setting
3 Wire cutters for trimming wire
4 Woodcarving tools for carving custom indents into wood, to make a die for sinking metal
5 Scissors are an essential tool for model making, and for cutting tape and sheets of wet and dry paper
6 Scalpel for model making, and general use with softer materials
7 Snips for cutting solder pallions or rough cutting sheet metal

A NOTE ON FILES

When choosing your file for a specific purpose, make sure it is the correct cut (determined by the number of teeth) for the job in hand. For example, a bastard file is rough cut and will remove waste metal quickly, but it will cut deep grooves in the final surface. The no. 1 cut file is less aggressive, and the no. 2 cut is finer still, for a smooth cut. The half-round file has the most versatile shape for filing as it can work into curves as well cutting a nice straight edge or plane. I always pick the half-round file as my default file for this reason. The cutting teeth on a file point forward so that the cutting action works on the "push." Drawing the file backward against the material will only blunt and clog the teeth, so try not to get into this bad habit.

Escapement files, riffler files, and slotting files are a useful addition to the toolbox; once you have them, you'll wonder how you ever managed without them.

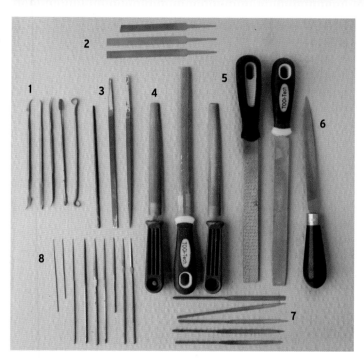

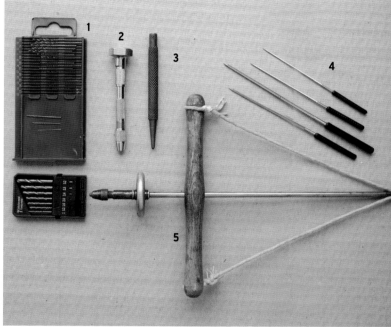

FILES

1 Rifler files have curved cutting surfaces for getting into difficult places

2 Slotting files are super-thin files with cutting surfaces on all sides, and can be as thin as 0.4 mm

3 Large square files, great for filing grooves

4 Large half-round files, from left to right: no. 2 cut smooth file; bastard file; no. 1 cut medium file

5 Large flat files, from left to right: bastard file for fast removal of material; raspy file for use on non-metalic materials (e.g. wax, wood, plastics)

6 Fine half-round file for gentle filing of silver

7 Needle files, various shapes, for small jobs

8 Escapement files for very fine work

HAND DRILLING AND HOLE SIZING

Small, precision holes are often best made using hand drilling tools. This bow drill was the first tool I ever bought; it's still one of the most used tools in my box. The pin vise takes drill bits and burrs and can be used for precise and subtle work, for example when cutting a seat for a stone. It's good to have a range of drill bits in your toolbox, but a set of broachers will provide the means to make any sized hole if you need an unusual measurement.

1 Drill bits, from 0.3 mm to 3.5 mm

2 Pin vise for holding bits and burrs

3 Center punch for marking the hole position before drilling

4 Broachers for expanding holes

5 Bow drill

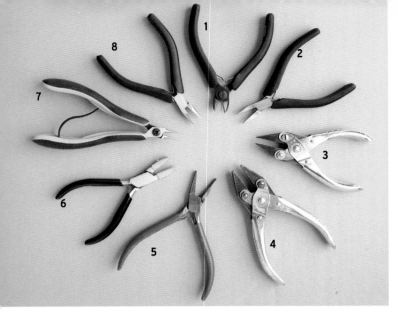

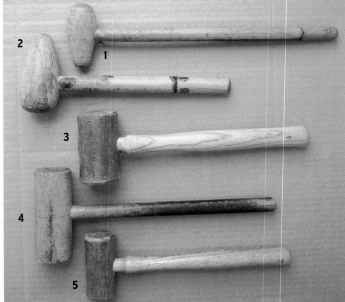

PLIERS

Gripping, twisting, bending, tweaking, and cutting—pliers get lots of use in day-to-day making, so it's important that they should be well made and comfortable to hold. More expensive pliers will have beautifully finished jaw surfaces that will leave minimal damage on your metal.

1 Wire cutters
2 Flat-nosed pliers
3 Snipe-nosed parallel pliers
4 Flat-nosed parallel pliers
5 Half-round pliers
6 Nylon-tipped pliers
7 Round-nosed pliers
8 Snipe-nosed pliers

MALLETS

Mallets made of wood, leather, or nylon will push metal with minimal surface disturbance. The impact of a mallet will also depend on the type of material it is made from. Boxwood mallets are the hardest, while rawhide mallets provide a more gentle impact. Generally, mallets are used in conjunction with a steel block for flattening, or with steel mandrels and formers for shaping metal.

1 Small bossing mallet
2 Large bossing mallet for dishing metal
3 Large rawhide mallet for low-impact shaping or flattening of metal
4 Boxwood mallet, which has a harder surface and a sharper impact and will stretch metal slightly; good for resizing a ring on a mandrel
5 Small rawhide mallet for gently making metal flat

HAMMERS

When two items collide with force, the softest of the items in the equation takes the main impact. So steel hammers, made from a hard metal, will dent, squash, and thin softer metals such as brass, copper, and silver. Every hammer has a specific job in jewelry making, and should be used for no other purpose; the surface quality should be kept pristine as dents and marks to the surface will transfer to your precious metal with every blow.

1 Planishing hammer for smoothing the surface of metal
2 Large raising hammer for stretching and thinning metal
3 Small raising hammer, also great for texturing
4 Ball peen hammer—I call this a jobbing hammer, for doing any old job
5 Large planishing hammer
6 Ball hammer for shaping and texturing
7 Chasing hammer for use with chasing tools
8 Riveting hammer

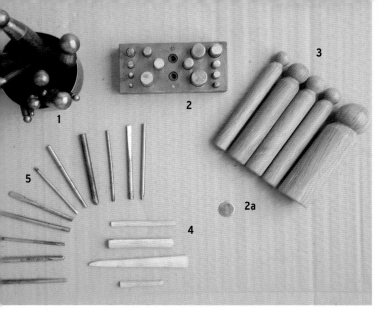

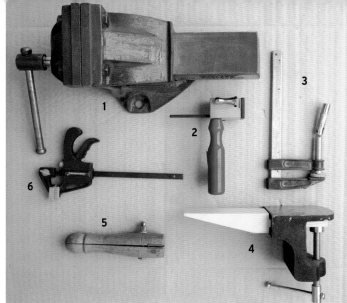

PUNCHES, FORMING, AND CHASING TOOLS

These tools are for indenting and forming metal and can be made from steel or hardwood, with steel having a harder and more cutting impact than wood. Use in conjunction with a steel hammer for maximum impact, or a mallet when lighter force is required.

1 Doming punches for curving metal
2 Disk cutting set (see 2a)—an easy way to prepare circles for doming
3 Wooden doming punches have less thinning impact on metal
4 Hand-made wooden punches for gentle shaping
5 A selection of hand-made punching and chasing tools for repoussé (working metal in relief) and similar processes

CRAMPS

1 Bench vise for holding tools, or your work. Line the jaws with a small sheet of latex, wood, aluminum, or copper to protect tools or work from damage. (Consider how else you might utilize the forceful squeeze that it is able to exert.)
2 Tube-cutting jig to assist in holding and cutting tubing
3 Metal quick-release cramp
4 Portable bench peg with in-built steel block
5 Ring vise for holding rings and other small items
6 Plastic quick-release cramp; it has a firm but gentle holding action

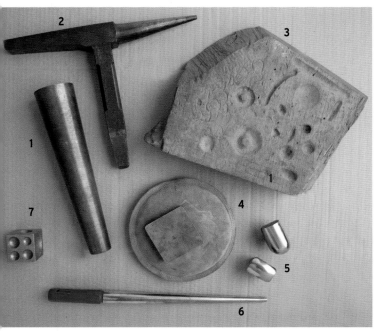

STAKES, MANDRELS, AND FORMING TOOLS

As well as using traditional stakes and mandrels for shaping metal, it is also possible to make custom shaping blocks from hardwood.

1 Arm mandrel for shaping bracelets; try to avoid using hammers with a mandrel as the surface easily dents
2 Anvil stake, useful for flattening, curving, and thinning metal
3 Custom-made indents in a wooden block for forming irregular shapes from sheet metal
4 Steel block with a leather sand bag to help quieten the hammering process
5 Curved stakes for shaping metal
6 Ring mandrel for making rings round and gently stretching them in size
7 Brass doming block for forming hemispheres from a disk of sheet metal

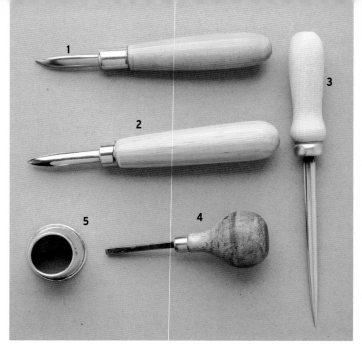

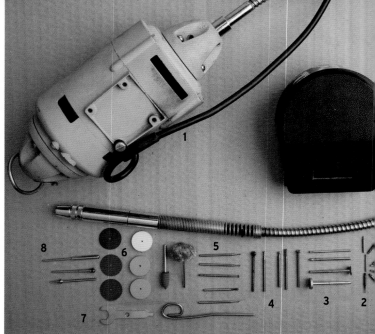

STONE SETTING

These tools are used at the very last stage of making. When stone setting, make sure that these tools are highly polished, with no sharp edges, and exert controlled force to avoid damaging the surface of your nearly finished jewelry.

1 Curved burnisher, good for getting into small areas

2 Straight burnisher to smooth over the pushed surface and to bring back shine

3 Long burnisher for longer sweeping, burnishing action on metal

4 Pusher to press down a bezel or claws

5 Loupe (to check how well you have set your stone!)

PENDANT DRILL AND ACCESSORIES

I use this versatile tool for grinding and polishing; the drill is controlled by a foot pedal, and bits and burrs are interchangeable in the handpiece. The pendant motor must hang freely when in use.

1 Pendant motor, foot pedal, and handpiece

2 Dental bits and burrs for grinding

3 Diamond-tipped burrs for grinding

4 Wax burrs

5 Small burrs for stone setting

6 Separating disks and polishing wheels

7 Spanner and locking pin for changing burrs and mandrels

8 Split pin, screw top, and threaded mandrels for use with emery papers, separating disks, and polishing wheels

FLUXES

Flux forms an essential part of the soldering process. Its job is to protect the metals from oxidizing while heating. There are many types of flux—each one has specific applications.

1 Borax is the most versatile of the fluxes and works well under most conditions, handling up to 1740°F (950°C) in temperature

2 Tenacity™ no. 5 is specifically designed for working with higher temperatures and is the flux of choice when silver soldering with steel; the fumes are toxic, so work in a well-ventilated area

3 Auflux is a liquid flux that is intended for use with gold; it tends to bubble less than borax and so it makes it easier to see what you are doing when applying heat

4 Fine watercolor brush for applying solder and flux

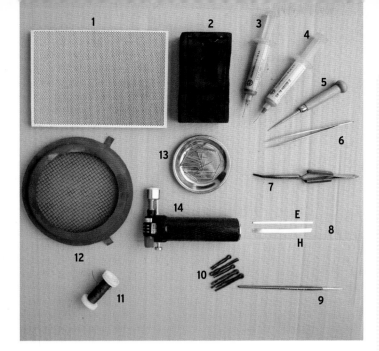

SOLDERING

Pay good attention to health and safety when using heat processes (see right).

1 Honeycomb soldering board for the even distribution of heat

2 Charcoal block, provides a protective atmosphere that reduces firestain on metal

3 and **4** Tubes of solder paste in hard (H) and easy (E)—these tubes have ready-mixed solder with flux and provide a handy dispensing method for applying solder to wires and other fiddly joints

5 Soldering pick to pull solder along a seam

6 and **7** Pointed tweezers and reverse-action tweezers for handling parts while heating

8 Hard silver solder strip (H), distinguishable from the easy solder strip (E) by being the wider of the two

9 Very fine watercolor brush for applying flux and solder

10 Split pins are very useful for holding items together for soldering

11 Steel binding wire for binding items together when soldering; remember to remove all traces before pickling

12 Wire mesh for heating metal from the underside

13 Pins for use with the honeycomb soldering board, to assist in positioning metal when heating

14 Small gas torch suitable for heating and soldering small jewelry items

SOLDERING AND SAFETY

Before you start soldering, read through the following safety guidelines. Anything that involves working with a very hot flame is potentially hazardous, and you need to be properly prepared.

- The room you are working in should be well-ventilated.
- Clear the soldering area each time before commencing work. Keep glass and plastic out of reach of flames and reflected heat, and keep a fire extinguisher handy.
- Make sure you've read the manufacturer's instructions and safety precautions when using items for the first few times. This is especially important when it comes to the soldering torch. It needs to be assembled properly, and you need to understand how to turn on and turn off the gas (and/or oxygen) safely.
- If you are soldering using oxygen and gas, make sure that you keep any grease or oil away from the oxygen bottle—the combination of oxygen and oil is highly combustible.
- It's advisable to wear a face mask while soldering. When flux is exposed to high heat, it smokes and this can irritate the airways. Always wear safety goggles. You should wash your hands after you have finished.
- Don't work with bare arms or legs—make sure they are covered, and wear shoes that cover the whole of your feet. Tie long hair back. Remove any jewelry that may get in the way, including bracelets, dangly earrings, and long necklaces, and don't wear scarves when soldering.

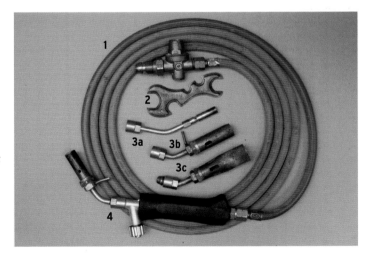

GAS TORCH

It is essential that your gas torch can provide a wide range of temperatures, and that it can sustain these temperatures for long periods. I like to use this propane gas torch that takes a range of nozzle sizes for flame control.

1 Pressure regulator—these are normally set at 4 bar

2 Spanner for changing nozzles

3 Range of torch nozzles, suitable for (a) melting, (b) soldering silver and similar metals, and (c) annealing

4 Latex hose and torch handle

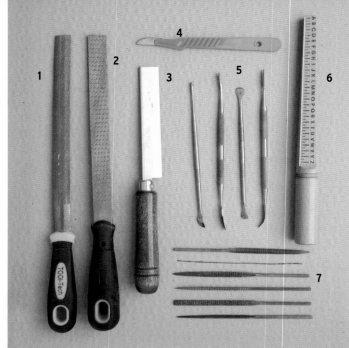

DELFT CASTING

This form of casting provides a great way to make use of your old silver scraps. When melting silver for delft casting, to reach temperatures of 1652°F (900°C) plus, you will need the largest nozzle you have on the gas torch. Pay good attention to health and safety when delft casting; there are possible dangers from fire and fumes, and the risk of skin burns.

1 Crucible for melting silver
2 Crucible holder
3 Delft sand (also described as clay)
4 Aluminum rings, used to contain the delft sand into which you make your mold

WAX WORKING

Wax is such a soft material to work with and the tools that we use need to be rough, or they will clog up. The medium requires sculpting and scraping actions, as well as melting.

1 Bastard file for smoother cuts on wax
2 Large raspy file for removing large quantities of wax quickly
3 Wax cutting saw for cutting slices from ring wax
4 Scalpel
5 Modeling tools for working wax; these tools can be gently heated in a flame to melt the wax
6 Wax ring sizing tool, the sharp blade scrapes the inside of a wax ring to size as you twist the tool
7 Wax needle files, notice the rough cut of these files

SANDING

Sanding is the first and necessary part in polishing up your metal after any kind of working process. I like to use wet and dry papers (usually in a dry state) as they last a long time, getting ever finer with use. Feel the papers to tell how coarse they are. (On the back you will find numbers that tell you this information too, of course.) The lower the grit number, the rougher the paper. Scratches and file marks are ground out with a rough grit (240 or 320), and then the surface is worked with finer papers in sequence (600, 800, 1000, 1200) until you have the desired degree of polish.

1 Wet and dry papers, showing the back and front
2 Glass fiber tape, used to reinforce the wet and dry paper on the back; thin strips can be cut and used in the piercing saw frame
3 Polishing stick for getting into small areas
4 Large buffing stick with wet and dry paper glued to its faces
5 Round buffing stick, perfect for polishing up the insides of rings

POLISHING

There are several approaches to finishing the surface of metal. A high luster is achievable with rouge on a mop in the pendant drill, but it is also possible to wear the surface unevenly. Barrel polishing will provide an all-over burnished effect, but sometimes I find this too shiny and often I prefer to apply the final finish by hand.

1 Pumice is used to clean metal at any stage in the making, and can provide a pleasing satin final finish to metal, too
2 Fine steel wool (0000 grade) gives a bright satin sheen to metal
3 Chamois leather, dipped in olive oil and rubbed with rouge, will provide a good all-over shine to the surface of your metal
4 Bristle brush for use with pumice
5 An abrasive polishing block is an eraser impregnated with grit, and provides a satin finish to metal
6 Renaissance wax, applied to metal once the desired polish or patina is achieved, will stabilize and protect the surface
7 Commercially available polish-impregnated wadding is also an effective solution where a high shine is required

BARREL POLISHER

A motor drives two axles onto which a latex barrel can sit; inside the barrel, stainless steel shot is placed with water, soap, and hair conditioner (in order to make the water slippery), and your work. The barrel rotates on the axles, causing your work to tumble with the steel shot, and so a burnishing effect is created.

1 The barrel polishing unit–motor and axles
2 Latex barrel
3 Stainless steel shot

SAFETY

Many of the processes we use in jewelry making are hazardous. Never take risks with your health when you're in the studio. Simple precautions (see page 183) and adequate protective equipment can save your life.

1 Protective face mask, use when working with the pendant drill and other mechanized processes
2 Leather apron, provides protection from excessive heat and splashes when casting metal
3 Safety goggles–if you don't have a full face mask (1), these safety goggles will protect your eyes from hazards. If you wear glasses, be sure to purchase goggles that will fit over them!
4 Dust mask, especially useful when grinding and polishing with the pendant motor
5 Leather gauntlets to protect against extreme heat, e.g. when casting or when tempering steel
6 Latex gloves for protection against chemicals

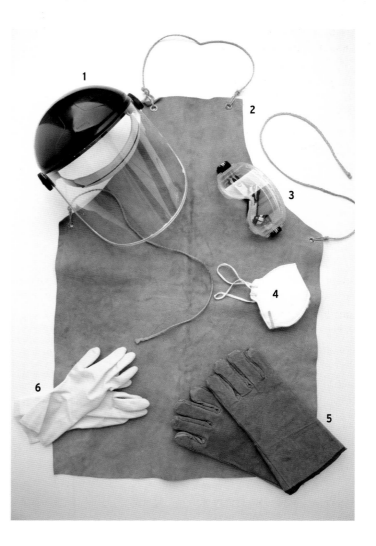

TEMPLATES

1 Pebble for Adjustable pebble necklace, pages 20–7

2 Small pebble for Adjustable pebble necklace, pages 20–7

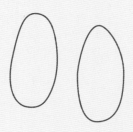

3 Flower for One-part die forming, pages 158–9

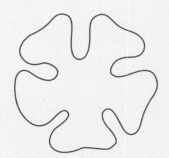

4 Taurean base unit for Playtime, page 174

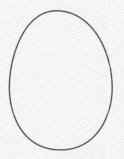

5 Armadillo shell for Evolution, page 175

6 One-piece pin, pages 98–101

7 Pewter and acrylic pendant, pages 102–107

8 Cactus box ring, pages 126–31

GLOSSARY

Annealing This is the process of heating metal (such as copper, steel, silver, and brass) to red hot (cherry red) to make it soft for working. Most metals can be slow-cooled in air, or quickly quenched in water after this heating, but care must be taken with steel and with some types of gold as this can affect the resulting hardness. (See Tempering, below.)

Buffing A process to give the final piece a smooth, highly lustered finish.

Burnishing To give the piece of metal a glossy, shiny finish by rubbing, usually with a burnisher or burnishing tool.

Casting Molten metal (or another liquid material) is poured into a mold to create a three-dimensional object. The process can be used to make one-off items; with careful planning, it is also possible to cast multiples of the same object. There are three main casting methods: cuttlefish, sand, or lost wax (see page 53) casting techniques.

De-burring The removal of sharp edges, air bubbles, and burrs on a piece of metal, usually with a file or with grinding tools in the pendant drill.

Enameling The technique of adding color to a piece of jewelry. Cold enameling refers to resin-based applications, while vitreous enamel refers to heat-applied glassy layers of color to the metal.

Etching A process whereby words, pictures, or pattern can be added to the surface of metal; the metal is selectively protected using a suitable stop-out, and then the object is immersed in an acid to dissolve any exposed surface, thus creating depth, texture, and contrast (see pages 132-9). Stop outs include nail polish, adhesive plastic, and PNP blue (for the photo-etching process). Commercial processes (photo etching and laser etching) can give more precise and repeatable pattern.

Fire stain A surface discoloration of sterling silver and other copper-containing metals, caused by the reaction of the copper element in the metal with oxygen. Unless removed, this discoloration can lessen the visual impact of silver. Where present, the gray stain can be readily identified under tracing paper.

Folding metals This process involves scoring and folding metal to create three-dimensional, geometric shapes from sheet metal (see page 164-9).

Forming Creating three-dimensional hollow forms from sheet metal using formers, punches, hammers, and mallets (see pages 154-63).

Fusion This is the way in which metals are joined together permanently by careful heating (see pages 146-53).

Keying a surface To rub a surface with wet and dry paper to make it rough, to improve the grip of a secondary substance (e.g. cold enamel or glue).

Married metals A soldered assembly of different types of metal sheet to create a single, multicolored (patterned) metal sheet, which can then be used to make a piece of jewelry (see pages 140-5).

Oxide A surface discoloration of metal caused by the chemical reaction of oxygen with the metal. Over time, silver will turn gray or black, and this process is speeded up when heat is applied; also metal can be treated with sulphurous oxidizing solutions to create this antique look, or to apply contrast to the piece.

Patination A controlled surface discoloration of metal, usually created using specific chemicals or compounds.

Pickling Used to clean metal and also remove excess flux after soldering. When metal is heated, oxides appear on the surface, which need to be removed. Chemicals, such as sulphuric acid, are used in this process. Citric acid is non-toxic and is a good alternative.

Polishing A finishing process whereby metal is made smooth or shiny using abrasives such as wet and dry paper, to remove scratches and imperfections. Wet and dry papers are worked through to make the surface ever smoother until the desired finish is achieved. A final high polish can be achieved using rouge and a mop on the pendant drill, on a bench polisher, or the piece can be put in the barrel polisher to give an all-over burnished effect.

Repoussé This is a metalworking technique where annealed metal is hammered into shape on the reverse; the metal is set into pitch or setters cement, and punches and chasing tools are used in conjunction with hammers to work a low relief design into it.

Reticulation This is a process of carefully controlled heating of silver, to bring the top surface of the metal to melting point, giving it a characteristic wrinkled appearance.

Quench A process used to cool a piece of metal down quickly after soldering. Using tweezers, immerse the hot metal into a container of water until cool enough to handle.

Tempering In tool making, the process of heating and quenching steel at specific temperatures to create the required hardness for its intended job. Red hot toolsteel, when quenched in water, becomes very hard and extremely brittle—it can shatter if hit with a hammer—so care must be taken to temper it correctly.

RESOURCES

Tools and precious metal supplies:

Rio Grande
www.riogrande.com
Precious materials including sterling silver tubing, solder paste, chains and findings, stones and beads, tools, enamels.

Boley GMbH
www.boley.de
German website supplying jewelry-making equipment, including Degussa flux.

Other materials:

Hallmark Metals
www.hallmarkmetals.net
Pewter, metal alloys, solder, plating metals and mold-making supplies.

Dipmicro Electronics
www.dipmicro.com
Press-N-peel blue transfer paper for etching.

Edmund Optics
www.edmundoptics.com
Liquid crystal (thermocromic) sheet.

Crystal Fit USA
www.crystalfit.com
Watch glasses.

Ultima International
ultimauk.com
For stockists of Ultima Red Ice fishing line.

Daiwa CorporationY
www.daiwasports.com
Contact for nearest stockists of Daiwa fishing line.

Sources of information:

Fairtrade and Fairmined:
Information about fairmined and fairtrade gold, and how to become a licensed fairtrade/fairmined gold jeweler.
www.fairjewelry.org

www.ganoksin.com
Jewelry-specific website containing information about processes and materials; worth signing up for the Orchid Digest, a forum for discussions about designing and making jewellery. (Worldwide, based in the USA.)

Society of American Silversmiths
The go-to resource for anything related to the art and craft of silversmithing.
www.silversmithing.com

Klimt02
An organization and website that offers space of knowledge, information, debates, and exchanges inside the context of contemporary jewelry.
www.klimt02.net

Recommended reading:

Lewton-Brain, Charles, *Hinges and Hinge-Based Catches for Jewelers and Goldsmiths* (Brain Press Ltd, 1997)

Lewton-Brain, Charles, *The Jewelry Workshop Safety Report* (Brain Press Ltd, 2002)

McCreight, Tim, *Hot and Cold Connections* (A&C Black, 2006)

Olver, Elizabeth, *The Art of Jewelry Design: From Idea to Reality* (North Light Books, 2002)

Olver, Elizabeth, *Jewelry Design: The Artisan's Reference* (North Light Books, 2003)

Untracht, Oppi, *Jewelry Concepts and Technology* (Doubleday, 1982)

Young, Anastasia, *Gemstone Settings: The Jewelry Maker's Guide to Styles and Techniques* (Interweave Press, 2012)

Young, Anastasia, *The Workbench Guide to Jewelry Techniques* (Interweave Press, 2010)

Places to visit:

Museum of Arts and Design
2 Columbus Circle, New York, NY 10019.
www.madmuseum.org

National Ornamental Metal Museum
374 Metal Musuem Drive, Memphis, Tennessee.
www.metalmuseum.org

Fuller Craft Museum
455 Oak Street, Brockton, MA.
www.fullercraft.org

INDEX

ACKNOWLEDGMENTS

Author's acknowledgments

Thanks to Judith More at Fil Rouge Press for her vision and to both Judith More and Jenny Latham for their generous support and patience throughout; to Stanza and to Amber for putting up with long days and late nights; also to Stanza for his creative input, and for the use of his photographs.

Thanks to Nora Fok, Henri Fernandez, Imogen Belfield, and Louise Loder for their inspirational contributions to this book.

Thanks to everyone at Flux Studios—members present and past, and to the students here too, for their interest and encouragement.

Thanks to Alex Yule, Becky Dockree, Bev Holden, Natascha Kotsopoulou, Yuki Sasakura, Sarah Eyton, and Nic Webb for the use of their beautiful work for illustration purposes.

Special thanks to all my family for setting me on this creative path, and their encouragement along the way; to my mother, Jane, for all those delightful clay-filled childhood play-days in her workshop, and to my father, Robin, who showed me how to find my form.

Publishers' acknowledgments

The publisher would like to thank Gerard Brown for the photography; Gaye Allen, Simon Goggin, and Dave Jones for design; Kathy Steer for editing; Anna Osborn for proofreading.

Picture credits

Key b = bottom, m = middle, l = left, r = right, t = top
Imogen Belfield: 88, 89; Sarah Eyton: 63 mr; Henrietta Fernandez: 66, 67;
Simon Goggin: background images on pages 16-17, 28-9, 38-9, 48-9; Nora Fok: 82, 83, 87bl, mr, br; Vicky Forrester: 8, 9, 18, 19, 28, 30, 31, 40, 41, 50, 51, 183br; Louise Loder: 74, 75mr; Shutterstock: 175tl.

Portrait of Vicky Forrester on page 7 by Stanza
www.stanza.co.uk
Tableware by Jane Forrester at www.bandonpottery.ie

All other photography by Gerard Brown.

ABOUT THE AUTHOR

Vicky Forrester is a graduate of Camberwell College of Arts (University of the Arts London) and Goldsmiths' College (University of London) and has been involved in the contemporary jewelry field for 23 years. She has been teaching and mentoring students in jewelry since 1995. Vicky's work has been exhibited extensively in the UK and abroad through various specialist galleries (Electrum, Lesley Craze, Flow, ProArte Monaco and many more). She makes one-off pieces to commission, also producing limited-editions. Her jewelry is held in private collections and examples of her work have also been published. Vicky is also the founder and director of Flux Studios. Flux Studios aims to bridge the chasm arising from the decline in opportunities for new makers to establish their businesses, and for the public to engage in jewelry practice. Her motivation to set up Flux Studios arose in response to her extensive experience as both maker and tutor of contemporary jewelry.

Find out more about Flux Studios at www.fluxstudios.org
Find out more about Vicky Forrester at www.vicky-forrester.com